Library of
Davidson College

JOYCE'S IRITIS AND THE IRRITATED TEXT

The Florida
James Joyce
Series

The Florida James Joyce Series
    Edited by Zack Bowen

*The Autobiographical Novel of Co-Consciousness:
Goncharov, Woolf, and Joyce,* by Galya Diment (1994).
Shaw and Joyce: "The Last Word in Stolentelling,"
    by Martha Fodaski Black (1995).
Bloom's Old Sweet Song: Essays on Joyce and Music,
    by Zack Bowen (1995).
Reauthorizing Joyce, by Vicki Mahaffey (1995).
Joyce's Iritis and the Irritated Text: The Dis-lexic Ulysses,
    by Roy Gottfried (1995).
Literary Idiolects: Joyce, Milton, and the Theory of Influence,
    by Patrick Colm Hogan (1995).

Joyce's Iritis and the Irritated Text

The Dis-lexic *Ulysses*

Roy Gottfried

UNIVERSITY PRESS OF FLORIDA
Gainesville · Tallahassee · Tampa · Boca Raton
Pensacola · Orlando · Miami · Jacksonville

Copyright 1995 by the Board of Regents of the State of Florida
Printed in the United States of America on acid-free paper
All rights reserved

00 99 98 97 96 95   6 5 4 3 2 1

Library of Congress Cataloging-in-Publication Data
Gottfried, Roy K.
Joyce's iritis and the irritated text: the dis-lexic Ulysses / Roy Gottfried
p. cm.—(The Florida James Joyce series)
Includes bibliographical references and index.
ISBN 0-8130-1404-2 (alk. paper)
1. Joyce, James, 1882–1941. Ulysses—Criticism, Textual. 2. Authors and readers—History—20th century. 3. Visual literature—History and criticism. 4. Novelists, Irish—20th century—Biography. 5. Joyce, James, 1882–1941—Health. 6. Iritis—Patients—Biography. 7. Reader-response criticism. 8 Intertextuality. I. Title. II. Series.
PR6019.O9U65324   1995
823'.912—dc20   95-4682

The University Press of Florida is the scholarly publishing agency for the State University System of Florida, comprised of Florida A & M University, Florida Atlantic University, Florida International University, Florida State University, University of Central Florida, University of Florida, University of North Florida, University of South Florida, and University of West Florida.

University Press of Florida
15 Northwest 15th Street
Gainesville, FL 32611

To my parents

CONTENTS

Foreword, *by Bernard Benstock* ix
Acknowledgments xi
Introduction 1

CHAPTER 1 Iritis as Cause and Effect 8
CHAPTER 2 Illness and the Magnification of Letters 22
CHAPTER 3 The Complicit Reader and Joycean Dis-lexia 43
CHAPTER 4 The Poet's Picture Puzzle 57
CHAPTER 5 Identity, Intertextuality, and Infection 95
CHAPTER 6 Ghosts, Sounds, and Errors 127
APPENDIX What Joyce Saw in *Ulysses* 161

Notes 167
Bibliography 179
Index 185

FOREWORD

Bernard Benstock

In *Joyce's Iritis and the Irritated Text,* Roy Gottfried applies a practiced eye and a high-powered lens to Ulyssean details and steps back to view the larger patterns that the details create. He focuses on the alphabet *letter* in relation to the epistolary letter, the printed *character* in relation to the personified character—relationships that result in the Joycean mosaic in *Ulysses.* Even subparticles as small as bits of broken type are under scrutiny, from which he expands outward centrifugally to encompass major aspects of the text. The particles are reassembled to make a study of both stylistics and thematics, the pieces returned to the pattern that makes up the sum total of its functioning parts. In doing this Gottfried employs an individually developed methodology composed of classical philology—the rhetorical systems that Joyce himself had studied—and contemporary linguistic approaches. Between Joyce's own inflamed eyes and many a reader's irritations with *Ulysses* Gottfried builds an intricate bridge.

ACKNOWLEDGMENTS

I have benefited from the sharp-sightedness of many; what is clear in this work is due to them, what is unclear all to my own limitations. Foremost, I cannot fully express my gratitude to the late Berni Benstock for his insight and support, his many comments and corrections. In this book, whose focus is on absence and what is not seen, each page is a reminder of loss, and Berni will be sorely missed. I am grateful to Michael Gillespie for his judgment and balanced vision. To my colleagues I extend my thanks: Vereen Bell for encouragement early on, Mark Jarman for his sensibility, Jay Clayton for his advice. My student Gian Balsamo gave clarifying attention to vague ideas. Particular appreciation is due to Walda Metcalf and the editorial staff at the University Press of Florida, whose scrutiny of the manuscript was much sharper than my own.

The myopic concern for this project was sustained and even aided by my dear wife Mary and tolerated with good will by my sons Oliver, Teddy, and Henry. I dedicate the book to my mother and father, describing them (somewhat as Stephen describes his parents) as the woman who gave me my eye color and the man, my nearsightedness.

INTRODUCTION

Much like an object placed at the focal point of vision measured in an eye examination, *Ulysses* is placed at the juncture of convergent but different perspectives, related but often at cross-purposes: as a work, it stands at a particular place in Joyce's physical life; as a text, it stands in mediation between the lines of sight of the author and the reader. It is a product of Joyce's increasing difficulties in seeing; it is a source of much confusion to the reader. *Ulysses* is hard to read in part because it is an object difficult for the author to see and in part because it is made difficult to see *by* him. The debates about what is to appear in any edition only confirm that it is hard to see what is to be read. In each case, as a product of creation and as a problematic book to be read, *Ulysses* is also an object meant to be seen, and seeing is a process of considerable challenge for Joyce and for his readers. (And, moreover, the reasons for that challenge are similar.)

It was Joyce's exclamation "My book will never come out now"[1] that moved Sylvia Beach to offer her aid in publishing *Ulysses*. His plaint at first glance seems to be that of the unknown and thwarted artist and seems much like his character Stephen's comment in "Proteus": "Who ever anywhere will read these written words? Signs on a white field" (3.414–15). Yet Joyce's actual statement is a deeply layered one that at first only appears to have an ulterior motive in getting help; it is rather a statement closely connected to all that *Ulysses* is as object: a visible product of his careful creation, a text of very questionable "signs on a white field" seen by a reader.

A book "comes out" when it is published; behind Joyce's provocative statement was his recognition not only of this obvious fact but of the etymology behind the word *publish*. Coming out in public means that the work emerges from the private, hidden writing of manuscript and typescript: it goes from unclear handwriting to black, printed signs on a white page; it further emerges, in the case of the earlier appearance of *Ulysses*, from the narrow field of the literary magazine. Being made public, the work consequently has a wide audience: a book does not exist until it is out in the world, open and evident in black and white to those who try to read it. Yet it is in coming out and being made public that Joyce has sought to obscure all sorts of things, in mysteries not only of meaning but also of simple letters and words on the page. As a true and essential Joycean paradox, *Ulysses* is best hidden and opaque when and only when it is most available as questionable "signs on a white field."

Yet its appearance in public as an object is accomplished and confirmed by its being a product. Tellingly, Joyce called his effort not the general "work," as he did later for years with *Finnegans Wake*, nor the generic "novel," but rather by the term that denoted its nature as a commodity, a "book." First, a book is the result of a commercial process; it is offered to the public as a product; second, the book that comes out by this financial process is a product itself of the mechanical process of printing. Printing, Joyce knew from his own bitter experience, was a long and convoluted process, whose result as a physical object could be subject to errors.

In order for a book to come out, it must unavoidably but also welcomely be caught in a matrix of commercial values, each objectified. Beach's plan for publishing *Ulysses* in several formats was most certainly more an economic than an aesthetic choice; the necessity of an advance subscription to capitalize the printing did not absolutely require a selection of editions. The range of prices was determined by how much the purchaser received in material value other than the intrinsic worth of the novel's art: signed and numbered copies on the best Holland paper cost more than unsigned works on the next grade of *vergé d'arches*, followed at the bottom of the list with unsigned works on heavy stock but otherwise unremarkable paper. This last was called, with no apparent irony, the "cheap edition." The price difference between the best and least works was more than double; however, in either edition, what actually appeared—that is to say, the physical texts themselves (in their pagination and words, according to the brochure, "all unedited and unexpurgated")—were, of course, identical.

Such commercial attention to material goods was carried even to the superficial and visual qualities of the book. The choice of Marcel Darantière as the printer of *Ulysses* was colored by the hues of aestheticism; one fame of the printer was his publication of the works of Huysmans, lending the odor of Des Esseintes bibliophilia to the publishing endeavor: the book would be attractive. The dandyism was continued in another way: Joyce fretted at some length about the color blue for the cover paper of *Ulysses*, paying a good deal of attention himself to what is only the *superfacies* of his art.[2] The surface of a book may cover meaning, but surfaces, such as the face, are the first thing seen. The book as material, physical object was likely Joyce's primary aim in its coming out.

The book is a product that appears before the public, published for its members to buy, on various grades of paper between aesthetically chosen covers. Yet the physical object of the book in hand contains only the material within it, those signs that are themselves the material product of a mechanical process; and that printed material Joyce wished to have work a particular effect on his reader. There is no clearer recognition by Joyce of this material status as object of his text's coming out, so as to be seen and received by his readers in a particular way, than in the pains he took with the last page proofs. Joyce, the one who had trouble seeing, was concerned with what the reader would see. He gave scrutiny to details that refer not to the inspired artistic creation of his work but rather to the mundane and mechanical, visible details of its printing. While it is true that Joyce made substantive additions to the novel at all stages of the process, even up until the last minute, the final page proofs show a detailed attention to what would be evident to the sight of his readers. In order for his text as an object to have an effect on his reader, Joyce must have it carefully edited and represented. This care demonstrates his sense of what comes out by a mechanical process, what appears on the printed page. In his introduction to the Rosenbach manuscript, Harry Levin observes that "despite [Joyce's] failing eyesight, he cherished a Mallarméan feeling for the appearance of type upon a page."[3] Joyce was concerned to see what appeared in *Ulysses* and concerned with what and how the reader would see it when it came out.

Even something so small as the potentially various forms that simple letters could take when struck in print mattered to him. In the reproduction of the flyleaf of one book in Bloom's mantelpiece collection, *The Short but yet Plain Elements of Geometry,* Joyce was at pains to have the printer reproduce the antiquated orthography of *s;* he carefully struck each letter in the copy and indicated what he wished to be seen on the page: "Si possible employez pour ces lettres l's ancienne en forme de '*f*.'"[4] In another place where the formidable abilities of Darantière were challenged by the expanding dimensions of Joyce's text, as in the case of the intended diacritical marks in the Slavic name "Prhklstr Kratchinabrichistich" in "Cyclops," Joyce offered an imaginative solution to get his desired effect: "Employez peut-être des accents circonflexes invertis."[5] Letters were never a simple matter for Joyce, and he gave them, despite his poor eyesight, minute scrutiny.

As with the letters, so too with the spacing and blocking of his text, its arrangement on the page. While attention to this issue seems to be a matter of artistic integrity and thoroughness, it is oddly tangential, as its purpose is highly formal and thus primarily visual; but it demonstrates Joyce's concern for how the reader would see the text. Joyce indicated places where paragraphs should go in the final stages of the page proofs; twice in "Wandering Rocks," where a change in the text evokes large-scale changes in space and time, he indicated where the text should be broken up by inserting a paragraph mark and noting in the margin, "nouveau paragraphe."[6] In "Sirens," with its fugal form, he was careful to mark the end of the introduction with its statement of themes and differentiate it from the body of the chapter, making a space where a printed form would replicate the laws of music. That change in the page proofs, however, would leave a widow line, violating a law of print that should also be honored. So Joyce combines his obedience to two arts, printing and music, by a Solomonic correction of meaning and method both: "Laissez ici une espace sans astérisques. Mieux serait commencer plus bas page 245 enfin l'espace se trouve après la 1ière et 2ième ligne de page 247."[7] Such detail seems fastidious, even too scrupulous, for an author with lofty aims for his work; yet no such detail of the appearance of the text when noticed would go unnoted, although, in the press of time and the complexity of the process, Joyce would overlook many. His attention indicates how he understood that letters must appear as he intended them when they came out on the printed page. Joyce saw and saw to every letter, in no small measure because letters are the most fundamental objects on the page.

The dates inscribed on the last page of that book, "Trieste-Zurich-Paris, 1914–1921," frame the entire work of imagining, writing, editing, and proofreading the novel—every letter, all efforts that were necessary to make it "come out." Beginning in November 1917 and ending in November 1921, a span of forty-eight months, the eighteen chapters of *Ulysses* were written at a pace of approximately one every two months and three weeks (although Joyce's actual composition was far less measured).[8] The proofreading lasted six months (concurrent with the composition of the last chapters), beginning on June 11, 1921. In that hectic pace of composing and correcting over the five years from 1917 to 1922, Joyce suffered eight separate episodes of attacks in his eyes, at least one a year and with two taking place in 1917, an average of one every seven and a half months. There is, therefore, another frame for the production of the final object of the book, one in which illness as well as artistic effort is a measure.

Thus it is that even as *Ulysses* came out as an object, it was seen in all of its stages of composition and printing by a writer with limited sight. What could Joyce make of the making of this text he saw so diligently into its final form as visible object to be read? And what could he make the reader make of it? For all the attention to the form of the novel as it comes out, there is a compromise on both sides of the object, in the interchange of vision between making it and seeing it. The text was out of focus for the artist, and he makes it so for the reader. Joyce's bad eyesight when he was writing and proofreading *Ulysses* is a model and a method for the uncertainties within the work; and consequently, and most important, his illness is a model and a method for the reader's encounter with the text, an encounter initially and extensively visual.

It is therefore the final and most pertinent issue, when Joyce wished his book to "come out" from the process of financial backing and mechanical production to be an object promoted and sold, that he wished it to appear to be seen, as seeing was an activity problematic for Joyce. It is only when *Ulysses* has thus "come out" that the most crucial quality is completed, a quality on which Joyce set the greatest store: coming out makes the book an object of sight to others. With this visible aspect of the received object, the unsettling enterprise of reading the Joycean text can be undertaken. Only when Joyce's book has come out to sight, as a product that can have an effect on the reader in its reception by being read, can it enter into the processes of meaning by being seen and misseen by the reader. Joyce will bedevil the reader's view of it, as *Ulysses* appears slightly out of focus for author and reader. The two lines of vision meet there on the page in the very objects of the words and letters: the weak vision of the artist and the weakened one of the reader, affected by the careful process of coming out.

The systemic uncertainty and obscurity of *Ulysses* for every reader may be best understood by simple premises about the physical object of the book and the physical limits of the author's seeing it. An examination of Joyce's vision and its limits will give a model for how *Ulysses* works, through an analysis of its smallest parts, which activate the process of misseeing and give it the most basic, if unsure, of foundations on the page: that place where the least level of the letter looms large to Joyce, as it must to the reader. An awareness of the obscured view of those objects printed on the page gives a sense of how the reader is made limited and unsure in reading the text: such a perspective demonstrates the way in which Joyce translates his physically disrupted experiences of observing the text, with every letter a physical challenge, into the reader's imaginatively disrupted experience of reading the text, with every word as an enigmatic challenge. Joyce's vision was physically disrupted; the reader's, cognitively. They meet in the difficulties of seeing.

This study therefore locates the difficulty of reading *Ulysses*, its density and opacity, in two sites. The first is Joyce's eyesight, which, it will be argued, was far more compromised and complicated than has been hitherto acknowledged. Joyce wrote and proofread all of *Ulysses* with vision blurred and impaired by iritis, which necessitated his using a magnifying glass to enlarge words, separating them out of context and even making prominent the individual letters in them. Eye difficulties are enshrined in *Finnegans Wake,* but they are not recognized as crucial to the creation of *Ulysses;* they are as pernicious in the text as glaucoma itself. The opacity of *Ulysses* is thus of a different order from that of the *Wake,* especially as the novel depicts a realistic world and is grounded firmly in the visual and graphemic.

The second site of the difficulty in reading *Ulysses* is a result of the limitations of Joyce's eyesight: the letters on the page, seen as magnified and deceptively separate by Joyce, are unstable and uncertain, making an irritated text. The reader is affected by the object, is made to engage the uncertainty not as an intellectual construct alone but first as a physical uncertainty. This study examines the ways in which the indeterminacy of the text proceeds from the small differences and slight opacities of simple letters at the most basic level in the large novel, and thus this visual indeterminacy precedes those hermeneutic uncertainties of other analyses. By the confusion, blurring, deception of letters, reading is undermined and the reader is made complicit in Joyce's illness. That is the ultimate result of the object of *Ulysses* and Joyce's engagement with it. As the reader is challenged to make meaning by reading a text of letters unsurely seen and deceptively irritated, the reader is infected with a particular kind of Joycean dis-lexia. This term is used to emphasize the disjunctive and disruptive quality Joyce created in the text; it is also used to distinguish this effect from actual clinical dyslexia and yet to suggest a strong analogy, to be discussed later.

This dis-lexia of the irritated text has several extended consequences. As the letters on the page are unstable in their form and identity, the identity of all elements made from them is suspect: that of the individual words, that of the characters, that of text and intertexts. The reader's own identity is also challenged by being infected by dis-lexia and by being disoriented in reading; one particular reader of Joyce (Oliver Gogarty) so affected is examined. The ways in which the typesetting and editing of *Ulysses* were influenced by Joyce's irritated text are also considered.

CHAPTER 1

Iritis as Cause and Effect

This study starts from a simple premise and a simple focus, although simplicity is always deceptively rich in Joyce: that Joyce's eyesight was compromised throughout the entire creation of *Ulysses;* that, as a consequence, the text is unstable and obscure in ways not fully recognized; and that the place of that instability is found in the very objects at which Joyce had to peer myopically through opaque spectacles and with a magnifying glass, the letters he wrote and saw printed on the page. The eyesight and the writing share a density, an opacity, that destabilizes the text; its surface, in turn, as the reader's object of sight, compromises the act of reading. Readers, even editors, have been affected. The opacity of Joyce's vision makes the particular density of *Ulysses.*

The consequences of Joyce's visual limitations to the text are real, although difficult to measure. It cannot be ascertained how restricted his vision was, how he saw or failed to see when working; yet there are indications of his methods in his remarks or those of his friends that suggest that he saw small elements and that he magnified words so that they became separate and discrete, even truncated, with their least parts, the letters, foregrounded to him. The consequences of this foregrounding are significant. Letters become magnified both in size and in importance. A text unstable in its smallest elements, those letters usually taken for granted, is made denser in uncertainty and obscurity as language is destabilized in its foundation. The effect on the reader of the text thus disrupted is great: reading is made discontinuous and fragmented at the level of the merest elements—and this in a text that is held to depict realistically and densely a world of verifiable order—so that the limits of Joyce's own vision are replicated, making any and all readers empathetic with and symptomatic of his handicap.

In November 1921, Joyce writes to Harriet Shaw Weaver about the first edition of *Ulysses:* "[I must] hold on till all the proofs are revised. I am extremely irritated by all those printer's errors. Working as I do amid piles of notes. . . . I cannot possibly do this mechanical part with my wretched eye and a half" (*Letters* 1:176). This letter seems to be one of many Joyce wrote to Weaver, plaintive and pathetic, yet it brings some particular notions to the fore. It shows that even after the publication of *Ulysses,* Joyce was concerned with the details of the text, in which printer's errors at that late stage must have been only minutiae of a lexical sort, their correction "mechanical." After the book was in print, Joyce still sought to set right its smallest elements, not the sorts of additions or complications that characterized his other efforts, but mere corrections. He had done such correction in the earlier stages of printing, those of the placard and page proof; he was also frequently correcting simple features of print—noting bad font, widow lines—those smallest and most superficial elements on the page. In this letter to Weaver, Joyce acknowledges, with his desire for correction, the presence of errors, and his illness seemed to insure that such errors would persist. Joyce would want his text free of unintentional errors so that he would have it filled with intentional ones.[1] If the printer's errors were ones of omission, there are also errors of commission; and the former should not get in the way of the latter, should not keep the reader from being confused and handicapped by those errors created by the artist.

Yet, as the letter suggests, the presence and persistence of error, intentional or not, in Joyce's text are connected with Joyce's eye problems. He called his debilitating episodes of inflammation "attacks," as if to suggest a plot against his artistic efforts, assaults on his creativity and his person; and Joyce was always eager to believe in plots. The two, text and illness, are cathected: it is no coincidence that Joyce uses the verb "irritated" to describe his response to the inability to correct; it seems to echo the cause of that inability, his iritis. At every stage in its long progress, from conception through composition to completion, the making of *Ulysses* was clouded with episodes of eye attacks: its history is parallel to Joyce's pathology. While the *Wake* is acknowledged as a book of the dark of Joyce's near-blindness,

Ulysses should be seen as the book of his impaired and compromised vision. From the first attack, while Joyce was beginning the whole enterprise in 1917, to a crisis while he was writing "Circe" and proofreading the last pages of the final chapters in 1921, illness and art went apace.

It is this fact that highlights the particularity of *Ulysses*. It is an aspect given full play in the night of *Finnegans Wake*,[2] but it is not considered a factor in the book of a Dublin day. Despite incapacitating illness, when the eye attacks were so severe that Joyce was not only blinded but had to be immobilized, Joyce by himself saw *Ulysses* through writing, revising, and correction. *Ulysses* is unlike the earlier works, which Joyce wrote when his sight was only myopic, not imperiled, and which he did not take through excessive revisions and stages of proofreading. *Ulysses* further is also unlike the *Wake*, even though the strain on Joyce's eyes during its creation plays a role similar in kind if not in degree: the last work was sometimes dictated to others, and proofread in parts by Stuart Gilbert and Paul León;[3] and it is clearly a book dominated by the dynamics of the dark as well as by the complexity of symbol and sound. *Ulysses* is unique: it is a book of the day, about a world observed and observing; and it is at the intersection of the rising complexity of Joyce's writing and the diminishing powers of his vision, a tension that needs fuller consideration. While written with compromised vision, it is a book that presents exact descriptions of the observed empirical world. The many sharp details in it are achieved with vision that was blurred and limited; the text appears clear, but close scrutiny uncovers many opaque elements. Like the conflict between Joyce's wish to have a text with intentional errors yet also a text that had unintended ones, *Ulysses* stands at the spot between stability and instability, deception and clarity, depiction and erasure.[4] It is a text that unsettles the reader insofar as it is more confused and complex than the earlier works, yet it still retains a view of the material external world (rather than the collapsed interiority of the *Wake*). It is a site where the text is unraveled as the eye becomes unfocused. The reader, trying to see, may be irritated by the text, may be challenged in ways similar to those in which Joyce's sight was disrupted. *Ulysses* seems out of focus in small ways—not the entire text, nor whole pages, but rather in sections and small places where those errors in printing are often made, the small places of single letters. The opacity of *Ulysses* is found in unexpected sights and unexpected sites.

This is the unexplored connection between the particular complexity of

Ulysses and the fact of Joyce's illness; and it is more than an analogy. Joyce himself made the connection: he writes again to Weaver with a history of the complications of his eye troubles, such as operations and unsuccessful remedies, to say the issue of iritis "is almost as complicated as *Ulysses*" (*Letters* 1:201). The famous photographs taken in Paris after 1924 by Gisèle Freund have imprinted on the mind's eye the image of a bespectacled Joyce with eye patch and opaque lens: it is a picture of a man with impaired sight using prosthetic devices, a picture that presents to the viewer a visage as hard to read as the texts he wrote.

From Zurich in the early years of the composition of *Ulysses,* Frank Budgen described Joyce as a creator with impaired sight. Budgen noted in 1919 that Joyce's "method of making a multitude of criss-cross notes in pencil was a strange one for a man whose sight was never good. A necessary adjunct to the method was a huge oblong magnifying glass."[5] This magnifying loupe made small parts of the large work leap out from the page, increasing their size and the difficulty of going over them.

Joyce needed to undergo an iridectomy in August 1919. Budgen remarks that when he first met Joyce, "he had undergone the first of his ten operations"; and he describes an exchange with him about some of the pencil notes Joyce had made. When Budgen complained that he couldn't read "one complete word" on the notepaper, as "there [were] about a dozen words written in all directions, up, down and across," Joyce offered him the glass and said, "A few letters will do if you can't read a whole word." Thus in the very act of notation and that of composition Joyce saw words in any order, separated into discrete yet confused elements, and was satisfied (by necessity) with a part standing in for a whole, a fragmentation and substitution in which vision and then meaning are decentered. Much as Joyce must have seen those jottings, Budgen as reader was forced to adumbrate a word from what parts of it could be seen, by guesswork and magnification. Budgen goes on to describe his attempt to read with Joyce's glass, making him participate in the process, a fellow sufferer: "But [the glass] magnified also the pencil smudges and made the labyrinth of pencilled lines bigger but not clearer, so I had to give it up after sighting and reporting several foggy shapes of letters which, however, were sufficient to give him his bearings."[6] Joyce would have to be satisfied with parts, reading imperfectly; the "foggy shapes" Budgen saw only reproduced what and how Joyce read, fogginess as a symptom of iritis and glaucomatous vision.

The date of this account corresponds to *Ulysses* at its earliest stages, and it demonstrates how the text is compromised by Joyce's sight in particular ways. First, the note taking, a fundamental feature of Joyce's mode of composition, is in its nature a fragmentation and abbreviation. Joyce's myopia would influence his tendency to see primarily small parts; iritis would blur, obscure, and make opaque the whole visual field; and glaucoma would limit his sight by narrowing that field of vision. Joyce saw all things written, even his own handwriting or works in print, as familiar yet unclear: they would be separate, discontinuous, limited; they would be broken into parts, the smallest elements foregrounded and magnified into blurred prominence. Parts would be missed, blocked out, unseen; intuition and guesswork would read out even a word, as well as a phrase or line. (Joyce's choice of notes and notebooks as a method of abbreviation may have been due less to his need for speed and concision than to his wish to assemble small units that would be more easily recognizable by limited vision.) Discontinuity, irritation, imprecision, deception, incompleteness are all equally the symptoms of his illness and the features attendant on the creation of his text; they are also the features of his or anyone's reading of it. Any small portion of a text must be given minute scrutiny; reading it requires a slow and deliberate pace, going carefully up and over each letter. Such an attempt to focus on and traverse every letter accounts for the insistence and prominence of the graphemic quality of *Ulysses,* although the work is heavily laden with the echoes of voice. By *Finnegans Wake* the darkness of Joyce's sight and the night within the text will allow the phonemic to take equal place in the reader's response. The still essential nature of what is on the page and the disruption of the smallest elements of language, fragmented and blurred, also contribute to placing *Ulysses* uniquely at the juncture of Joyce's work. When Joyce seeks to put the language to sleep in *Finnegans Wake,*[7] he has done so because he has shut his eyes. Joyce's impairment and the devices to remedy it, the frosted lens and the magnifying glass, brought him actually face to face with the letters on the page of his own composition; holding his face right up to his text, he was literally confronted with the literal. Joyce's handicap brought him right up against that of language itself.

The difficulties and severities of Joyce's illness should not be diminished, even if they have not been stressed as an essential part of the texture of *Ulysses;* vision always compromised as myopic, frequently totally useless, often impaired, would be an acute trial for someone not a writer. Yet the uses of adversity can be fortuitous, if not sweet. Joyce's illness throughout the work on *Ulysses* made him read physically so as to be aware of the inchoate and deceptive nature of all language. Its obscurity matched that of his own sight. Not only would he know the opacity of a text and of language, but most particularly he would be aware of the instability and density of the smallest sign of language, the letter itself. As he could see only shapes and shadows and parts, as Budgen described, he could not help but deconstruct language at its foundation as he tried both to write and to read it. Joyce's handicap made him a poststructuralist as both reader and writer. The opacity of language was met and exceeded by the opacity of his sight as he tried to read letters one by one.[8]

Yet here arises another paradox for which *Ulysses* serves uniquely as a point of focus. Even as it is written and read with a sense of the limit and disruption of the smallest and most unstable part of language, it is written to depict accurately and fully a world to be observed, filled with characters who do the observing, a world where the objects encountered have a materiality that evokes the features of classical epistemology. Materiality as Aristotle described it and the empiricism consequent to a materialist view are issues at odds with compromised eyesight and deconstructed language, yet they were issues congenial to Joyce. While destabilizing the language of the text—indeed having the language of the text destabilized for him by his vision—Joyce still sought to depict in detail the world of stable material, physical objects (just as, despite his handicap, Joyce sought to live and write in that world).

This conjunction of poststructuralist practice of language (if forced upon Joyce by his disability) and a classical set of assumptions about the material world—that is, the combination of the language of the text and the text's depiction of the reality of Dublin—is another unique space in *Ulysses* where two different lines meet. As with the other conjunctions described above, such as that of *Ulysses* at the point of increasing verbal density yet decreasing authorial eyesight or that between unintentional errors and intended ones, it is a space rich with depth and possibility. With all its converging issues, it is a stereoptic space, one formed by the multiple lines of sight. And into that space between author and text, between the language of the work and what it seeks to describe, and quite actually between the pages of the book, the reader peers, engaging all these lines of sight. For, while on those pages of the book the destabilized language is presented fragmented and opaque, yet the pages themselves and the dark imprint on them are conspicuously material objects for the reader to confront, literally, with a face close to the page. The reader's experience of the text and the world within it is wholly and primarily visual. As Stephen says of the world on Sandymount Strand, a world he claims exists even when he does not look at it, the page is what "you damn well have to see." Joyce disrupts the surface of the text and the process of reading so that the reader's vision is disrupted. Thus the reader of *Ulysses* confronts the pages in print in much the same way as Joyce wrote and saw them, with a sense of the foregrounding of parts of words, with the looming up of enlarged fragments. The reader is thwarted in reading, facing a text that is obscure and opaque on its very surface, the reading eye moving slowly and unsurely, peering at smallest differences. If the book is a world, then the reader must move through it as Joyce did in the real world, interruptedly, in obscurity, with magnification. If Joyce's iritis made him write a text with difficulty and with impediment, producing a text that was unstable in its errors intended and those not, that text in its turn makes the reader affected by that illness, and symptomatic. Much like Budgen, who tried to read Joyce's notes with that magnifying glass yet found himself peering and seeing unclearly as Joyce always did and thus became briefly complicit with Joyce's handicap, so the reader is infected by the text into irritation.

The process of competent reading has always been thought to be a smooth and progressive activity, but certainly a text as dense and complex even at the thematic level as *Ulysses* is one that does not subscribe to easy lection. Moreover, as will be described in the next chapter, Joyce further challenges reading at its most fundamental level, the way in which words are processed, so that even the least part of the reading endeavor is unsure. The discontinuity of Joyce's vision makes a discontinuous text, one that becomes, with its parts opaque and obscure, nearly unreadable.

The symptoms of the reader's view of the text might be described by analogy to another clinical impairment that would answer to Joyce's illness. Joyce's illness was physical; the reader's has no such basis. The reader's handicap lies in the processing of the text. The text evokes all the responses suggested by the notion of irritation: a stirring up, a provoking, an excitation, an annoyance, and a vexation. All these terms could, and indeed have, been used to describe both *Ulysses* itself and the reading of it. Yet this study wishes to focus on the fact that the text of *Ulysses* is so vexing precisely in ways that unsettle the eye. The reader always reads haltingly, stopped frequently by the confusion of discourses, the question of who speaks or what is described. Pauses must be made for reflection and orientation in a slow pace of reading, and the words "reflection" and "orientation" show their origin in visual activity. Simple words often arrest attention—some unfamiliar, such as the "felly" of a wheel (6.490); some newly minted by elision, such as "cuffedge" (1.106).[9] Yet it is not the semantic level nor even the thematic level that is the source of such interruptions and vexations in the reader's sight; the smallest elements of the large work are particularly obscured and oblique. The very slight clues of letters that give normal reading its impetus to move the eye ahead by leaps across words and lines are vexed and changed by Joyce. And as his myopia and magnifying glass made him see letters as separate and highlighted or his iritis failed to let him see some at all, so his text thrusts letters into prominence or obscures them for the reader. The single stroke in print of the letter *l* comes to mind despite its thin presence on the page: the confusion of "world" and "word" and the misprint of "L. Boom" for Bloom, confusions that draw upon the central tension of language and representation, are brought into focus by a simple letter. The examples involving this letter are obvious, entered into the thematics of the novel, but there are many other letters making words of questionable meaning, small differences that provoke the reader in the processing of the lines on the page. All errors within the text are only shadows of errors possible through the reading of the text. Once it is vexed and irritated by such details, the eye is always cautious and suspicious, reading ever more slowly, seeing words separately and letters discretely, so that letters and disrupted words untie and unite the surface and the substance. (An irritated eye would begin to notice that "unite" and "untie" in this previous sentence are anagrams.)

As an introduction to this disruption of letters in the reader's processing of the text, an instability of a lexical sort to go along with even as it precedes those instabilities both metatextual and thematized long recognized as part of *Ulysses,* another kind of introduction should be scrutinized with Joyce's magnified myopia and opaque iritis. Any reader, beginning the novel for whatever time, is struck by the Latin phrase in the fifth line, "*Introibo ad altare Dei*" (1.5). No matter how familiar with the metatextual facts of the Mass (a familiarity now waning), no matter how conversant with the thematics of Mulligan's joking and his parodic Black Mass in "Circe," each and every reader must be struck in a visual way by the phrase as it stands out prominently on the page: the foreign language makes evident the alterity of language, and the italics in particular underscore as alien the material aspect of print on the page. The setting off of the line by the dash that Joyce characteristically used to indicate dialogue is a further visual mark; when he argued with Grant Richards for the dash in the printing of *Dubliners,* Joyce claimed that inverted commas were "an eyesore," a rather prophetic phrase, and one that asserts the effect of print on the reader. Later in "Circe" when the Mass is parodied, the connection of these scenes is reinforced by something also visual: because a Black Mass is an inversion as well as a perversion, Mulligan speaks another invocation: first, one inverted in value—"Introibo ad altare diaboli"—and then one that is in English but further disrupted by being printed backwards: "Htengier... Dog Drol Eht" (15.4708). Thus the two scenes are mirrored to the eye in a way that especially involves the sight of language on the page, its status purely as signs of letters, foreign, highlighted, and inverted.

Yet there is more along these lines of the disruption of letters. The text describes Stephen entering Nighttown chanting "*the* introit *for paschal time*": "*Vidi aquam egredientem de templo a latere dextro*" (15.74, 77). The word "introit" visually echoes the opening of the novel: it is a substitution. Indeed, the word "introit" is the definition of the introductory part of the liturgy in which the priest speaks in the first-person-future tense, "introibo." At Easter the usual introduction that Mulligan speaks is replaced by the one Stephen intones. Church ritual and grammar both unite these passages, where the reader is aided by metatextual information. Yet substitution and transformation are part of the irritated and irritating nature of Joyce's words printed on the page. While "Telemachus" has *introibo* italicized, "Circe," with its particular formal aspects, has "introit" in Roman with the surrounding text in italics. The mirrored inversion between the opening of the novel and the fifteenth chapter is reinforced in a way that is primarily visual. The reader's eye is forced to confront this near-similarity even as memory may unite the different contexts: the sight of different sites of the material on the page is put to some vexation and disturbance.

However, the passage with Stephen intoning the "introit" continues to vex the eye. What Stephen chants immediately following the italicized "stage directions" (the substitution for the usual "*introibo ad altare Dei*") adds to the disruption of letters, causing the eye to read slowly, unsurely, and magnify letters that would otherwise go by unimpeded: "*Vidi aquam egredientem de templo a latere dextro.*" The first word here acts as a signal that sight is to be affected, and a particular portion of this whole sentence seems disturbingly similar to the reader's uncertain eye. It seems itself to make a substitution and a transformation of the opening of the novel, even as the phrase substitutes in the liturgy for the one Mulligan speaks. The sentence maintains the alien quality of language set in italics and further inverts the letters from "Telemachus" from *ad altare* to *a latere* (and as the initial part of *dextra* seems mirrored in *Dei*), from *ad altare De*i to *a latere de*xtro. Where the first chapter has "ad," "Circe" has "a"; though the prepositions are antonyms, their visual similarity is asserted, and a gap appears with the lack of the *d,* a sort of obscure spot in vision like that caused by iritis. Moreover, when once challenged in stability, being disrupted and fragmented, several other letters begin to be less clear, defamiliarized to the eye and subject to slippage. The *d* of *ad altare* by inversion seems to reflect unclearly the *b* in *Introibo;* the *q* in *aquam* mirrors the *g* in *egredientem*. Once subject to a myopic scrutiny in a mistrustful pace of reading, the text, which has already thematized substitution, irritatingly begins to become blurred and obscure. The disposition of letters is transported and repositioned over several hundred pages of text; reading at either site is halted and challenged. Rather than merely processing the lines and reading past the words, the reader is forced into pausing; the sight of the text is unsure: *latere* is nearly an anagram of *altare*. Yet in the fact that it is not an anagram lies the vexation; the resemblance is close but not total, reflecting a puzzling incompleteness and unreadability, if one understands the purpose of reading as to make meaning and similitude and not to find small difference.

There is, of course, something of a puzzle in an example like this. Both the passages are first puzzles regarding material extrinsic to the text, the liturgy of the Latin Mass, and next puzzles regarding material within the text, the thematics that connect chapters. But at the most fundamental level, their puzzles are ones of the material intrinsic to the status of the text, that of the letters that make it up. Such a connection between "*Introibo ad altare Dei*" and "*Vidi aquam egredientem de templo a latere dextro*" seems mere ludic play of the anagram, of the sort enshrined continually in *Finnegans Wake* but somehow not so elevated in *Ulysses.* Yet such near similarities and vexing inversions are crucial to *Ulysses,* more crucial because they do not occur in nearly every word, as in the *Wake,* but often enough, if unrecognized, to disrupt reading;[10] and such opacities and blurrings of words are crucial to Joyce, as the play of letters is backed by the pain of his eyesight. To him the lexical connection of the two phrases was evident because of his disability and his myopia and because of the agency of the palliatives used to remedy them, the opaque lens and the magnifying glass.

An anagram, moreover, like the mirror-imaged letters *d* and *g,* is a turning of letters that suggests a revolutionary disruption, one fundamental to every glance at the text and to the very status of the text, one that undermines the smallest element and thus, inescapably, the whole. The revolution of Joyce's word may well start and end with the letters he saw and wrote unclearly.[11]

Such a revolution, filled with instability and inversion, challenges not only meaning but authority. Because of the opacity and deception of letters, even the authority of editorial decision is undermined by uncertainty when it seeks to choose a reading. To an uncertain (and suspicious) eye, the letters *g* and *d* have a deceptive similarity, and two words made from their slight difference are "goner" and "doner." They constitute the crux of an editorial decision (and an editor is a reader who is also uncertain about letters, and whose "reading" in turn affects all subsequent readers). The Random House editions (1934, 1961) have "One whiff of that and you're a goner" (102 [1934], 104 [1961]); the Rosenbach manuscript has, in Joyce's hand, "one whiff . . . and you're a doner."[12] The Gabler edition restores the earlier reading on the grounds of the manuscript (6.612), yet the hierarchy of texts may be less at stake than the anarchy and the literal "revolution" of the letter in space. Thus if Joyce is to transform and reform letters in the text, disrupting the surface and the reading of it, the very status of authority is questioned, and the very limit of what could be right or wrong, written and read, is obscured. The presence of either "you're a goner" (RH 102 [1934], 104 [1961]) or "you're a doner" (6.612) cannot be considered as a matter of error when the features of disruption are prominent. Thus no amount of careful consultation of typescripts or editions could ever provide a stable text because that text is subject to flux and uncertainty at the smallest level of the letters in every word in it.

Meaning is thus dislocated on the page particularly within the simple letters in the line; the normal processes of reading are disrupted; and the presence of obscured and deceptive letters causes a dis-lection that runs through the entire work, both adding to and undermining it.[13] Indeed, it is from the very primacy of the smallest sight cues of letters, essential and opaque, that all of the disruptive incompleteness of *Ulysses* is derived. The reader can glimpse hermeneutic gaps only after reading over those lapses and lacunae within the words on the page.[14] Interpretative confusions come only after visual ones. *Ulysses* may, as critics claim, teach us to read it, but it also teaches us to unread. If the text of *Ulysses* is unreadable, it is so first because each word resists being easily read.

This essential importance of letters themselves, disruptively appearing and disappearing on the page, goes unrecognized in current critical readings, even as it underlies them. It is the poststructuralist notion of language that allows the recognition of the disfunctional features of words, but rather than attribute the disjunction to the function of discourse, such disfunction should be seen as more basic because it belongs to the enterprise of the letter itself. The burden of language's opacity, its *différance*, is borne by the letter and not the sign. Cultural studies, which discuss texts likely seen by author and character in order to consider the ways those texts are dialogically engaged, overlook the fact that any text, from canonical to popular, is recalled precisely in quality as printed, visible lexical material—that is, cultural artifacts are included in a work as much for their visual artifactness as for their cultural value—and all texts read and seen are subject to limitations of vision.[15] Similarly, reader response criticism and studies of style are concerned with the reaction of the reader to parts of the text or other models of language but neglect the essential fact that any reading of Joyce is hindered by the surface he is at pains both to highlight and to obscure.[16] That is, poststructuralist analysis, reader response, stylistic, and cultural criticism all are about what is seen and read but neglect the fact that what is seen and read is itself reducible—and reduced by Joyce—to the most literal, the irritated letters, obscure and opaque, at the lexical level.

It is in this destabilized myopic level of letters that the very vexing, if unnoticed, confusion of such letters as *b* and *d, q* and *g* become highlighted, as the eye, once irritated by the text, becomes increasingly unsure. So Joyce's disability creates a text to be read similarly in the disruption of its letters: the lection of *Ulysses* is impeded by dis-lection. The reader becomes complicit and symptomatic with Joyce's iritis, irritated and vexed into reading a text unstable and unclear in its smallest elements. Joyce's disability lay in the production of letters, disparate and obscure; the reader's difficulty lies in the processing of the letters, magnified and opaque. Joyce's iritis makes for an irritated text; the reader, irritated by those lexical features, is confronted with a sort of Joyce-induced dis-lexia, a way of trying to read the text by misseeing and misreading the words on the page. The reader experiences almost clinical problems such as confusions of letters, their inversion in different axes, a general distrust of what is to be seen. It is through this dis-lexia, the unsure and incorrect glimpse of words and their parts, that the reader is made complicit and symptomatic with Joyce's eye troubles.

It is not even polysemy that defeats unitary meaning; it is polylexy. The surface of the *Ulyssean* page is unstable, not immediately as a *Wakean* one, but when close scrutiny is applied to what appears insidiously transparent; uncertainty stalks the very letters. There is not only "dislocution" in *Ulysses,* as Fritz Senn calls it, a disruption of the space of the text (location) and the discourse of it (locution);[17] there is also a disfunction in its most basic part, the lexical one.[18]

Forced by an obscuring of what is seen on the page into the metaphoric effect of a disability in reading, the reader will be prone to errors and unclarity. The reader must be more than a restitutor of the meaning of the text, the lector as rector;[19] the reader can only with suspicion and extreme difficulty make connections, and these will be undermined with inaccuracies. If the ideal reader for the *Wake* is an insomniac, the ideal reader for *Ulysses* is handicapped. Such errors are the very ones Joyce would wish to keep in his text to make the reader a fellow sufferer. Thus it is clear why Joyce complained to Weaver in that letter of November after the publication of *Ulysses* about the printer's errors he wished to correct. The book published was out in the world for all to read; printers' errors would not do, as they were only "mechanical," not artistic, not intentional, not symptomatic. It is the tyranny of the body that the very illness Joyce would exploit to destabilize his text in an intentional way would also keep him from correcting the unintended errors. Errors in words and letters might be portals of discovery for the reader of *Ulysses,* but they have to be made by the artist, not artisan printers, and they have to speak for the artist's suffering; and that for Joyce meant not only exile and putative penury but the "wretched eye and a half" of his illness.

The status of error here separates *Ulysses* from the other texts of Joyce, again making it a pivotal point of vision. A single letter, missed or repositioned, precludes error in the earlier texts. All their letters must be stable. For example, it matters to the plot and its denouement in "The Dead" whether Gabriel or Gretta asks the bottle maker at the furnace whether the fire is hot: the earlier versions have "he called out to the man"; the corrected Dublin holograph, "she called..."[20] Error is not possible in *Finnegans Wake*, where all meanings are potential. When Wayne Booth queried exacerbatedly why the text should read differently "Brimgem young, bringem young, bringem young,"[21] he asked for a certainty that the *Wake* never would offer. The fact that *altare* and *latere* are near anagrams is enough in *Ulysses;* the space of not limiting the possibilities is necessary for obscurity. Yet individual letters in *Ulysses* do not have the weight or symbolic resonance that they do in *Finnegans Wake*, as sometimes representing sigla or symbolizing concepts such as the *chi rho*, indicating a particular error such as Piggot's forgery, or marking large oral changes in language. Such Wakean confusions of the letters *p* and *k* or *l* and *r* are part of the complexity of the text, being enshrined and long recognized by criticism.[22] Yet these pairs are substitutions with a historical oral component that further sets the later text apart from the earlier. A phrase such as "pristopher polombos" (*Wake* 120.02) is readily converted because of the oral feature of the change; by contrast the substitutions of letters in *Ulysses* such as *t* and *b* (in *introit* and *introibo*) are primarily graphemic in function, being vaguely similar to sight (in a spatial axis). Joyce put the language to sleep after *Ulysses* because he wished to shut its eyes to the visual function of language;[23] limitless ideas and sounds can come through dream vision. The instability of *Ulysses* is an obscurity that is held in tension by sight made imperfect and confused. That instability continues outward to the sight of the text and sights depicted within it: the letters of the text are to be seen, but not fully; in focus, but with blurred parts; clear, but magnified and discrete, as Joyce saw with his iritis, to make an irritated text.

CHAPTER 2

Illness and the Magnification of Letters

Joyce's eyesight was a constant liability in his life. From the incident at Clongowes of the breaking of his spectacles, substantiated in biography if fictionalized in *Portrait*,[1] it is evident that he could only peer unaided at writing close-up, and even then what he saw was compromised: "He had tried to spell out the headline for himself though he knew already what it was.... But the lines of the letters were like fine invisible threads and it was only by closing his right eye tight tight and staring out of the left eye that he could make out the full curves of the capital" (46). The autobiographical connections between Joyce and Stephen are tenuous, yet the issue of weak eyesight is indeed one element that they shared. Ellmann notes that Joyce, while needing glasses, did not wear any during his Belvedere and University College days, with the result that his nearsightedness became part of his personality, although Ellmann's explanation seems to make vanity the cause rather than the more likely penury.[2] Joyce's first date with Nora, set for June 15, 1904, was threatened by his weak sight, so the date commemorated by the physical text of *Ulysses* comes about delayed by difficulty: "I may be blind. I looked for a long time at a head of reddish-brown hair and decided it was not yours. I went home quite dejected" (*Letters* 2:42). Absence and blankness obscure his vision even of the desired object. Joyce was always aware that he could not see well and aware that he missed seeing certain things.

Not coincidentally, Joyce began to wear eyeglasses again at the time he began writing fully and productively. When in "Circe" Stephen makes reference to his lost glasses, Joyce draws an autobiographical chronology: "Must get glasses. Broke them, yesterday. Sixteen years ago. . . . Ineluctable modality of the visible" (15.3628–31). Various issues are embedded in this comment, certainly in the phrase "ineluctable modality of the visible," coming from someone as myopic as Stephen (who at Bella's cannot bring the match to the cigarette under his nose); but there is also a series of wry jokes in Stephen's reference to sixteen years. For June 16, 1904, the date of the scene, there is the missed glimpse of Nora. From 1904, sixteen years back yields 1888—debatably, given Joyce's changing of the chronology of the *Portrait,* the time of Stephen's spring term at Clongowes, the scene that describes Joyce's distorted view of the letters of his own writing seen up close. Sixteen years back from the date of the writing of "Circe" in 1921 yields 1905, the date John Lyons gives as the time Joyce began wearing glasses.[3] Thus writing, biography, and optics are connected.

The composition of all but the three initial stories of the *Dubliners* follows in rapid succession from the year 1905, as though the remediation of his vision enabled Joyce to work. Of his weakened eyes, he writes to Stanislaus from Trieste, "I was examined by a doctor of the Naval Hospital here last week and I now wear pince-nez glasses on a string for reading. My number is very strong—could you find out what is Pappie's."[4] This interest in the strength of his prescription seems to be a sort of Oedipal competition with the father and a nod to biological necessity (the "man with my eyes" as Stephen puts it in "Proteus"), but certainly that notion of "strength" describes the necessary degree of magnification that enabled him to write; what remedied Joyce's vision at the outset of his career would bring the written word more immediately and larger to his sight.

Yet Joyce's eyesight was to be handicapped and limited even further by illness. What myopia required enlarged, iritis and resultant glaucoma would blur and restrict. Iritis is a painful viral inflammation of the colored part of the eye (in Joyce's case, the left) that causes blurred vision. During an episode the pain is so severe as to affect both eyes and cause incapacitation, necessitating immobility, usually in a completely darkened room. The effects of such attacks are cumulative, causing a progressive blurring due to secondary glaucomatous scarring, making the lens opaque; the result is a restricted and clouded field of vision and a diminished discernment of light and dark.

Joyce's first attack of iritis occurred in Trieste as early as 1907, and he attributed it at the time to his having spent the night inebriated on the damp pavement.[5] Rheumatism was a likely cause; another possible cause was syphilis.[6] The second attack, somewhat ironically, arose in 1909 while Joyce was in Dublin for the second of his visits having to do with the establishment of the Volta cinema. There was another attack in 1915 in Zurich, after Joyce had completed *Portrait*, that Ezra Pound, now sponsoring Joyce, noted "incapacitated him for work for three or four weeks."[7]

The composition of *Ulysses* in all of its stages was clouded for Joyce by occurrences of such eye attacks, so much so that one might consider both the art and the pathology to be related. Not a part of the composition or correction of the text was unaffected. Between the years 1917 and 1922 Joyce suffered episodes at strikingly regular intervals of at least once a year, twice in the first year he was at work on *Ulysses*. Indeed, the attacks seemed to cluster around the completion of several chapters, as if the effort of working were the cause (a fanciful diagnosis Joyce himself held). The effort of writing *Ulysses* was measured on the body by the twisting effects of the illness; the somatics were turned into signs. Recovering from an episode, Joyce described himself tortured by pain, though less so than earlier: "I am now more like a capital S than a capital Z."[8] It is worth noting that the only letter Stephen could make out without his glasses in *Portrait* was a *Z*: the title of the essay he was to write was *Zeal without prudence is like a ship adrift* (46).

Ominously for a man given to superstition, an attack occurred in January 1917 at the onset of Joyce's work on *Ulysses*.[9] Gorman remarks as an understatement that "he worked [on *Ulysses*] under difficulties."[10] Of this attack, Joyce wrote to Miss Weaver, "I have no pain but the consequences this time seem rather serious—but I hope always that an operation may be avoided. I can read and write however and am continuing my book at the usual snail's pace."[11] It is precisely the snail's pace that might have triggered an attack, yet it is also the pace at which letters can be seen up close. At this stage, the work on the book included much of the composition of "Telemachus" (which was to be completed and sent to Claud Sykes in November)[12] as well as attendant note taking. It was this method of taking notes that Budgen noted "was a strange one for a man whose sight was never any good," adding that the "adjunct to the method was a huge oblong magnifying glass."[13] This magnifying loupe made just such small parts of the large work leap out from the page, further increasing the size and presence of the written letters beyond what Joyce's prescription for myopia had done. The size also accounts for his snail's pace in reading. Joyce's will to work was strong, but his hope of avoiding an operation was futile; he needed to undergo an iridectomy in August of that year, 1919. Budgen remarks that when he first met Joyce, "he had undergone the first of his ten operations." It was then that Budgen complained that he couldn't read "one complete word" on the notepaper, as "there [were] about a dozen words written in all directions, up, down and across," and Joyce offered him the glass, saying, "A few letters will do if you can't read a whole word." What is most pertinent here is that in the act of notation and likely that of even the initial composition of *Ulysses,* Joyce was writing by seeing words highly foregrounded in size and displaced in space, viewing separated letters as discrete yet confused elements—a discontinuity that matched the opacity and blurring of his vision, an absence into which meaning is projected.[14] A word was adumbrated from the parts of it that could be seen; guesswork and magnification produced the material of the written text. As Budgen said, the glass only "magnified also the pencil smudges and made the labyrinth of pencilled lines bigger but not clearer, so I had to give up after sighting and reporting several foggy shapes of letters which, however, were sufficient to give him his bearings." Joyce could see only parts, reading imperfectly the shapes of words made foggy by his blurring glaucoma. Limited in sight, he had to be content with all that must be glimpsed or guessed at, the blind spots that make the opacity of language most evident and magnified.

Joyce's writing and illness continued apace. In June 1918 he informed his agent Pinker, "I have been laid up again with my eyes" (this was during his work on "Hades");[15] in February 1919, to Mlle. Guillermet, "I have been ill again with my eyes for the sixth time"[16] (while he was writing "Scylla" and "Wandering Rocks"). As if to add insult to injury and to reinforce the importance of the visual to a man who sensed its aesthetic importance and felt its physical impact, during 1918 and 1919 Joyce lived at 38 Universitaetstrasse, a building that had an optometrist as a tenant in one of its streetfront stores; a picture shows signs reading "Augen Optik" and "Brillen" large enough to have been visible to Joyce each time he returned home.[17] The *Joyce Archive* reproduces a notebook of Joyce's whose cover has just this address; this is likely to be the notebook of which Budgen speaks.

The move to Paris, though an impetus to his art, accelerated Joyce's attacks of iritis; while the climate in Zurich was often unfavorable to his condition, that of the colder and damper French city was worse. Soon after his arrival in 1920, he had yet another attack, this one while working on "Oxen" and "Circe." He also succumbed in September 1921, writing to Larbaud that he was "nearly dead with work and eyes."[18] He claimed that Circe, on which he was writing, was seeking her revenge, but it should be noted that he was reading final page proofs, under the pressure of time, as well. Lucia Joyce's eyesight, too, became increasingly complicated at this time by an aggravated strabismus, a fact that would add to Joyce's sense of the difficulty of seeing in general and make him further aware of another problem in particular, that of a doubled or crossed image.

Certainly as early as 1917, then, Joyce was aware of the image that floats between the eye and its object; and for a writer, that object is the page itself. He writes to Harriet Shaw Weaver to note his slow recovery, "In these circumstances I have not been able to do very much with my book *Ulysses:* but I have done what I could."[19] What he could do was confront, magnified and up close, language as an opaque and dense form. So writing and reading were conscious efforts for him. Straining at parts of words with a glass, sitting in a darkened room where the only sight he could see was the image of his own writing in his mind's eye, when he came to write the presences of the words of his novel, he was aware of the fragility of reading (his characters' and his readers') and the visual disfunctions to which it is subject.

Joyce was both forced by his illness as much as disposed by his artistic method to confront right up against his peering eye the particular opacity of words, disrupted into the smallest elements of letters and mere shapes, magnified greatly, discontinuously foregrounded and obscure. Blurring and blind spots only made evident and stressed repeatedly to him the deceptive similarities of letters. And the letters he wrote and read were additionally distorted not only by his handicap but also, further, by the instruments he used to remedy his vision: the spectacles for myopia, the opaque lens for the eye sensitive with iritis, the additional magnifying glass.

It is just such deceptive qualities of letters in their forms magnified and diminished that are tested by the ophthalmological examination for visual acuity, and Joyce had seen many examination charts in his life. Indeed the symptom of his text may be the pathology of his eyes. While there appears to be no set series of letters employed in the charts that are used to test vision, what was established as standard by the Dutch ophthalmologist Herman Snellen is the visual angles of one minute that give the chart its characteristic appearance of letters in proportion, starting at the top with one large letter, followed by the next row of two, then three rows of proportionally smaller letters, and so on.[20] In order to test the acuteness of recognition, Snellen chose "as a unit of comparison the recognition of letters seen at an angle of five minutes." He goes on to describe his test: "We have adopted as proper objects square letters, the limbs of which have a diameter equal to one-fifth of the letter's height. As the limbs and subdivisions of the letters measure one-fifth of their height, they present themselves at an angle of one minute; for instance, our letter *C* shows an opening, as compared to the *O,* of one-minute visual angle. In testing accuracy of vision, we accept perfect recognition and not uncertain perception of letters."[21] Thus what is true of these charts, regardless of some variation in the letters used, is the fact that the letters are repeated throughout the rows and that letters are chosen for the small differences in shape between them; hence the frequent appearance in American and English ophthalmics of such similar letters as *T* and *P, F* and *E* and *Z.* Someone straining at an eye chart (as Joyce most certainly did) would be confronted with an awareness of how letters, when stared at, have deceptively similar shapes, with only the smallest variations in form creating large differences in identity, and as well with an awareness of how some letters are "correct" or "wrong," what Snellen called "perfect recognition and not uncertain perception." Joyce specialized in the uncertainty. Also evident at the examination is the repetition of the possibilities of letters, a repetition of their forms both genuine and imagined, as some letters are repeated and yet some letters only appear to be repeated to eyes that are not "perfect." The eye examination constantly evokes error by the deception of small differences in letter shapes.

So the act of writing, the acts of reading (text and eye chart), and the presence of illness for Joyce concern the issues of what is to be seen in print as similar, discontinuous, present and absent, all within the possibilities of the materiality of letters. Joyce's condition, with his weak eyes and the need for frequent professional consultation, would have borne him unexpected fruit from his pain. Joyce repeatedly experienced the ophthalmologist's techniques: discrete letters, whole lines (and words halved or broken up, letters reversed), images cast by the light of the ophthalmoscope on the eyeball, which in the healthy eye gives a ghostly and mortal reflected image of the blood-filled arteries at the back of the retina on the forward surface of the corneal lens. All these techniques he also made his own as the form of irritation: highlighted letters and figures, words and sentences twisted, broken up, elongated. All *Ulysses* is an eye examination; its disruptive and empty lexical surface is always to be read with uncertain perception.

In his own text Joyce took pains to correct errors where he intended accuracy, those printers' errors about which he complained to Weaver in the letter after the publication of *Ulysses*. Joyce was aware of what could go wrong with letters, so he took care to set his text right. And he did this at a level of the text and in a stage of production less artistic than earlier levels and stages, almost wholly surface—the final page proofs. Here are examples of the meticulous care Joyce took with his work, and this care came at some cost, as he made these kinds of corrections at a time when he was pressed to finish writing the last chapters of the book itself and was further hampered by another attack of iritis of the sort that was always brought on by overwork and excess reading. The proofs are dated "4.xi.21"; Joyce had an attack in September.

Throughout his readings of the earlier chapters, when time was less pressing, Joyce repeatedly marked letters that printed uncleanly or had broken fonts; this is a tedious task for a man of limited vision and a testimony to his concern for the surface as much as the substance. Even at a point in proofing when he was concerned with a substantive addition to the text, adding the name of "Borus Hupinkoff" to a list in "Cyclops" (in a note that has prompted much comment from John Kidd) by means of a card to Darantière's assistant, he adds in a postscript that "the letter 'f' appears to be imperfect often in the type."[22] More interestingly to the point here, Joyce often noted and marked on the same page the bad fonts of letters quite similar in appearance: for example, on one page proof of "Cyclops,"[23] he corrected *h* three times for being imperfectly struck; he corrected one *h* in place of a misread *b* and one *n* for a *u*. The similarity of these letters in appearance shows the scrutiny to which he subjected the very surface of his text, as well as his awareness of the resemblance of several letters to others.

The physical appearance of the type was a material concern. For the creation of the capitalized headings in "Aeolus," Darantière's typecase often lacked sufficient blocks for rare letters repeatedly set; instead, the typesetters would put an empty barred space (=) as a reminder to take other blocks for the letters when they became available. Throughout "Aeolus," Joyce patiently and repeatedly supplied the missing letters in the text. (The printers would again need to place the barred space for letters when longer passages of italics were struck in "Nestor," "Aeolus," or "Circe"; Joyce caught most of the omissions in the first two chapters and some in the last, but by that time he was involved with many other tasks.) Joyce wanted his letters to be seen as standing out on the page, even to the point of indicating that an exclamation point in a headline in "Aeolus" be struck more sharply ("plus fonce"); he noted the same typographical effect and correction ("Imprimez ces lettres . . . plus fonces") in the "Ithaca" depiction of Bloom's kinetic poem whose first letters make up the anagram "POLDY."[24] An anagram, after all, is simply a jumbled version of writing, a disorder of letters like that created for the eye chart to stand out in opacity and magnification. Thus the plasticity of letters, jumbled, discrete, and highlighted, and their deceptive similarities of forms and shapes would come to Joyce as both the effect of his illness and the consequence of his practice: *b, h, n,* and *u* are all similar. He would be aware of the deception inherent in letters, the useful ways in which they could be exploited with the various mistaken possibilities of their forms.

Such possibilities of form are an idea from Aristotle that is present within *Ulysses*. The passage from "Proteus" in which Stephen, walking the beach with eyes open and closed, makes his famous comment "ineluctable modality of the visible" is often cited as a paradigm for the novel; certainly Stephen's comment "thought through my eyes. Signatures of all things I am here to read" (3.1–2) makes this connection evident, as the comment is frequently treated as a metaphor for the act of reading the novel *Ulysses*. Yet attention should be refocused on the passage as a description of the *product* of what is seen as read, "signatures" being the result of the act of writing, and all letters "signs" of what must be seen in order to be thought about. The passage speaks to the sense of language's protean change, not only in diction (as Stephen says, "trudges, schlepps, trains, drags") but particularly in its form as sign. It is a change that Joyce experienced when he tried to read signatures through his weak eyes. All acts of reading inscribed in *Ulysses*—and they are legion—are primarily and foremost acts of seeing what is to be read, seeing an object that is dense in print to think through the eye. What is consequently "ineluctable" for Stephen, the writer, and the reader is the inevitable and necessarily visible component of what is written and read, and written to be read. And more: the operative word in this passage is "modality." Foremost, it describes the variety of what is visible, a fact underscored by Stephen's recognition of both sign and signature. What is seen is to be scanned as meaningful, but what is meaningful and visible can take many forms, especially when distorted by vision. Modalities are the logical possibilities that lie inherent, in the Aristotelian entelechy of form, in the visible signs that are the universe; yet modalities are also the possibilities that more basically lie within the letters on the page, those most visible if overlooked signs in fiction that create the universe of the novel, those twenty-six letters containing the infinitude of word forms, all lying possible within them. Modalities are those deceptive similarities of letters, the small differences in their shapes; they allow the possibility of confusing *h* for *b* or *n* for *u* in the page proofs (as Darantière's printers did and as Joyce corrected). Such modality is the result of Joyce's illness and allows him the opportunity to manipulate what is seen on the page, to change the possibility of letters, to change form and meaning in what is read. Modality is the challenge to the particular act of reading itself. The "modalities of the visible" speak both to the effects of Joyce's illness and to the qualities of his text.

Indeed, when one stands back from the page, a dispassionate glance at *Ulysses* suggests how frequently simple letters are foregrounded in a text of long and large dimensions.[25] Any text that plays on the obvious inversion of *god* and *dog* as in "Proteus" or with the invocation "Drol eht" in "Circe" has put foremost an awareness of the modalities of letters and their disjunction in a text, turning letters backward and forward in possibilities and with purpose. The reader's eye goes to school, for example, in that intentionally misleading chapter "Wandering Rocks," in a description of concurrent action: "[Rode] the honourable Gerald Ward A.D.C. From the window of the D.B.C. Buck Mulligan gaily, and Haines gravely, gazed down" (10.1223–24). The honorific title and the abbreviation for the bakery are genuine details of the novel's verisimilitude, but their magnification makes them prominent and gives them a contiguity that adds an additional meaning (a contiguity enforced to the eye by the grammatic and visual parallel of "gaily/gravely"). Somehow the eye, from long training (scholastic as well as optometric), expects to see A.B.C. from the first phrase,

B and *D* slightly similar in shape. The second abbreviation seems almost right: "D.B.C." Of course, by the end of the pairs the eye does have the elements of the sequence A.B.C.D., even if in disorder (and the eye chart tends to repeat letters in certain patterns of disorder). The reader would want to put things right because the text has clearly irritated his eye; and the text provides the means for him to do so, by the magnification of letters.

Often there is a literal diversion of letters in disarray: the Hely's sandwich men parading through the text play with the order and synchronicity of both the text and the material of the alphabet. At one point all the letters are present with the particular markers of periods to suggest their visual presence and their effect on Bloom's thinking: "H.E.L.Y.S. Wisdom Hely's. Y lagging behind" (8.126). At another time, by way of the part that suggests the whole, as Joyce would grasp while attempting to read, just one board, "apostrophe S had plodded by" (where the marker ['] is reproduced to greater density by the word [8.155]). Further on are two other appearances in an extension of all the letters to form a strained continuity: "H.E.L.Y'S filed before [Boylan]" (10.310); and "H. halted and four tallhatted white flagons halted behind him, E.L.Y'S" (10.1237; Random House 1961 has both appearances as "E.L.Y.'S." [227, 253]). This jumble of letters, familiar to denizens of the streets of Dublin, is a paradigm of the juggling of letters on the page of Joyce's Dublin, and their extension over the space of pages of text suspends, prolongs, and undercuts meaning. Hely's store is unclearly presented by signs that have no intrinsic meaning (why are the letters separated by periods, for example? Bloom notes that the ad "doesn't bring in business"); and their disarray adds additional difficulty in reading.

By writing in the margins of the galley proofs and placards and in the spaces between lines, Joyce makes *Ulysses* one-quarter greater in bulk, in its palpable density, complicating reading by sheer volume. As *Ulysses* is to be seen in print, that print occupies space and weighs upon the reader; volume is a sort of magnification. There are words that call attention to this density of material by the repetition of letters: "wavyavyeavyheavyeavyevyevyhair" (.809), "endlessnessnessness" (.750), "wayawayawayawayaway" (3.404), "Waaaaaaalk" (.25). These words take up space in the text and impress themselves upon the reader as weighty, printed matter; they add letters to letters in an imitative but redundant elongation and extension of the act of reading, as if they themselves were part of an eye chart. They magnify how much is to be looked at.

In a similar manner but to opposite effect, the text offers the density of too much material to the eye so that meaning cannot be extracted from reading. The letters foregrounded on the page begin to be opaque, impenetrably dense. The headlines "K.M.A." and "K.M.R.I.A." in "Aeolus" (7.980, 990) may stand for and deflect Myles Crawford's imperative; they draw attention to the intriguing power of letters and retain some sense of their meaning. Yet the list of the abbreviations of priests' orders and the honorific titles in "Cyclops" may stand in for real institutions, but in their multitude they present all the modalities of the alphabet, too many to make any sense, overwhelmingly adding to the opacity of the text. The eye is distracted as they blur and become indistinct. ("Amongst the clergy present were the very rev. William Delaney, S.J., L.L.D." [12.928] and "sir Hercules Hannibal Habeus Corpus Anderson, K.G., K.P., K.T., . . ." [12.1893]).

The modalities of letters of the alphabet are infinite, as the list of societies and honorifics palpably illustrates, even though they proceed from only twenty-six possible shapes. Take as example the first thing seen within the text of *Ulysses:* "Stately, plump Buck Mulligan came from the stairhead, bearing a bowl of lather on which a mirror and a razor lay crossed" (1.1–2). What is there in it, among a host of other things long noted by critics, what is material and visible, are nearly all the letters of the alphabet: to be precise, twenty-two out of the total, constituting a large majority—nearly 85 percent. Unobtrusively, the first sentence, read closely and at a snail's pace, offers to the eye all of the potential of written language; all the possible forms at the disposal of the writer are on view to the reader. Some are nearly in sequential order "St*a*tely . . . Bu*c*k"; the rest are there, if disordered, even the rare *y,* in "lay," and the *z,* in "razor," both near the end of the sentence as in the alphabet. However, within this presence, certain letters are noticeable by their absence, as if omitted from the line of sight; the missing four are infrequently used ones—*j, q, v,* and *x*. (By contrast, the second sentence of the novel contains just over half of the total letters, sixteen; it shares the same four missing from the first but lacks common letters [*b, c, f, k, p*] and the rare *z*.) Another sentence, chosen by *sortes Joyceannae,* yields similar results; longer sentences, after all, contain many possibilities: "Bare clean closestools waiting in the window of William Miller, plumber, turned back his thoughts" (8.1045). Twenty letters are present here (some making a repeated pattern of similar shapes—*wi*ndow/*Wi*ll*i*am *Mill*er). Along with the same four letters missing here as in the first sentence, the *y* and *z* are absent. Yet even the gaps in the opening sentence of the novel are reconstituted by the text as it moves through its lines; any reading of *Ulysses* is often delayed and disrupted (as with the disjointed and highlighted Hely's men); its linguistic level read as story gives back what was missing from its lexical level as letters. The items described as "crossed" on the mirror in the first sentence give another word for the letter *x* missing from the presented alphabet; it appears out of absence by the magic of the other, present letters put together. Another letter missing from the near-total is the *j*, that presence always and everywhere absent in the text that signs the doubled initials of the author's identity; it is to be found some four lines later on in "jesuit," a meaningful substitution. The two remaining absences, *q* and *v*, appear restituted a few lines later; the discontinuity made by absence in the first sentence is restored by the continuity of reading further toward another site and thus sight in the text. *V* appears by line 10 in the word "gravely," an encrypting and entombing of a sort of absence; that rare *q* comes in by line 15 in the word "equine," which etymologically indicates its classical and hence epic origin.[26] The first appearance of the *x* as a letter is much later, in lines 51 and 53, where it appears in "Saxon" and "Oxford," words of history and power.

History, power, the Mass, all the metalinguistic issues and institutions in the opening of the novel, all its status as a created world, even its institution as text, are to be represented, literally, by the letters on the page. And it is the letters that are a real magnified power in *Ulysses*, letters that are the smallest parts of the world of the novel but enlarged in consequence: they are the very primal matter of the book, in the terms of Aristotle so dear to Joyce, from which the final, if questionable, form of the novel is derived. The letters are small matter that matters: the ongoing debate about the synoptic edition is, after all, finally one that turns on the issues of which letters make which words and where. The initial sentence contains all the matter of the matter of the text fundamental both to its status as text and to the act of reading it, what is to be seen foremost and originary to the meaning of *Ulysses:* which letters are present and which are absent; which hidden and discontinuous ones are made present in a later place or page by the continuity of reading. The first sentence demonstrates all the issues of what is to be *seen* imperfectly and incompletely in the novel.

(The name of the tower, Martello, provides a sidelight on history and power, but as a consequence of the prominence of single letters. According to the *Oxford English Dictionary*, it is an Anglicized version of the placename Mortella in Sicily, where such towers resisted the firepower of the British Navy. Yet the change is more than linguistic imperialism; the transposition of the letters *a* and *o* is a disruptive move, resembling the tests of an eye chart and opening up the possibilities of error.)

The possibility of error in spelling depends on which letters are "right" and which "wrong" in a way that resembles the possibilities on an eye chart. The consequences of mistake are correspondingly large: mistakes of a letter are magnified in consequence. If a change in spelling complicates the process of reading a text by making that text disruptive and disfunctional on the reader's seeing it, causing the eye to substitute "Mortella" for "Martello," misspelling adds even further difficulty, as it produces errors of seeing of another kind. Some, such as Martha's fortuitous error of the dropped *l* of "world" and "word," open up a universe of material: its consequence is magnified as is the individual letter itself. Other errors limit and question. Molly, perhaps self-conscious about her inabilities at diction and orthography, thinks of writing a note: "your sad bereavement sympkathy I always make that mistake and newphew with 2 doubleyous" (18.731–32). Here a reader finds a confusion and proliferation of signs and numbers, "2 doubleyous." Moreover, even as Molly sees in her mind the very corrections of her error, the text obligingly depicts the letters struck but obstinately confuses the eye. To the errors of spelling within the text are added those of printing, highlighting it, too, as a perilous entity. The botched line of type from the *Telegraph* account of Dignam's funeral is the most evident example, the most famous of all the *hommages* in *Ulysses* to both its own existence on the printed page and the inaccuracy of that existence. The obituary notice is reproduced in italics to stand out on the page (16.1248–61): the *l* dropped from Bloom's name looms large to him, even while it creates another character, "L. Boom"; and the passage also awards the nonattending Stephen two letters of academic distinction, "Stephen Dedalus B.A." (Bloom attributes the error in the line to his having called Monks; Darantière's printers, Joyce must have thought, were similarly distracted.) Such errors within the text only reflect the ones that irritated Joyce in the printing of his own text.

Another form of foregrounded letters that have an unstable identity is the italics of foreign phrases, dialects, or jokes that are signs of their own evident existence as language, inscribed as textuality. The additional letters, strange to the eye, and the other font make them disruptively and challengingly unlike the surrounding text; the highlighted letters have an alien aspect, defamiliarizing what is the limited extent of the alphabet. In the passage from "Proteus" in which Stephen considers the visible world, he cites from a variety of foreign phrases—among them Greek (*oinopa ponton*) and Latin (*Omnis caro ad te veniet*) in the same paragraph (3.394, 396); their very strangeness suggests the material of language as language, and their appearance in italics also demonstrates that Stephen is seeing them in his thought as written texts. That the Greek is in italics in the Roman alphabet and not the Greek one is a further distraction and complication. This is the image of language as alien, difficult to read; Joyce knew that this presentation and disruption must be visual, the material shape deceptively the same in words and form.

As individual letters are highlighted and subject to disruption, so epistolary letters, being made up of the writing and reading of individual alphabetic letters, seem very likely sites for confusion.[27] The letter magnified will have its disrupted effect most strongly in a form of all letters. As these epistolary letters appear in the text, read by both character and reader, they stress the presence of alphabetic letters and their disruption; much of the correspondence sent and received in *Ulysses* is rife with confusion and error from the unstable individual letters within it. Martha Clifford's letter has its prominent confusion of the *l* dropped from "world" into "word." It too is due to a "mechanical" error, a jump of the hand between two lines of the typewriter, *l* just below the *o*. Yet the consequences of so small an error are greatly magnified: a whole universe is at stake, or a value (as *l* was also used in older typewriters for the numeral one). The postcard Breen receives makes its own disruption between the visible signs *U.P.*, which may be incorrectly transcribed by the text, and their possible meaning, as the letters play with the aural quality of the tension between graphemic and phonemic function—"you pee."[28] This postcard presents not only a question of the recipient Breen's potency but a visual statement of the potency of letters.

Bloom, answering Martha in the Ormond Bar, seeks to disguise his identity by distancing and defamiliarizing not only his name but the letters used to sign it: "Remember write Greek ees" (11.860). His answer, as it can be reconstructed from his comments, many times uses the letter, as may be expected; once, he corrects himself: "No, change that ee." A different sign is used for a common letter to add mystery and otherness, highlighting again the unstable prominence of the letter. Unstable as well is the hangman's epistle from "Cyclops," likewise reproduced in full for the reader to see. In addition to its comic style, there is a visual comedy in its disruptive lowercase letters and lack of punctuation: "*i have a special nack of putting the noose once in he can't get out hoping to be favoured i remain*" (12.428–29). Particularly magnified, the foregrounded aspects in these examples of letters are evident as signs that are not easily read and likely misunderstood.

When "unlocked" in "Ithaca," Bloom's dresser drawer makes prominent, among other things, some hidden correspondence whose dense depiction in alphabetic letters reveals the tensions and confusions that produce an irritating text. One letter is from Milly, written when she was young, "an infantile epistle" and counterpart to that day's birthday thank-you. There are also three typewritten ones—"addressee, Henry Flower, c/o. P.O. Westland Row, addresser, Martha Clifford, c/o. P.O. Dolphin's Barn" (17.1797)—to which Bloom adds the one received that day. These letters are kept privately, as they are of a secret and emotional nature; hidden from view, they are unlocked to the reader's eye by being presented by the text, made to stand out prominently from the page by their representation through means of fragmented wording, abbreviations, and capitalized letters.

This correspondence Bloom has secreted away is contained in a drawer, an actual physical object in the world of the novel yet an object represented by a word that has occasioned a pun in "Circe" about Bloom's secret life. When Gerty MacDowell says to him, "you saw all the secrets of my bottom drawer" (15.384), the word "drawer" is punned as an article of woman's underclothes (and there is much grammar in that word "article"). This polysemic paranomasia in turn opens the field of play to reveal in the word two other pertinent issues. The first is the representational nature of language: "draw" as used to mean "sketch" or "depict," as the epistles are represented within the text. The second is the self-referential quality of all printed language: "draw" in its etymological sense of "pull," as galley and page proofs are pulled, those final physical objects that make up a book to be read. (In French, the language of the printers who produced *Ulysses*, derivatives of *tirer* ["to draw"] are used for Joyce's command to the printer to set the proofs ["tirez"] and for the dash that Joyce uses to set off spoken language [*tiret*].)

Once unlocked, these texts of correspondence deserve closer scrutiny, that of the myopic glance and the snail's pace. Milly's letter, preserved probably for a decade, is a relic of a text whose status represented on the page attests to its staying power for Bloom (in Bloom's memory) as well as the permanence of black ink. "An infantile epistle, dated, small em monday, reading: capital pee Papli comma capital aitch How are you note of interrogation capital eye I am very well full stop new paragraph signature with flourishes capital em Milly no stop" (17.1791–94). This juvenilia might well serve as a paradigm as well as a relic. All its imprinted, scriptible visible features are noted: capitalization, punctuation, paragraphing, signature. It is an "infantile epistle" because it is a sort of embryonic form of all possible texts.

In addition to the letter from Martha that contains the error of "word" and "world," which Bloom received during the events of "Lotus Eaters" (and which is itself depicted there twice—once read by Bloom and hence seen by the reader, once remembered and depicted in the narrative), Bloom possesses three other, undepicted letters from her hidden away in this drawer; and the text presents all these letters not in their form as epistles, as in the crucial missive of the morning or Milly's above, but rather in another highlighted form of alphabetical characters whose meaning is itself hidden and private, that of a cryptogram regarding their authorship. The pattern of these cryptic alphabetic letters leaps out from the page and causes the reader to puzzle out what appears before his eyes rather than to simply see the mailed and received correspondence as transcribed or represented. Thus the figurative function of language is displaced by its status as aggregated letters, jumbled and magnified. The mysteries of various letters in *Ulysses*, mysteries that include mistakes, are here valorized as the cryptic nature of all letters. What is revealed by this encoding is less the density of language than that of the alphabet itself, a feature most evident to Joyce's peering eyes:

the transliterated name and address of the addresser of the 3 letters in reversed alphabetical boustrophedonic punctated quadrilinear cryptogram (vowels suppressed)

N.IGS./WI.UU.OX/W.OKS.MH/Y.IM: (17.1799–1801)

First, the subterfuge of the cryptogram obscures identity and meaning temporarily, substituting for Martha and her address other letters in a determined and increasingly complicated pattern. Meaning is to be hidden from Molly, presumably, but accessible to the reader because the rules and the solution—all in letters—are both provided. Moreover, the ruse draws particular attention to the visual and encrypted nature of all texts by persistent assertion of mere alphabetical signs. (And the reader remembers that Bloom seeks to defamiliarize his answer to Martha by "Greek ees.")

In draft versions, what appeared in the text was also a code, but a simpler one—a cipher, not a cryptogram: "the name and address of the addresser of the 3 letters in reversed alphabetical cipher, Nzigsz Xornuliw, Wloksrmh Yzim."[29] Most probably, Joyce made the change to add additional layers of ludic, encrypted complexity, but the change stresses even more the density of letters and print and creates a disruption in the normal direction of reading. (The fact that the denser puzzle was added in the very last stages of page proof is further evidence of Joyce's attention to details of printing, that part of the enterprise, seemingly less creative, that most makes manifest the surface of letters and is the final thing seen. This change was made on January 27, 1922.)[30]

There is a programmed, intentional difficulty in reading these letters of and about letters, Milly's juvenile note and the cryptogram; that difficulty, however, does not reside in deciphering their meaning but rather in the simple act of trying to read them. Meaning is not locked up in them; in this regard the missives are omissive. Milly's note, after all, is phatically empty; its real function is as an exercise in the act and the form of writing, much like a mechanical copying of letter shapes in penmanship. Moreover, her letter practices the most formal features of writing, capitalization, paragraphing, and punctuation. Similarly, the cryptogram is not a search for meaning but rather the defeat of it by redundancy: the answer is present in the text before the puzzle is given, the solution appearing before the question—hardly a problem to solve under the circumstances. Its substitution is purely systemic.

In both Milly's note and the puzzle, what is unlocked therefore is not meaning. Nothing is represented; all that is actually unlocked is the basic presence of the alphabetical letters themselves in the various scripted or printed forms they can take, the possibilities of what can be done with the alphabet. The real function of these secreted treasures is to magnify the importance of the smallest units at the lexical level of a large novel. What is ultimately made evident in the close scrutiny of the unlocked letters in Bloom's drawer is the density and nontransparency of those more basic letters of the alphabet; the letters stand out in their smallest lexical units and in their presence as form rather than in any meaning or representation. These are the very features most evident to Joyce in his illness. They are dense and irritating, resisting and thwarting reading. Yet there are fruits and simple moments of recognition that derive from this disrupted and impeded reading, a close sense of what is possible for the reader in liability and limit. What will become clear—or as clear as possible, given the confines of the opaque nature of the disrupted text—are the features attributable to and discernible in the misworking of irritation; what is evident are the discontinuous and simple pleasures of impeded vision.

Milly's letter has its imprinted, scriptible features noted as a symptom of reading difficulty; this difficulty is a fact particularly noticeable because it has no message but just the form of a message. Yet its stultifying simplicity makes a paradox: when a phrase such as "note of interrogation" or "stop" is written out so that the figure of the question mark or the period is made into other letters and is built up apparently into discourse, the importance of the letter over the sign is thus stressed to the point of marked precariousness and redundancy. Continuing the expansion of the space of the empty message, a space filled by the opacity of the letters, the capitals in Milly's note are written out as words—"pee," "aitch," "eye"—indicating their status as letters. Here too is a strain on reading: the phonemic quality of letters is reproduced as a visible, lexical feature so that the graphemic and phonemic are confused.[31]

Finally, Milly's note might function as a message in a particularly striking way, drawing attention to the constant presence of letters that must be seen closely and magnified in importance. Certainly in the density of that "capital eye I" for the single-letter first-person pronoun is a tacit recognition by the author and for the reader of the property of writing as meant to be the focus of sight. Milly's letter, despite its communicative, phatic function (the "I"), is not described as "saying" but rather as "reading," something hidden away in a drawer but meant to be unlocked when seen by the "eye" affected by unstable magnification.

It has been remarked that Joyce added the cryptogram of Martha's name and address in the last stages of proofing to alter what was a simple cipher. This change is of course in the direction of greater density and complexity of the letters themselves. Yet to create either puzzle is to engage the text in play; but with an unpredictable, disordered view of the system of the alphabet, the ludic is inescapable and correspondingly denser.

The cipher:

the name and address of the addresser of the 3 letters in reversed alphabetical cipher, Nzigsz Xornuliw, Wloksrmh Yzim.

The cryptogram:

the transliterated name and address of the addresser of the 3 letters in reversed alphabetical boustrophedonic punctated quadrilinear cryptogram (vowels suppressed)
N.IGS./WI.UU.OX/W.OKS.MH/Y.IM

The complexity achieved by increasing the opacity and repositioning of the letters also has some felicitous moments of comic coincidence based on the essential and finite possible features of the changed letters. The earlier cipher resembled some of the Hungarian words within the text (because of the number of *a*s in the word "Martha," which become *z*s in the reversed alphabet), and when the text of *Ulysses* actually prints out Hungarian words in "Cyclops," one in particular stands out: *Marha* (12.560), the word for "cow." The denser cryptogram, by adding the pattern as "boustrophedonic" with the suppressed vowels and with the capitalization, creates the word "OX" and makes it stand out more readily. Thus the revision appears to provide a humorous gloss on the Greek "bous" hidden within the adjective describing the pattern. This gloss is possible by means of the substitution of letters and by possibilities of a sort of crossed reading—"OX" and "bous" within a word that means "crossing" and "turning." The reader's eye is teased into these possibilities by the enlargement of letters, here not only in their capitalization but by their consequential importance as puzzle.

This sort of chiasmal reading, by which letters bring often disparate elements into focus, is a feature of Joyce's irritated text that strains reading beyond the visible page. The letters seem to reflect other sights of the text and other texts, to the disruption of time and space in the reading process. Such a crossed reading is not an allusion, because it is only the constellation of letters that is the similarity, not context or even words. The importance of letters magnified brings disparate sites into prominence. The exotic word "boustrophedonic" itself is evocative of this sort of cross-reading, restricted (but appropriately so) to the sight of a site in Joyce; it seems to reflect across to his earlier book *Portrait,* where the phrases "Bous Stephaneforos" and "Bous Stephanoumenos" both appear on the same page (168). These earlier appearances contain even further possibilities for the twenty-six letters, in similar and strikingly uncommon groupings: the same *bous* in all three appearances is combined with *stroph-* and *steph-,* themselves deceptively similar to make "boustroph"edonic/"Bous Steph" aneforous/"Bous Steph"anoumenos. Obviously, the latter two are quite apparent puns on Stephen's name; but, conditioned by this crossing over, a reader can see back into the cryptogram the figure of Stephen obscured by the letters. (This crossed image is reinforced when Stephen remembers the phrase "Bous Stephanoumenos" in *Ulysses* [14.15].) The magnification of letters carries forward and backward in reading space and time and disparate sites of different texts. When it is remembered that the final text of the cryptogram in "Ithaca" was changed late in composition yet that it can jump beyond the text to an earlier work, using as a point of connection only the letters themselves, the far-reaching, excursive elements of irritated letters and their consequently disjunctive reading become apparent.

The addition of the cryptogram increases the density of the text by the compact presence and the sheer insistence of letters as such. Yet from this layering another density emerges, one not of meaning but of mistake. Joyce clearly marked the cryptogram on the page proof (even correcting a letter he himself had poorly transcribed),[32] yet even he, nodding, is subject to errors of misseeing. According to the given description of the "boustrophedonic" pattern, the letters for the word "Barn" should be reversed ("NRAB") to yield "MI.Y" (with the "vowels suppressed"). As the complexity of the verbal surface increases, so does confusion; here the actual letters Joyce himself wrote in his addition, "Y.IM.," are wrong. At this point the reader can see again the particularly two-sided consequence of Joyce's eye problems: the cryptogram is added to create a playful density of letters; yet as the text is open to such disruption and eyesight is fallible, error is inescapable. While Joyce controls the possibilities of the alphabet in creating the cryptogram, he overlooks his own mistake; he is both perpetrator and victim.

In the small compass of the dresser drawer are to be seen all the features of the letters and their highlighted disruption, the magnified consequences of Joyce's own eyesight: the possibilities of the visual form of letters; the challenge to meaning in the small scope of disrupted letters; the reader's sight on the page and beyond the page as a constant challenge to reading; the confusion of the graphemic and phonemic; the presence of errors intended and unintended.

While the act of reading the text by peering at it defines the role of the reader with the novel or the character as reader in the novel, the focus should also be on what is the visual aspect of the novel—not the act of reading *Ulysses* but what is there to be read. The visual field is primary here, but, like Joyce's, it is restricted; it impinges on and affects the act of reading. All acts of reading in *Ulysses* are foremost and essentially acts of seeing; yet seeing is fraught with handicap, as Joyce well knew, both philosophically and physically; if Shakespeare is bawd and cuckold, Joyce was victim of his illness and perpetrator of its effects on his reader.

CHAPTER 3

The Complicit Reader and Joycean Dis-lexia

Errors in seeing originate with the handicapped Joyce, such as the unintentional error for the transposed "Barn" in the cryptogram. Those errors in seeing within the text by the characters themselves are intended paradigms of the writer's weakness, his irritation and limit. The characters similarly interpret letters incorrectly, projecting meaning from obscure and incomplete elements; they too seem influenced and affected by the author's vision. And as every error by the character is clearly one that is also by necessity committed by the reader, as every error of the character is imposed upon the reader, so the reader is inescapably drawn into misreading and ultimately made complicit in the author's weakness.

Walking about, Bloom has a "throwaway" placed in his hand by someone identified by letters, "a sombre Y.M.C.A. young man" (the redundancy of "Y.M." and "young man" included); the very name of the handout, the "throwaway," suggests that it is a text of limited and inconsequential value, and Bloom's glance at it leads to misunderstanding: "Bloo. . . . Me? No. Blood of the Lamb" (8.8–9). From a slight glimpse of a visual sign, Bloom projects a meaning for the text that corresponds to his view of the world: he reads himself in the text because he feels somehow the subject of much Dublin discourse (as is confirmed by his sense of the watch's marching cadence in "Circe": "Bloom. Of Bloom. For Bloom. Bloom" [15.677]). The reader sees in a similar confusion, as the letters on his page of the novel contain the character's name—"Bloo . . . M(e)." Both are wrong. Bloom corrects his mistake by closer scrutiny of the throwaway: "No. Blood of the

Lamb"; the reader, scrutinizing and projecting over a longer text, will see other such mistakes as "Bloowho" (11.86) and "Bloowhose" (11.149) in "Sirens."

Bloom, ever the active reader, is also and inevitably a misreader and thus a shadow and paradigm for the author and his audience.[1] As he walks toward the Ormond Bar, Bloom's "dark eye read Aaron Figatner's name. Why do I always think Figather? Gathering figs, I think" (11.149–50). In Bloom's answer to this self-posed puzzle is the essential coupling of activities, "read" and "think." What arrests Bloom here, both visually and mentally, impeding his progress, is the tendency of the eye to develop the modalities inherent in language in print by the act of reading: very small elements are used to leap toward meaning. The *n* and the *h* are similar enough in the possibilities of their form—they seem to fit the requirements for the figures on the eye chart—that the eye mistakes them, especially when the mind can provide by thought a context for the misreading. To unify writer and character in this error, this letter pair of course exactly repeats the confusion of the type font Joyce noted in the page proofs of "Cyclops." Bloom's sharpness of vision seems in question, especially as he seems to repeat this mistake ("why do I?"). Yet such an error on Bloom's part is an essential discovery in the act of reading any printed text, the book no less than the sign denoting and hence advertising the jeweler's shop. Joyce's visual weakness includes misreading as probable meaning, error as possible interpretation. Bloom has been tricked by the possibilities of language and by the power of seeing. Joyce's playing with letters within words (and words themselves) causes an immediate discontinuity of reading, but that discontinuity imposes on any reader the need to establish—even if incorrectly—continuity and context: the presence of the mistake requires the reader to connect one sight with another site of absent meaning so as to make continuous at the level of thinking what is discontinuous at the level of seeing.

That what Bloom reads is a shop sign only reinforces again the facts that for Joyce, any of a variety of printed materials constitutes a text of meaning, and his text is constituted of a variety of materials. A shop sign is an item in the street, and seen, like the customhouse clock, it can lead to an epiphany. It is worth remarking that Stephen in *Portrait* feels that "every mean shop legend bound his mind like the words of a spell" (178), and the *legend*-ary aspect of those signs as to be read is reproduced in *Ulysses;* while the "bare clean closestools" in the shop of the plumber catch Bloom's attention (in the random sentence compared with the one opening the novel), his eye is caught by the repetitive patterns of the written legend "William Miller, plumber." With the Figatner legend, the act of Bloom's misseeing is rich with suggestion of the power that print occupies in the mind like a spell. Trying to be a conventionally competent reader, he projects meaning derived from his previously existing understanding of letters and the world; it is just such a reader that Joyce knows will be disrupted and handicapped. Not only does Bloom make a simple-minded mistake creating a context ("gathering figs"), he also has a text envisioned within that context: the harvesting of fruit is the intent of Agendath Netaim, the planter's company, whose claim Bloom has read that morning in the circular. Moreover, it is quite likely that his eye catches the name of the diamond setter because of a conflation of other related and suggestive but not fully present associations. "Aaron" and "jeweler" (two words presumably emblazoned on a sign or shop window) evoke an ethnic sense (Moses' brother and Jew) that meshes with the gathered fruit of Palestine and that must appeal to Bloom's identity, thus reinforcing the arresting of his "dark" eye (itself an ethnic marker). Additionally, although less strongly as a sign of meaning than as a mark of the visual field, the double vowel that begins the name Aaron also works the effect of stopping the eye. Figatner is indeed a Jew in Dublin, but his existence in whatever form is at the least a printed construct made up of the letters that present him incorrectly and suggestively to Bloom's eye and the reader's (and to Joyce's eye, the one that was not "darkened" by illness).

Another example of Bloom's observations of letters, and the limits of both his vision and his understanding, involves his trying to read the text of the letters on the priest's chasuble in All Hallows Church: "Letters on his back: I.N.R.I? No: I.H.S." (5.372).[2] He confuses them in no small measure because he initially missees them, as the priest, kneeling and rising, would cause his garment to fold and turn. (Bloom, being on the pulpit, or left, side facing the altar, would see the *I* clearly but would see the next letters less so: an example of an imperfect text imperfectly seen.) Yet Bloom's misreading is suggestively a disfunctional one because he mistakes letters that are similar in shape, *H* and *N*—again as in Figatner, again the very ones Joyce took pains repeatedly to correct in the page proofs of "Cyclops." From his confusion and then correction, Bloom then proceeds to misunderstand (with Molly's help) what the initials mean; he goes awry even when he recognizes the correct letter: "Molly told me one time I asked her. I have sinned: or no: I have suffered, it is. And the other one? Iron nails ran in." Letters detached from their context in one language might make a statement in another. Indeed, the text suggested by these letters is various, either the abbreviation in Greek letters of the name Jesus or several Latin mottoes. If it is the name, identity is questioned; if the motto "In hoc signet . . . ," the sign is destabilized. In all cases what is obscured to Bloom is the letter, capitalized, abbreviated, and magnified in importance.

Bloom's observations involve the act of seeing, and his object—even when it is, as with Stephen's epiphany, a clock—brings him to other ends. His moment is not intellectual but experiential, but it, too, is subject to error. Bloom walks the streets of Dublin, but what he sees there brings about revelations different from those that Stephen enjoys. "There's a little watch up there on the roof of the bank. . . . His lids came down on the lower rims of his irides. Can't see it. If you imagine it's there you can almost see it" (8.560–63). Stephen can "almost see it," but Bloom's eyes can see only so far, and what he looks at is the physical world. The sciences of optics and astronomy connect here for him: he "held out his right hand at arm's length towards the sun. Wanted to try that often. Yes: completely. The tip of his little finger blotted out the sun's disk. Must be the focus where the rays cross" (8.564–60). This experiment with stereoptic vision, a sort of do-it-yourself parallax, is concerned with the physical world, not the world of epiphanic illumination; and, characteristic of Bloom, he has his facts wrong as he misunderstands what he sees. His irides will adjust to admit only a portion of the sun's rays (and the reference here is to that portion of the eye that, inflamed, was so troublesome to Joyce). The sun is not blotted out by his covering the spot where its rays cross into his eyes; rather his finger covers the degree of arc on the horizon occupied by the diameter of the sun. What he has measured is not the distance of the star but the distance between the eyes on his own face (an act of self-definition in a physical way). Where the lines of the eyes cross is the focal point of sight, and for readers, what is placed at that juncture is the text.

The reader by himself is made to misread *Ulysses*. During the apocalyptic burning of Dublin in "Circe," a regiment goes into action: "*Gallop of hooves. Artillery. Hoarse commands*" (15.4662–63). Projecting the notion of cavalry from the first phrase, "gallop of hooves," as Bloom projects

"Figather," the reader expects the last phrase to be "horse commands," assuming a simple contextual meaning. Yet the intrusive presence of the additional letter *a* subverts that meaning, and the tension caused by its presence in the phonemic, the polysemic, and the lexical all coalesce to impede reading. Every stage of the reader's understanding is undermined. The simple, small addition has caused irritation and confusion.

The reader assumes competence as regards seeing and interpreting the status of the text as everywhere and constantly aware of its own textuality and materiality: he knows how to read the unraveling deconstruction of lines like these from "Ithaca" in which a Dublin street address and a cliché juxtapose each other into humor: Bloom "had marked a florin (2/-) with three notches on the milled edge and tendered it in payment of an account due to and received by J. and T. Davy, family grocers, 1 Charlemont Mall, Grand Canal, for circulation on the waters of civic finance" (17.980–84): "canal, circulation, waters." A reader can reasonably project meaning according to theories of reading and do so even with the polysemy of the text. Yet when the reader encounters in the span of three lines "the superstition of the populace" and "the envy of opulence" (17.845, 847), he begins to doubt his eyes. If the text of *Ulysses* is unreadable, it is so first because each individual word resists being easily read. Like Joyce, the reader must go at a snail's pace, must be irritated and confused: he is a fellow sufferer (as well as a fellow believer in hermeneutic uncertainty). Again, another dynamic and another density is involved when, in the space of less than a page in "Sirens," the text posits disruptive possibilities to the reader's eye with similar signs: as "By Cantwell's offices roved Greaseabloom" (11.185), Miss Douce "with grace of alacrity towards the mirror gilt Cantrell and Cochrane's . . . turned herself" (11.214).[3] The plasticity of the lines, the amalgam of "greaseabloom," and the imitative, inverted syntax of Miss Douce's reflected turning are familiar parts of Joyce's lexical surface, but the parallel of Cantwell/Cantrell works by means of some other quality of the text (in addition to being coincidentally facts of Dublin life, the names of liquor distributors and products). What these words present to the eye is the deceptive modalities of letters, the uncertain supplementarity that lies within the opaque material of language printed on the page. A change in just one letter, *w* to *r*, transforms into instability two words in the lexical surface to produce uncertain polylexy: Cant*w*ell, Cant*r*ell. In a third instance, another actual shop sign in Dublin, "Elvery's Elephant house" (6.253), is likely to create confusion by the similarity of its letters. Different form and lessened meaning are the consequences of the magnified and important possibilities within the alphabet; as a result, reading, based like Bloom's Figatner on projections of what is seen, is thwarted and made disfunctional by the prominent density and the consequent important opacity of simple letters. The reader seems unsure of what is read. There is a certain unclarity to the text, even in uncomplicated contexts, as if the reader's eye were troubled with illness.

A different kind of uncertainty appears in a scene in which the factual aspects of history and journalism, two genres that depend on record, are also questioned. The puzzling use of letters creates a reading that seems to have no substance or material, probably a joke on the characters as well as on the reader. Myles Crawford's recreation in "Aeolus" of the coded information on the Phoenix Park murders conveyed by Gallaher through the printed page of the *Weekly Freeman* is disfunctional and deceptive:

> Have you [the paper] of 17 March? . . . Take page four, advertisement for Bransome's coffee, let us say. Have you got that? . . . T is viceregal lodge. C is where murder took place. K is Knockmaroon gate. . . . F to P is the route Skin-the-Goat drove the car for an alibi, Inchicore, Roundtown, Windy Arbour, Palmerston Park, Ranelagh. F.A.B.P. Got that? X is Davy's publichouse in upper Leeson street. (7.651–69)

It should first be noted that Crawford is not using the actual paper of Gallaher's account. His date, March 17, is symbolically suggestive of a clichéd sort of Irish nationalism but not accurate; he fails to indicate the year, and even if it is 1904, the newspaper would have been lying around for three months, a fact that does not say much for the archival. Moreover, it is clear that the advertisement chosen is only used as an example ("let us say") and not the one actually employed by Gallaher. Yet the confusion of the newspaper's date and choice of ad is only compounded by the confusion caused by the letters named for the encoded message. T and c are certain to appear in an advertisement for tea and coffee; a and b are also in the word "Bransome"; f and p are possible; but k is unlikely, and x strains credulity. Even were Crawford to mean metaphorically "X marks the spot" of Davy's publichouse, then all the other letters in the ad would have their literal existence challenged. The letters as markers are not only of questionable meaning but also of questionable presence; separate letters lose meaning when seen disparately, as Joyce saw them. Crawford's audience—and Joyce's—is misled and made to misread.

In one fundamental sense, everything that is written hides meaning: the cryptogram that obscures the letters from Martha is a reminder that all *gramma* is *crypton,* and all reading is in some measure an act of puzzling out meaning encapsulated by symbols. Those symbols, however, are held to be stable. Reading is thought to be a process by which understanding is projected from the slight clues and sight cues of the fixed identity of letters, by the certain substance of their very lexical nature. The reader reads what appears in the book and processes it into an understandable whole; this is an apparently simple dynamic, yet it is a process fraught with possibilities of error, especially from seeing. Current theories of reading suggest that a competent reader proceeds from a brief sight of the text and projects a strategy "which process[es] very little of the vocabulary and punctuation in a text and which rel[ies] on a careful selection and continuous synthesis." In fact, these theories suggest, the reader tends to predict meaning based on his prior knowledge of the world and the conventions of a text, so that meaning is "a sort of oscillation between prediction and confirmation. . . . The brain tells the eye what it expects to see on the page: the eye in turn confirms the prediction." "A good reader skips directly from distinctive features to comprehension as if letters and word shapes were merely slight clues."[4] These features, "merely slight clues," are the very things that Joyce had to have magnified for him by his glass and then had to read at the snail's pace; he magnified them in turn as he wrote, and their importance is not slight.

This smooth, interpolated process has an ideal (and idealized) hermeneutic; it is an accretive and hierarchical dynamic. Moreover, it is one that Joyce eagerly disrupts, as Bloom's Figatner is such a projected meaning but a mistake. If reading takes place as the brain tells the eye what to expect, Bloom disposes the order when he asks, "why do I think Figather?" Joyce disrupts reading to make his reader handicapped. It has been readily evident that at one large formal dimension *Ulysses* stands in contradistinction to the "prior conventions of a text" (whatever its very close resemblance to the reader's "prior knowledge of the world") so that it cannot be easily assimilated by the reader. Yet Joyce's challenge goes to smaller dimensions; rather than let the reader skip directly over the words, letters, and shapes merely as "slight clues," he wishes to have the reader arrested even in that simple visual process of reading and stopped by the cues to sight that are normally overlooked. The very letters of his text demand to be seen as "sight" cues; they are highlighted into prominence. Hence the cryptogram is capitalized to stand out on the page; thus Joyce fretted over the minutiae of the fonts of type, *h* or *b;* thus Bloom misreads the slight clue of "I.H.S." Letters both clear and confused make for error and puzzle, both of which cause the reader to pause over the material printed in the text, to see it as opaque and recalcitrant in not being easily processed or projected into a larger comprehension. Joyce makes the reader give the same attention to the lexical level as he did in both writing and proofing his product; by foregrounding the letters, he makes the reader see them separately, discontinuous, blurred. Misreading and miscuing, features of his handicap, appear in the text to prolong the act of reading and compel the reader to puzzle at and look at the text, thwarting reading speed and facile comprehension.[5] Reading is disrupted at its smallest level so that its supposed hierarchical order and its temporal causality are undermined: simple lection cedes place to constant dislection.

If the theories of reader competence presuppose the projection of meaning from a glimpse of visual clues, Joyce subverts those visual clues so that a process of misreading follows. The reader cannot predict meaning with ease but only with impediment. Such halting uncertainty and misreading—dislection—cuts into any unitary view of *Ulysses* on the page. As Joyce's eyesight—limited, channeled, opaque—offered him no large view, only the myopic partiality of small pieces glimpsed through his opaque glass, darkly, so the act of reading his novel affords only the small and separate pleasures of trickery and incomplete recognition because of the reader's misseeing and dislection of what letters deceptively hide and reveal when magnified.[6]

Reading thus imperiled is always excursive. To be discursive, reading would have to be accretive and directed, presupposing an order that Joyce does not permit. To be excursive, reading would transpose or move away from the text into disruption and discontinuity. As myopic focus must be given to the smallest unit of the text, so only small parts of the novel can be seen at one time. Reading with a magnifying glass, as Joyce did, would increase a diachronic view of the work; rather than enlarge whole lines in synchronic order, the glass would isolate parts of lines including those above and below. As Joyce saw in fits and starts, in parts and pieces, so Joycean reading jumps and turns. It moves in reading time and space, sharing elements from his clinical illness. It will confuse sound and sign, the graphemic and the phonemic, always to produce small sights of focus, of critical attention.

The letters of the text, irritated by Joyce's iritis, infect the reader with Joycean dis-lexia. This study uses the term "dis-lexia" to distinguish this feature of *Ulysses* from the clinical disorder of dyslexia (the "dis" reflecting all the disruption and confusion that Joyce works into his text and the sight of it; the "lexic," like the clinical term, pertaining to the letters themselves). Yet the analogy has the limited merit of bringing issues into tangence as regards what is seen. Joyce, of course, was not a dyslexic, yet his vision was impaired, and his limited eyesight is pertinent to the prominence of letters as discrete, disjunctive, and opaque on the page of his novel. As iritis and glaucoma caused shadowy blurred vision, as his frosted lenses made letters appear opaque and unclear to him, and as the magnifying glass he used made him see letters up close, separate yet deceptively similar, so all these features are presented to the reader. As processing a text is the role of the reader, dis-lexia thus is a useful term for how the reader is made complicit with Joyce's limited vision. As Joyce had trouble seeing his text to write it, so the reader has trouble seeing the text to read it.

Clinical dyslexia is neurological rather than optical; and, as neurological, it pertains directly to the reader's cognitive processing of a text. Moreover, it causes problems like Joyce's symptoms and their effects on the reader: the transposition of letters in space;[7] the disposition of sequences;[8] the confusion of graphemic and phonemic errors.[9] (One theory of dyslexia suggests that it is caused by the inability of one eye to dominate in reading and suggests the remedy of covering the stronger eye to strengthen the other in what is termed "monocular occlusion." Joyce was an unsuccessful practitioner of this method long ago.) The term for dyslexia current in Joyce's time was "word-blindness," the first part of which would seem to pertain to his art and the second to his condition.

There is a further effect of the text on the reader, another consequence of the magnification of letters that Joyce needed in order to see his text and then reproduced within it for the reader to confront: it is the importance of the foregrounded, unstable letter to the status of the "world" of the novel, its representation of material reality. Dis-lexia on the part of the reader affects that component of the reader's experience of reading that evokes the material world. If hypothetically unencumbered reading competence requires a previous understanding of the world (as noted earlier, the reader tends to predict meaning based on his prior knowledge of the world), so Joycean dis-lexic reading will require uncertainty about it. As Joyce's view of the actual, material world he inhabited was limited and compromised by his illness so that he saw only light and shadow or missed seeing, so too is the reader's view of that world of the material text (and the depictions in it).

This connection of Joyce's actual world and the reader's view of the world of the text is true, in part because of the autobiographical element in all of Joyce's work. Yet it is true in a most simple, palpable way. The text, created by Joyce, is the object that the reader sees: the reader literally confronts the book, face to face, holding it in hand, as the book has its own first-order reality as a material object.[10]

Even while undermined in both form and meaning, Joyce's alphabetical letters require and acquire their own substance by being presented in print. The irreducible presence and elemental density of letters (even when they are magnified) become firmly struck, ex-pressed and im-pressed in the final form of the novel. While matter and final form are ideas derived from Aristotle, the poststructuralist program of the letter seems at odds with these older notions of a sort of first-order reality of the letter; yet Joyce seems capable of sustaining a postmodernist practice along with classical ideas. Letters are matter, in no small measure because they are the actual reality of print that constitutes the text and discourse; irrefutably, the printed novel is a material object in the world, to be seen by the reader. Joyce displayed a minute attention to the visual form of his novel as it was printed; he was even concerned about the shade of blue to be used on its cover. His recognition of the importance of the letter and its necessary formal features, this lexicality, is nowhere better seen than in the scrutiny he gave to the last page proofs, as noted earlier. This is the place where his own attention is drawn to the particular visual and material character of letters, and it is an overlooked place and an unexpected attention. Despite distractions of illness or the writing of the rest of *Ulysses*, Joyce saw to the smallest and densest part of his endeavor. (The appendix will consider what Joyce saw in that first edition.)

One reason Joyce was concerned with what the reader would see on the page was that he had theorized in his early years that the aesthetic object was to be defined as what was to be seen. Joyce's aesthetic in the years before the composition of his works is often primarily concerned with sight; oddly enough, when he wrote both the Paris and Pola notebooks in 1904 and 1905, he needed glasses but did not wear them—not, as noted, until late 1905. As articulated by Stephen (if subscribed to first by the young Joyce in Paris and Pola), much of this aesthetic resides in the realm of the visual; it is concerned with "seeing." (One must remark that these ideas are inscribed in notebooks, those forms of discontinuity and fragmentation; they appear under the heading of "Aesthetics," as if the young Joyce wished to include the diphthong as a way of making his notions themselves more visible and enlarged so he could better see them. "Esthetics" is the spelling used in *Portrait*.) The expression of the notion of epiphany in *Stephen Hero*, whatever else its validity may be for an understanding of Joyce's work, is also concerned with sight: Stephen says of the Ballast Office clock, "I will pass it time after time, allude to it, refer to it, catch a glimpse of it. It is only an item in the catalogue of Dublin's street furniture. Then all at once I see it and I know at once what it is: epiphany" (211). The aim, of course, is knowledge, the "seeing" as apprehension, but all the intellection begins with a visual act, as the glimpse is a necessary precondition of all thought, even if compromised both in vision and subsequently in thinking.

The notion of beauty, derived from Aquinas, is similarly concerned with the essential property of sight: *Pulcra sunt quae visa placent.* As Stephen glosses to Lynch in *A Portrait:* "He uses the word *visa* . . . to cover esthetic apprehensions of all kinds, whether through sight or hearing or through any other avenue of apprehension" (207). Yet Stephen, in his wish to discourse broadly, embraces too much—Aquinas uses *visa* unambiguously for the act of seeing and understanding; and it is such seeing, as both visual and cognitive act, that plays to Joyce's concerns. The examples Stephen gives are all things to be seen, grasped in the act of intellection because of their very visible material substance.

The application of these ideas to the book as material object and to the act of reading is obvious. The things grasped in intellection by the power of the visual are things of the world "presented in space," as Stephen says, objects such as the clock or basket that decorate—furnish, even—the house of fiction in the wordy world of the novel. In order for one to see, there must be an object, and for the novel, what is to be seen is what is on the page. The book as object also occupies that space in the world; it comes to hand and yet causes errors through the reading of it in time.

Yet in all these ideas and scenes sight is compromised: Joyce needing glasses when he wrote the Notebooks, having iritis as he worked on *A Portrait;* Stephen needing glasses as he discusses epiphanies and art (could he, with his myopia, see the clock or the butcher boy's basket?). And Joyce's theorizing is destabilized even further: while it relies on physical objects—busts, lice, cows, excrement—for definition, it is an aesthetic that Joyce resolutely practiced on verbal constructs and that he used to produce art present as the material artifact of the pages of a book. His theories are subject to the confusions and deconstruction inherent in all language, and especially those confusions and that instability that Joyce experienced when he peered at and magnified what he had written.

That disruption of letters, their opacity and confusion, which undercuts the theory of the beautiful as visual and intellective, also undercuts what is presented as material and actual within the novel. The "world" depicted aesthetically by language is unstable because of the opaque nature of alphabetical letters that do the depicting. Martha Clifford's letter to Bloom, seen in the text, has its own materiality complicated by being encrypted; yet it initially makes through error its own destabilizing of the "world" through the "word." As countless critics have noticed, this fortuitous error inscribes the tension between representation and language's nontransparency, as that mistake clearly destabilizes the figurative nature of the fictional world as precariously presented by discourse. Yet the scrutiny of myopia and irritated magnification focuses on one smaller and essential element in this split: what disrupts both "world" and "word,"[11] representation and discourse, is a single letter. The letter is essential to both, but it is something more basic and more fundamental than either. The confusion in Martha's note to Bloom is caused by the addition of a letter; the addition creates a density of the alphabet within the word that parallels that density of the cryptogram, how the correspondence is represented or depicted in the drawer. Further, fortuitously, the additional letter is an *l,* as if to sign the disruptive density of the letter itself. Any letter is an essential fact in *Ulysses,* thus magnified into larger consequences. One might say that the mistake in Martha's letter is not the addition of a gratuitous *l* but rather the disruption of the element that stands precisely at the juncture of both depiction and language, world and word. The letter magnified has its own dire consequences; one might say that Joyce believed in *l.*

Indeed, the letter is so essential that it not only unmakes representation but even unmakes language as well. Both figuration and discourse are materialized and dematerialized literally by the elemental presence of a letter. Martha's note and its mistake are paralleled by a thought of Stephen within the text. When walking along the Strand and contemplating the visual aspect of a world conveyed by the trickery of stereoptic vision and imagination, Stephen opens his eyes to see that the universe is not a projection of his imagination; he remarks: "there all the time without you: . . . world without end" (3.27). He seems to posit a reality that is external to himself and existent separate from language, a reality that belongs to a hierarchical divine system of the sort engaged in by a conventional (unhandicapped) reader. Such an external reality is a notion from an older system of meaning about the nature of matter, particularly in Stephen, that is attributable to Aristotle. A reader of course knows that all Stephen's imagination and sight are themselves in a text and hence have no reality, no "world." Indeed, if he is so nearsighted as to need glasses, what does Stephen see on the beach but unclarity, and what does he hear but mostly sound? The reader, however, persists in "seeing" the world of the novel.

Yet Stephen's discourse itself may have no referential connection to the world he tries to see; there might even be, following the logic of Martha's error, no "word." Scrutiny and mistrust of the letters invites seeing that the words "you" and "end" may not only *not* be about the world ("world without end," "world without you"); they may not even be part of a discourse of words. If Martha's world contains an extra letter so that it betrays its origin in discourse rather than reality, "you" and "end" may not be representation nor even discourse but only the alphabet letters *u* and *n.* If the word with the additional *l* forms the world, such a "world" can exist lexically without *u* and *n.* The graphemic and phonemic collide at the level of the lexical to recognize the presence and disruptive possibilities of letters. The reader can no longer overlook the letters nor trust reading to go past or through them to refer to a material world but rather can only see the closed and self-absorbed limited view of magnified letters and restricted vision. Language may be inadequate to describe the world, but (as Joyce knew and practiced on his readers) sight is further inadequate to language.

Thus the world that Stephen claims to see all about him dissolves before the reader's eye, as it disappears from Stephen's when he closes his; yet it does not return, as it does to Stephen ("world without end" quoted from the liturgy), because the magnified letters obscure and make unsubstantial their own substance and what they seek to represent by depiction. The real, verifiable world from which *Ulysses* apparently seeks its verisimilitude thus always dissolves through unstable letters. The tension of the names Cantwell and Cantrell or that of Elvery's Elephant house are cases in point. Real entities in Dublin, persons and products, they still are unmade in their reality by their precarious similarity in a text that has foregrounded letters and made them opaque.

Thus the reader's view of the fictional world, like Stephen's on the Strand, is complicated by unclarity in ways that are similar to Joyce's view of the world and of his text. This fact makes the final stage in the reader's complicity with Joyce's illness. As Joyce's view of the page was irritated by iritis, so the reader's view is vexed similarly by magnification, by substitution or deception, by obscurity and disruption; and the world of the novel is reduced not to a clear Dublin day of verisimilitude (nor a dark night of dreamy worldscape) but to vague puzzle, shadow, and echo. These consequences of the reader's dis-lexia will be, respectively, the focus of the next three chapters.

CHAPTER 4

The Poet's Picture Puzzle

Remarking on Ben Dollard as he plays piano in the Ormond Bar, Bloom grants him his good points—"Decent soul. Bit addled now"— and suggests Dollard's Micawberesque impecunious optimism: "Thinks he'll win in *Answers,* poets' picture puzzle. We hand you crisp five pound note. Bird sitting hatching in a nest. Lay of the last minstrel he thought it was. See blank tee what domestic animal? Tee dash ar most courageous mariner" (11.1023–26). Dollard's addled state makes him, Bloom notes, a reader prone to error, and if the puzzles Bloom suggests for the weekly are hardly challenging to a reader more astute than Ben, they are suggestive of larger issues. Joyce himself once entered such a newspaper's puzzle contest in order to win a prize, answering the several questions correctly but losing because his entry, sent from Pola to London, was late in the mail.[1] He might have spared himself the trouble; his novel has the same features as a puzzle.

"Poet's picture puzzle" certainly describes *Ulysses* itself. The poet is the maker, the craftsman, a term that embraces the image of the wily Daedalus, the self-portrait of the artist; and, as it particularly implies the ideas of purpose and skill, the term "craftsman" also applies to Joyce's concern with the mechanical printing of his text. "Picture" suggests the verisimilitude of the novel, its apparent depiction of real life. "Puzzle," coming last, as the nominal, adds a gloss to both previous terms, in part undermining art and turning the poet-craftsman into an intentional trickster, unclear and unexpected in *Ulysses* if an expected presence in the *Wake*. A puzzle is a problem, an enigma, and particularly a vexation. Puzzles to be read make eye problems of the sort that the "poet" of *Ulysses* enshrines in order to make the reader resemble him in his difficulties.

A puzzle brings reading to a halt, requiring a closer scrutiny of the text, a peering at small elements, as the letters are disengaged from the easy process of reading. Just such an example is "see blank tee what domestic animal?" The first words have a dissociated meaning; they are present not really as words but instead as letters *c* and *t* to be read as words rather than as the constitutive parts of words. The last two words are denotative, descriptive, and nominal; they contrast with as much as define what precedes them. All *Ulysses* is like this example, a tension between letters and depiction, the truly literal and the figurative.

"See blank" also suggests an opaque quality. *Ulysses* is a text that makes even simple words problematic and disfunctional in reading, such as spelling hat "ha" (4.70, 5.24, 11.876) and bat "ba" (13.1117). Readers sharper and less addled than Dollard have been puzzled by the facts of what is depicted in it: who was M'Intosh, and how many lovers does Molly have? All such problems as these not only are not to be solved by the act of reading, but many of the puzzles are to be found within the text of what is read; indeed they are caused by the very text itself. Things that seem clear are often puzzling when viewed myopically and dis-lexically. The hidden packet of Martha's letters, encoded in the cryptogram, is such a lexical puzzle, and it even contributes to error.

Thus any and all puzzles (those direct posed ones and other deceptive ones) magnify letters separate from context, foreground them as a diversionary move from and at the expense of the narrative level of reading: depiction and meaning give way to deceptively diverting signs. And when readers remember that the novel has depicted in its fourth chapter Bloom's own "domestic animal," "see blank tee" cat (whose language is also rendered in strange letters), they become aware, if they were not already, that the novel's every depiction is puzzlingly made up of letters and lacunae.[2] The pictures conveyed by narrative, where the reader engages the "world" of the novel through easy reading, are put at cross-purposes by a puzzle of letters, just as any disruption of letters is itself at odds with reading. The depicted reality of the text is destabilized by the presence of all letters because all are puzzling when highlighted and made separate, irritated into confusion. The reader's experience of the text, his being in its world, is compromised, brought up short to emulate Joyce's being in his own uncertain shadowy world.

The entire text is just such a puzzle, as well as an eye examination, of objects and characters depicted through words, and incomplete words at that; some elements are presented clearly and some are not. Some letters are not there but are to come, as in the modalities of all possible letters of the alphabet within the first sentence of the novel. The text is further disjunctive: its puzzles and answers both lie in the reader's dis-lexia, and meaning is suspended or rendered problematic and irrelevant. Some letters are given and some withheld—the dash and the blank are as meaningful for the solving of the obvious picture puzzles as are the letters present: much meaning in *Ulysses* resides in the space of absence, the blank and the dash, the space between letters of a word as well as the spaces and pages between the appearances of words in the text. Additionally, the blank and the dash are terms of the printer and the typist, terms that indicate the material quality of what is presented on the page and how. Moreover, the letters that are given in the puzzles Bloom offers present other issues to the irritation of the reader: that they are additionally read as sounds confuses the activities of reading and hearing. It is not incidental that Joyce chose, among the various ways to represent the third letter of the alphabet, including the phonetic "sē," a version that reads like a verb for and an imperative to the reader: "see." What is to be read and solved is something to be puzzled at when seen, something dis-lexic and unclear.

It is at this juncture of puzzle and picture, disruption and deception—and the hint of the tension between phonemic and graphemic—that *Ulysses* is distinguished from *Finnegans Wake*, even though both texts were affected in increasing degrees by the pathology of Joyce's eyesight. The *Wake* has no narrative representation, or perhaps (and better) it is all narratives; *Ulysses* has one that seeks to adhere to specific place and time, nearly the classical unities (this is another gloss on the former's being a book of the night and dark and the latter one of the day and putatively clear). The words in the *Wake* pertain to all possibilities; those in *Ulysses* pertain at first to the world being depicted. Thus it is that words in the *Wake* seem foreign immediately to the eye, but those in *Ulysses* seem at first to be clearly recognized. Many words in the *Wake* are hapax legomena; those in *Ulysses* appear more than once. Words in the *Wake* must be unpacked, with a variety of meanings to be extracted from them, all pertinent to the no/all narrative. Words in *Ulysses* seem to pertain to narrative and representation and facts, yet when looked at closely they begin to blur, lose definition, and become obscure. The words of *Ulysses* are more insidious precisely because they appear to be clear when they are not; those of the *Wake* have the forthrightness of their own obscurity. In the latter work, a pun is apparent immediately as a word that is more than one thing: "breadchestviousness" (156.14), for one, requires unpacking. It has something perhaps to do with a bread chest and, by extension, with the pyx; it suggests deviousness and other material qualities of trickery. The context from The Mookse and the Gripes about the "Filioque" controversy might (just) aid the reader most distantly in hearing in the word the Russian for "procession of the Holy Ghost." The reader of the *Wake* knows at the very least that, at first glance, this word is problematic.

If words in the *Wake* are most often puns, for which various meanings are clearly possible (many aided by sound), those in *Ulysses* are puzzles, in which meaning is hidden and masked. A puzzle of a word (not the same thing as a word puzzle) is one that is not apparently packed and impacted at first reading. Stephen, looking out from the Martello Tower, sees the bay as "a dull green mass of liquid" (1.108). The image is recoverable, as metaphor creates words that strike the reader with layering that can be understood. "Mass," of course, is the physical opposite of liquid, but it is a word that suggests that Stephen does not see very clearly, and it always seems to have a religious echo (especially as Mulligan has just completed his parody of the Mass). Stephen associates the bay with the bowl at his mother's deathbed, filled with bile. The sea, the bile, and the mother are connected; the word "liquid" seems to unite them all, apparently without vexation to the reader.

Later, when Stephen wishes to hear the "word known to all men" from his mother's ghost, he is thinking of mother love, *amor matris,* and especially a quotation from Aquinas, *amor vero;* these are connected in his mind with the phrase "love's bitter mystery," bitter like bile and the sea. The reader is troubled by the reference to Aquinas—in part, as shall be discussed in chapter 6, because the lines were dropped from the text, but particularly because of the letters in the Latin phrase. The bile bowl of bitter waters connects with mother and with love in various metaphoric ways, but least apparent and finally most puzzling is the connection of letters: "the mass of dull liquid" seems to contain the quotation "*amor ver aliquid aliqui.*" What was a mystery of love is a puzzle of letters. (By irksome reinforcement, when in "Circe" Stephen sings the introit "*vidi aquam,*" he reinforces the scene from the morning when he was looking at the water, and the directions for his singing, quite troublingly, are "*aliquantulum.*") The word "liquid," initially a seemingly transparent picture, becomes a puzzle through the vexation of reading the text.

"Poet," from Greek, and "picture," from Latin (with an obvious gloss on *ut pictura poesis*), are classical in origin, evoking the classical epistemology of reality and depiction; "puzzle" has no clear etymological origin, so it appears to upset and invert in genealogy the words that precede it, just as the puzzle undoes the representation and the status of the poet. Thus the phrase itself ("the poet's picture puzzle") seems to reproduce what is unique about the text of *Ulysses* in bringing together disparate ideas—those of the language of classical philology and philosophy with those of contemporary deconstruction. The studied alliteration of the phrase "poet's picture puzzle" foregrounds one letter as if to magnify the essential purpose of any letter: stressed in repetition, the letter is a reminder that all the puzzles of *Ulysses* have their origin in the etiology of Joyce's iritis and in the ways in which it is reflected in the intentional vexation of the text, whereby and wherein what seems to be clear and understandable—say, a cat or the sea—becomes blurred, obscured, and puzzling. The world of the text, apparently without you and without end, is just another word, without *u* and *n*.

Genealogy requires the tracing of one set of phrases in the order in which they appear in the novel to see, as if in a case study in ophthalmology, the dis-lexic origins of disjunctive parts of letters as they make up what becomes a puzzle. Stephen in "Proteus" imagines a visit to his uncle Richie Goulding; this scene of Stephen's imagining already unhinges narrative presentation as it realistically depicts a visit and then unimagines it precisely in its "seeming" depiction ("Am I not going there. Seems not"). Stephen imagines his uncle saying to him, in a not-real offer of nonexistent food, "We have nothing in the house but backache pills" (3.98). The fact of Goulding's sore back becomes a notion that attaches itself to his appearances in the text, as the realistic object of the legal bag forms part of the depiction of his character. So much seems the stable function of narrative. Bloom, thinking of Goulding in "Hades," remembers the legal bag and additionally notes, "that backache of his. . . . Thinks he'll cure it with pills. All breadcrumbs they are" (6.61). When he meets Goulding and eats with him in the Ormond, Bloom observes him closely in a telling description: he "saw the tightened features strain. Backache he. Bright's bright eye. . . . Pills, pounded bread" (11.614–16). Bloom continues to think about the nostrum (a false remedy much like Stephen's imagined visit), but he particularly diagnoses Goulding's ailment as Bright's disease, in which the kidney is affected by alcohol consumption, resulting in pains in the back and a brightened luster in the eye. Bloom makes a simple association of the disease and its symptom—"Bright's bright eye"—although he errs, as Bright is the name of the physician; but his association is enforced by the repetition of letters. (It is not at all coincidental, it must be observed, that the eye is indicated as a symptom in this configuration of words.) Last, in "Circe," Goulding, clasping his hand to his back, is quoted as saying, "Ah! Bright's! Lights!" (15.516). The phrase in and of itself is puzzling in meaning; if Goulding's disease were to make him sensitive to strong light, he would resemble Joyce. Yet there may be no specific reference to this phrase; it is a sort of empty place, a puzzle without first seeming to be one. It may only have behind it the forcefully puzzling aspect of letters. Goulding's apparent echoing what Bloom has said ("Bright's bright eye"), making a connection between eyes and light, is present through the variation that comes from the possibilities in the forms of the letters *b* and *l*. Letters when highlighted shed light on the obscure and puzzling.

With the idea of discovery, Goulding opens that indispensable part of his identity, the legal bag, to reveal "*tightpacked pills*" (15.503). While enough meaning has accrued in the narrative depiction of these issues for the reader to recognize that "tightpacked" refers to Bloom's belief that the medicine is nothing other than rolled up and compressed bread crumbs and that "tight" also refers to the condition of Goulding's back, there is an additional meaning that comes from the appearance of letters: constellated together throughout the text, separated by the spaces of pages as lines are separated by space and size in eye charts, are various words with letters deceptively similar to the ones in this phrase to account for what becomes its puzzling effect. To wit, "t*ight*packed *pills*" reveals "br*ight*backpills," itself a condensation of "Bright's backache pills," through the same configurations of *ight* in "bright" "light" and "tight"; the similarities of *b* and *t* and the deceptive inversion of *b* and *p* in "back" and "packed"; and the mere repetition of *pills*. (The word "pills" in *Ulysses* is subject to several deformations, once derived ["110 Pills"] from "Post No Bills" [8.101].) What is seen in such examples, if they are stared at closely enough, is just this puzzling packing of the possibility inherent in the deceptive forms of letters, in visible if disjunctive pieces, reconstellated in disruptive parts. Pertinent to the "poet's picture puzzle" of crafted intent, all these phrases appear in the manuscript from the earliest stages of the novel's composition. Gabler projects the phrase "tightpacked pills" in "Circe" from a lost manuscript, corroborating its presence in the Rosenbach fair copy that Joyce himself wrote out.[3] The draft of "Circe," it should be noted, was written during the eye attack of 1921. Thus this entire essential cluster running throughout the book was not a late addition but an essential and original part of the puzzle as much as the narrative of the novel. Indeed the narrative level of depiction, the facts of Bright's disease, the nostrum, and Goulding are all secondary to the puzzling deception of letters.

The list of Molly's lovers in "Ithaca" is a case in point about some item that appears at first to be clear and to refer to something within the text, yet that becomes on scrutiny clouded and uncertain. The list has always had a questionable status as information, filled as it is with names that come from comment, surmise, and comedy. But lists are items meant to be seen and thought about;[4] and, while they are thought about and paused over, the problematic aspect of the basic, lexical level becomes apparent: perhaps there is the foremost challenge to its meaning. Among the names are the following in sequence, which suspiciously share identical parts, first in suffixes: "Christopher Callin*an*, Leneh*an, an* Itali*an* org*an*grinder, *an* unknown gentlem*an*" (17.2137–38). As the repeated part, *an*, begins to move into other positions within the words, this repetition undermines the meaning of the list by giving it its own generative logic; as well, it has its own rhythmic connections, a sort of "love's old sweet song." As reinforcement of this lexical cluster, earlier in the list there is "Bernard Corrig*an*" and later "Alderm*an* John Hooper . . . Father Sebasti*an*"; there is also a visual and echoic similarity in "Benjam*in* Dollard and Sim*on* Dedalus"—variations of letter shapes. All the identity of these lovers is called into dispute by letters that list them; what purports to be a meaningful series is made difficult by the disposition of its smallest parts. While Irish names have a tendency to end with *an*, Boylan and Mulligan are missing from this list; and while the indefinite pronoun is common, the additional presence of "an Italian organgrinder" and "an unknown gentleman" reinforces a puzzling and gendered quality. To top off the disruptions, the entire list ends with "and so on to no last term"; its factual aura dissipates into repetition, alliteration, even a near palindrome—"on to no."

If what is not immediately apparent can become so on myopic inspection, some puzzling material is immediately evident, such as the line of type that sets Dignam's name and sits quite noticeably and obtrusively foregrounded in the text: "mangiD kcirtaP." (7.206). Its first function is undeniably to present that particular density of print that Joyce must have encountered with his magnifying glass; its second function is to make disfunctional the act of reading that text, with the reversed words vexing the eye. In a novel of much similitude, however, this presentation of a "real" type as it is set is wrong; the letters appear as letters—that is to say, not as they would appear to a typesetter, to whom the letters themselves would also be backward and not only the name they spell out. (The endstop would similarly precede the letters, not follow them.) Why this is so suggests something about what Joyce wants to do with all the letters of his novel, complicating reading by puzzling the eye.

At a practical level, there is no type, hot lead or set letters, that reads forward in the case so that it prints backward on the page; there is no way, in short, to reverse the process of type into printed, visual words. But Joyce isn't really interested in the process of printing (the few details in "Aeolus" notwithstanding) so much as he is in the product, for the product is what is to be seen. Even in the handwritten Rosenbach manuscript, Joyce writes out the name seen backward with letters forward.[5] Had he wished to reproduce the image exactly, he could have done so there with his own lettering. Throughout the various proofreadings of Darantière's work, where no skill by the considerably skilled printer could produce the effect of backward type, Joyce was content to have the letters read correctly, making only emendations so that the final letters were capitalized rather than the initial ones.[6] Joyce did not trouble about the imaging of the letters because he was concerned less with the process of getting words to the page than with the process of reading itself, with the page as its object. And having the letters read forward and yet constitute a word backward maximizes the reader's confusion. Joyce knew that readers see letters forward and that they read forward, always looking ahead. Even the eye charts that he peered at so frequently tested the limits of acuity by offering letters similar in form—to wit, *T, P, Z, E, F*—jumbled, disordered, repeated, but rarely inverted and backward. It was their modalities that intrigued him, not their impossibilities, things that never were. The letters seen forward but making a word that has meaning only when seen backward is a prime example of the dislexia Joyce brings to each reader throughout the text. The metathesis of the letters (which Stuart Gilbert recognizes as a rhetorical figure)[7] is a transposition of meaning that is always present in this disfunctionally read text. The process of seeing with difficulty what is on the page and trying to anticipate what is to come, the essential act of the eye's involvement with the novel, is what Joyce makes irritating and puzzling.

As a side-glance, it might be remarked that, while Bloom sees his two shelves of books reflected in the front-room mirror, their titles as catalogued by "Ithaca" read forward normally (17.1361–1408). The details provided by the text stress the particular material quality of the books themselves, with color or condition of covers, and even reproduce the long *s* from both printing and script in the seventeenth-century inscription of one "rendered into Englifh" (17.1399).[8] Consistency is not Joyce's aim in these or any matters, but rather the playful and puzzling disruption of all possibilities of all that the eye tries to see.

One "backward" reader within *Ulysses* is the vision of Rudy, who, only because he is a ghost, can read both forward and backward. The backward-yet-forward name recreated on the page in "Aeolus" stands in for an absent, now defunct Dignam, so that the name itself on the page is a ghost of what it should be, a sight of something impalpable, a glimpse of what cannot be there. As such, it is a paradigm of all language in this novel whose author himself was subject to blind spots and absences and who sought to create the same effect in the materiality of print in words on the page.

This perplexing aspect of the visual text and its confused and complex reading surface is also brought before the reader by the presence on the page of other signs that are purely visual but are presented as if they were depictions of something thought by the characters. Here most evidently is applied the tension of the puzzling letter shapes and the unraveling picture of the novel, as these signs add to Joyce's disruptive reading dynamic of optical confusion. There is, for example, the presence of the ampersands as if they were words: "Maginni, professor of dancing, &c" (10.56, 1238). Molly's soliloquy, read as if spoken, contains a host of such conflations: she thinks of gifts at "Xmas" (18.453), a word that exists primarily as a written term. There are numbers that appear in her monologue as symbols, as in her puzzling over the meaning of the phrase to give "9 points out of 10" (18.269) or her thinking the adverbial phrase as "1st thing" (18.479).⁹ Surely a visual form thought as a word but depicted as a sign is something to stop the eye of the reader, make him halt in the process of reading, and make him puzzle out what appears to be presented on the page. When Molly thinks about preparing for Boylan's arrival, she remembers giving the coin to the one-legged sailor at "1/4 after 3" (18.344), yet she too thinks (on the same page, line 333) of the actual time of Boylan's arrival as "four." One way to account for this obvious inconsistency is, unsatisfactorily, to attribute it to Molly's feminine nature; another is to attribute it to Joyce's disruption of the logic of representation, a challenge to phallogocentrism in which Molly would share. Yet ultimately the reader should realize that she is remembering what she has *seen* written down in Boylan's letter. Readers have also only seen this time written out within the text: whatever issue there is as to the fact that a reader is not actually present to "hear" Molly tell Bloom the time she expects Boylan (as Kenner notes),¹⁰ he has seen the text where Bloom says, "at four she said," so that the time exists as something written out on the page, as it does for Molly in the letter. One may think in numbers if the numbers come, but, having seen a text, the eye remembers the shape on the page.

The text depicts an individual who executes a similar diversionary trick with letters. Bloom remarks on the doctor who "got fellows to stick [papers] up or stick them up himself for that matter on the q.t. . . . POST NO BILLS. POST 110 PILLS" (8.99). By altering letters only slightly, probably with plastered bills (Boylan, one ought to remember, is himself a billsticker)—B to P, "NO" to a cipher "110"—a new meaning is created, one that relies on the similarity of letters (and see Goulding's backache pills, above). Here is the advertised proof of the modality of the visible, the different possibilities inherent in the form of the letters in print; and because a doctor performs this disruption of unauthorized advertising, the ingenuity of the artist and the presence of illness both are aligned as the cause. (If Joyce's iritis had been a consequence of his inadequately treated syphilis, and if he had known of the cause, this small passage would have a certain poignancy.)

Certainly the text must be trying to puzzle the reader's eye and make unsure what appears factual when, during a conversation in "Aeolus," letters jump. Crawford is speaking of the great forefathers of journalism: "Then

Paddy Hooper worked Tay Pay who took him on to the *Star*. Now he's got in with Blumenfeld . . . Pyatt!" (7.686). All this lore is true. The "Tay Pay" is meant to reproduce the Irish pronunciation of T. P., the initials of O'Connor's name, yet the name already provides for the reader an association that Crawford goes on to make to another newspaperman, the French journalist Pyatt. In the very pronunciation of those initials as written out in the text, "tay pay" jumbled in dis-lexia produces "py(y)at(t)"—one missing letter, one extra. This example occurs in the chapter about print; the headline for this section, "CLEVER, VERY," is a hysteron proteron rhetorically in terms of its semiotics, but it is a literal puzzle to the eye, repeating the *ver*. This chapter has earlier shown Bloom watch the type being set for Dignam's obituary notice, where the displacement of the letters as a visual product aims both to underscore the materiality of printing and to undermine it as an object for the reader. The chapter also is one in which a mistake will be made that produces the "actual" line of jumbled type that "appears" in the evening's *Telegraph*. Jumbled letters are a fact of life in how a great daily organ is turned out and also in how a great modern novel is written; they are the inevitable puzzling free play of any text that Joyce embraces with his opaque eye and magnifying glass. That one of the headlines, referring to what was thought by earlier critics to be a central theme in this chapter and perhaps even in the book, is reproduced "HOUSE OF KEY(E)S" (7.141) is certainly a notice that Joyce literally publishes, to the effect that whatever seems to be of importance to the depiction of character or theme, what seems to be the clue to a mystery, depends on the visual in its presences and absences. All deciphering of picture puzzles needs a key, as does all reading of the disrupted and disruptive text, and the key embeds the necessary eye: just change the parentheses—k)*eye*(s.

The eye may be the key to what is hidden inside of and in parts of words; when something in the text arrests it, one can almost be sure that the catching is intentional, the work of the puzzling poet as the way to make the reader complicit in handicap and confusion. The eye sees in black and white on the page, closely, needing a prosthetic device, as Joyce did with the magnifying glass that improved his sight as the ear trumpet was supposed to improve weak hearing; as *Finnegans Wake* has it, with its emphasis on the aural, "he's seen it in black and white through his eyetrompit" (247.32). (*Ulysses* also relates impaired eyes and ears: "Old Mr Verschoyle with the ear trumpet loves old Mrs Verschoyle with the turnedin eye"

[12.1496].) The close, even mechanical scrutiny, however, yields the possibilities of trickery in the letters seen so near, their similar modalities leading to a trumping of the eye. This trickery of depiction has always been possible in the pictorial arts, even by the ancients, as Bloom is aware: "The Sacred Heart that is: showing it. Heart on his sleeve. Ought to be sideways and red it should be painted like a real heart. . . . Would birds come then and peck like the boy with the basket of fruit but he said no because they ought to have been afraid of the boy. Apollo that was" (6.954–59). By referring to Apollo, Bloom, like Joyce and the reader, connects gods and artists and recognizes the deceptive quality of all depiction. Yet the artist as writer can become a trickster too by using the deceptive modalities of the letters in a text that depicts in order to create a lexical trompe l'oeil. This very thought of Bloom about art plays just such a trick of the eye. The Bloomism of mistaking Apollo for Apelles is only one jest in the passage, an error as much of changed letters as changed facts. The artist whose work is alluded to is not Apelles but Zeuxis, so that in Bloom's mistake the reader's eyes run the gamut of names from A to Z. Straining with or without an eyetrompit to see such puzzles in and beyond the words of *Ulysses,* the reader tries to peck at some of the deceptively depicted "fruits" of meaning in the text but is alerted to the likelihood of trumpery.

When the odd and striking word appears, its purpose may be to introduce some realistic fact, but its effect is always comic, disruptive, and often purely visual; such is the tension between picture and puzzle. As the word seems to start out from the page, complicating what ought to be the facile activity of reading, the very deceptive, similar materiality of language is stressed; yet as the word stands out as a trick, the language also simultaneously dematerializes what is represented, the puzzle undoing the picture. Here is an example of the odd word that stands out in the text; its tricking effect works on the eye and on the mind, and meaning is extracted only after much vexation and jumbled difficulty. The text must be seen as disrupted and disjointed, with only certain parts magnified into prominence and importance, and those small enough. As Boylan is in the hackney car on his way to Molly, the progress is described thus: "By Dlugacz' porkshop . . . trotted a gallantbuttocked mare" (11.884). This last adjective certainly puzzles the eye and requires some thought for understanding by a process of exfoliation, thinking as well as reading: Boylan eyes a certain part of equine anatomy, the toff actually looking at the horse's "glossy rump" (11.525), hence "gallant/buttocked." There may be a sly glance at the *Dubliners'* "Two Gallants" in this ironic view of Boylan's view. (There may also be a reference in this rhythmical chapter to Stephen's thinking about prosody in "Proteus": "*Won't you come to Sandymount,/ Madeline the mare?* Rhythm begins, you see. I hear. Acatalectic tetrameter of iambs marching, No: agallop: *deline the mare*" [3.21–24]. The "agallop" and "gallant" echo each other in horseness because, as the reader hears, he sees similar signs.) Moreover, Boylan is on his way to see Molly, among whose prominent features are her buttocks, so that Boylan probably has them on his mind.

The diffused and highlighted reading sights and sites of these odd words span the novel and begin to slip, through difficulty, into error. "Buttock" is an inappropriate term for the hindquarters of a horse. The cab, we are told in the passage, is passing Dlugacz's porkshop (and thus the alert reader knows that it is on Dorset Street and just around the corner from its destination). In that shop in the morning, Bloom wished to watch the servant girl walk away, being especially interested in seeing her hips swing, "her moving hams" (4.172). The word choice there is obviously dictated by the setting and the chapter's symbol (the kidney) to be one regarding meat, but it too is somewhat inappropriate diction for that part of the human anatomy where the back changes name—as inappropriate in its own way as "buttocks" is for a horse; there is a puzzling quality to the word choices. In fact, they should be exchanged. And the mind does exchange them, after carrying over some two hundred pages of text, as the alert eye, emulating the magnifying glass, connects disparate sights and sites, focusing on the hind parts, and makes a playful response.

Yet there is even more behind this elaborate visual joke, something that gets to another part of the odd phrase "gallantbuttocked"—something uncovered, so to speak, by myopic scrutiny. Earlier, when Bloom enters the library after having made his examination in the museum of those seats of divinity, Mulligan whispers to Stephen: "His pale Galilean eyes were upon her mesial groove. Venus Kallipyge" (9.615). The perplexing adjective "gallantbuttocked" in "Sirens" has as one of its meanings, a meaning haltingly revealed to the eye by the modalities of letters, a literal transcription and translation of this Greek word: "buttocks" translates *pyge* exactly, and "gallant" transcribes (while changing) similar letters in *kalli*. A visual memory of the word Mulligan uses, if not of the anatomy it describes, reveals the humor behind this unique adjective. The foreignness of the

Greek phrase (a means of foregrounding the density of letters) begins to blend with the alien appearance of the neologism "gallantbuttocked." Nor is this mixture of ancient languages and uneven etymology so foreign to other parts of *Ulysses* (it is to be found in the phrase "poet's picture puzzle"): Joyce's theory about what constitutes *Moly* and its efficacy against syphilis depends upon a very loose translation of syphilis as derived from the two Greek words *su* and *phylis*, "swine love"; it is equally a visual joke, even if Joyce meant it as a serious contribution to a reading of the classics.[11] The combination of letters of different languages produces a confusion of registers in which to read.

In a seemingly perverse modality, "Venus Callipyge" appears in "Circe" (15.1705), offering another variation on this string. The use of the *c* might indicate a shift from the Greek kappa to the Latin hard *c*, thus mimicking by letters what the title of the novel achieves in shifting from the Greek to the Roman world. Yet this new sight of "Callipyge" suggests another; the word contains many of the letters in Calypso or Calpensis, thus making Molly the afterimage of all of Bloom's rear views. In their magnified importance, letters carry the weight of meaning.

Similar letters may make similar shapes—this, after all, is the point of the ophthalmologist's examination for visual acuity—but similar letters can also involve very different signs and sounds. In "Lestrygonians," Bloom creates a poem not much worse than Stephen's vampire poem: "*The hungry famished gull / Flaps o'er the waters dull*" (8.62–63); the italics serve to make the textuality of his endeavor stand out. He elevates his effort by remarking that "that is how poets write, the similar sounds." Immediately before noting the gulls, Bloom thinks about a brewery: "Vats of porter, . . . Rats get in too. . . . Imagine drinking that! Rats: vats." Similar sounds seem to be in his mind, but for the text, these thoughts are similar signs; while the first example is a poem in which the sound is stressed, the second is in prose, whereby the similarity is initially one of sight (thus raising the prospect of a tension between the aural and the visual). Earlier Bloom thinks of a marching cadence: "Table: able. Bed: ed" (5.73), which is both aural by rhyme and visual by repetition of letters.

Between these two examples in the text is a paragraph in which the issue of the appearance and form of letters on the page is raised by an odd configuration that catches the eye and buttresses these thoughts in Bloom's mind. Bloom is described in the third person: "Looking down he saw flapping strongly, wheeling between the gaunt quaywalls, gulls" (8.51–52). This sentence, coming from a consciousness other than Bloom's, is sophisticated in its style, and the sophistication is best seen in the way that its syntax replicates the action of the birds: the object of the verb "saw" is placed at the end of the sentence, allowing the various modifiers (participial, prepositional, adverbial) to come between and thus create the image of the birds' motion in a circular manner above the river, between its banks. Yet a closer glance reveals more in this sentence: the concept of *betweenness* raised by the birds' action and by the sentence's imitative syntax (as well as the idea of reflection in the water of the river) is continued by a repetitive pattern in the words of the sentence, a pattern exploiting similar signs: "walls, gulls." (This repetition obviously anticipates Bloom's poem with its "gull"/"dull" that follows several lines later; insofar as Bloom picks up the word "flapping" from this sentence for his poem, one can say that he is seeing his own text, the one he is in.) One might say that the "walls"/"gulls" pair is alliterative, but it is so less for reasons of sound than those of sight—as it were, restoring the visual and lexical component to the etymology of the word "alliteration"—*ad littera,* "to the letter." Joyce is specifically playing with the difference between sight and sound in letters, to the advantage of sight over sound on a printed page and to the confusion of the reader of them.[12] (Here is a major difference between *Ulysses* and the *Wake.*) The visual similarities in this sentence require a further sharp glance. No one hearing a poem with words pronounced "gŏnt" and "kē" in it would think the words alliterative in sound, but they are to the eye, close enough to tease the eye and to make the brain think "gaunt quay."[13] That they appear alike is a fact—or accident—of typology of the sort of possibilities of language that the disabled Joyce always saw in the modality of letters. Yet they are tantalizingly different in their dis-lexic reversing of the image and order of their signs: *g* and *q, au* and *ua.* The effect is to reinforce the bracketing *betweenness* that is reflected and replicated in the sentence's imitative syntax and to present again a visually disfunctional lexeme.

In another example, aggressively puzzling and strange words again trouble the eye and bring reading to a halt. In "Wandering Rocks," one character goes on in detail about a city council meeting concerned with the language question: "No quorum even and Hutchinson, the lord mayor, in Llandudno and little Lorcan Sherlock doing *locum tenens* for him. Damned Irish language, language of our forefathers" (10.1009–12). All this seems again factual for the reader: not only does this passage describe an actual meeting; it does so with much detail, appropriate diction, and a great deal of irony. The lord mayor was away in Wales, and Lorcan Sherlock did stand in for him; the terms "quorum" and "*locum tenens*" are correct for the deliberative procedures. Yet the puzzling aspect begins to come into focus: for a meeting on the Irish language, the language is aggressively un-Gaelic, Latin and Welsh rather. Moreover, the odd combination of "Lorcan" and "*locum*" seems to wish to catch the eye by modal similarity, a repetition of the unfamiliar, reinforced by the proximity of "Llandudno" (which itself is an odd word dis-lexic in its appearance). Joyce must have been pleased by the coincidence wherein "real events" are disrupted by language: first, that Sherlock was a substitute, and second, that the very words so nicely play off each other visually. He is not above using this concatenation again, as if by way of reinforcing its lexical oddness, repetition being a feature necessary for weak eyes: "Circe" describes how "*Harrington, late thrice Lord Mayor of Dublin . . . confers with councillor Lorcan Sherlock,* locum tenens" (15.1378–80). As noted at other points, because such "Circe" passages are always in italics, the second "locum tenens" is in roman, giving a reversed visual sign of lexical difference. Other letters have been substituted, as the Hutchinson of the earlier passages gives way to the slightly similar Harrington here; and if Harrington is the "late" mayor, and truly departed, then Sherlock is by necessity *locum tenens.* What is actually "holding the place," as the Latin says, is the humor of the information (who was mayor, when, and the other facts) and the particular visual joke that derives from similar letters, seemingly incongruous, which take up place and space in the text, puzzling and trumping the eye as it tries to proceed through the text.

As this last example illustrates, the modality of the same letters of the alphabet makes different words in different languages, increasing the implied tension of sight and sound and adding another register or context in which the eye can be trumped. Foreign words, as italicized or phonemically different from the surrounding text, are alien and estrange the reading process. The same alphabetical sign in a different language valorizes form and shape over meaning and confuses the reader, making uncertain what is read. One Italian cursing another in "Eumaeus" says "*Culo rotto*" (16.314), and Bloom does not understand. Yet in the same chapter, when Bloom thinks about the effects of inebriation on one person and he says of his "other gay doings when rotto" (16.1187), he uses the same word in a different language. Bloom's ear is unlikely to have made the connection, but the reader's eye must. Bloom makes another such connection between the same languages: when trying to remember the phone number for Nannetti, he recalls a number he associates with that of his friend Citron (7.219). Moments later, he remembers the soap, and he does so because it is what he redundantly calls "Citronlemon" (7.225), combining two languages into one jumbled word.

Stephen has a similar trick played in his thoughts in "Proteus," although, unlike Bloom, he is aware of the languages and of his punning. In that crucial passage when he thinks about how sight affects our sense of the world, Stephen considers Aristotle's distinction of "coloured signs" and bodies. With pedantic predilection, he alludes to Dante's praise of Aristotle: "*maestro di color che sanno*" (3.6). *Color* is the Italian pronoun, obviously, and it comes from an exact quotation, but it resonates as a visual pun in the order of Stephen's thought about sight and color. The British spelling (immediately before in "coloured bodies") and the American tease each other into supplemental play with the Italian word. The pun is of course aural (Stephen speaking to himself in the passage), but the first order of reality is on the page, where the eye sees the words and imposes meaning on them. And here the ludic poles are reversed: the eye sees apparently the same word (certainly the English reader would note the similarity—and Joyce also had an American for a publisher), but the mind later restores the difference.

Stephen himself is aware of making a joke, this one in French, which appears visually as well as aurally in the text. Remembering Paris and Kevin Egan's son Patrick, Stephen has the image of the young man as he "lapped the sweet *lait chaud* with pink young tongue, plump bunny's face. Lap, *lapin*" (3.165). The italicized last French word seems to echo both verbally and visually the English participle of the given past tense, "lapped." (Additionally, there is the visual enjambment of "young tongue.")

He may not be aware of making another such puzzle in the same chapter, "Proteus." Thinking about rhythm in the shortened metrical phrase "*deline the mare*" (3.22, from the passage quoted earlier in reference to rhythm and the rear image of the horse), Stephen introduces a word that stands out in italics. Because other such phrases in the same chapter present foreign languages, the reader's eye may be tricked into seeing the last word as the Latin for sea, *mare*. The two Greek words for sea have already appeared in the text in the first chapter (Stephen hearing them spoken by Mulligan) as *ponton* and *Thalatta* (1.78, 80), although to add confusion they are in the Latin alphabet. Stephen, deep in thought, may comically be oblivious to what is before his eyes all around him, the waters of the Irish sea. The reader's eye has been assaulted with words, all in Latin characters, from different languages.

Bloom is no less capable of such feats of language than Stephen. In worrying about the word *voglio*, Bloom is concerned as to whether the *g* that is present in the word is pronounced, elided, or silent and thus absent—a conflict of sight and sound; he questions the notions of the Italian language. He fails, of course, to ask Nannetti, although the only reason for believing the latter should know, apparently, is his name (Bloom, for example, does not know German). Bloom's failure surfaces in a scene in "Circe" when he asks the "Marion" who hums the duet from *Don Giovanni*, "Are you sure about that *Voglio*? I mean the pronunciati" (15.355). What appears to be an syncopic end to his inquiry and another failed attempt at certitude is really an elaborate series of continued visual puns on the Italian language. (As a speaker of Italian for so long, Joyce must have been particularly aware of the carryover between the two languages, in addition to his recognition of the modalities of letters.) The abscission of "pronunciati" opens the visual possibilities of letters into other languages. For one, the truncated word with its ending looks like any number of Italian words; in fact, it seems nearly as authentic as the word "Giovanni" that appears immediately before it. Moreover, it resembles at its end the name Nannetti, the name of the very man Bloom thinks could help him with the quandary.

Hebrew forms the basis for another trick of the eye. When Father Conmee belatedly attempts to read his breviary, he interrupts the tryst of Lenehan and the girl, both emerging from the woods after venery (and Lenehan's version of this interruption in "Oxen" is a good gloss on Conmee's obtuseness). If Conmee is oblivious to the reason the two are in the woods, the breviary is more aware, and so too is the reader with an alert eye; Conmee turns from the girl to the passage "*Sin:—Principes me* . . ." (10.204). The first word is a heading taken from the section designations of Psalm 119 and is a letter of the Hebrew alphabet; Conmee should hear it pronounced as *shin*. And what he reads is complicated by following the Hebrew with Latin, both italicized to suggest their alien quality to the surrounding text. Yet there on the page is a word that accurately describes in English what Conmee fails to recognize in the material world in front of him, even though the event is as plain as the letters on the page before him: *sin.*

In "Cyclops," within several pages there are two words of a particular exotic and Eastern suggestiveness: "Rahat" as a proper name (12.562) and "loquat" (12.1004). Their endings, with the same letters (*at*), give a particularly Arabic cast to their appearance, although the second word is a corruption of a Chinese one; and that Arabic cast fits neatly over suggestions of Gibraltar with its exotic trees and Molly, the context in which the second word appears. Yet the association of the word "loquat" with Molly has no real semiotic sense; it is a puzzle. Perhaps it is reinforced only by the lexical, visual similarity of the first part of "loquat" to "loquacious." The magnified and fragmented opacity of these letters makes for a glimpse of something not there in the text at that point; language makes present to the text what is absent.[14]

The astute if challenged reader should by now know that meaning is often hidden in the text of *Ulysses,* occluded and unclear, and must be sought everywhere by the process of reading with myopic scrutiny. What irritates the eye in the reading of *Ulysses* are words and letters seen there on the page and yet not seen. In short, Joycean reading is meant to be discontinuous, as was Joyce's sight, filled with gaps of uncertainty and obscurity. Here is a further challenge by Joyce to the normal process of the eye engaged in reading; and it is a further irritation because it occurs in two dimensions.

Current theories of conventional reading (discussed in chapter 3) suppose a ready extrapolation of meaning from a slight glance at a few words, a process that Joyce makes impossible by vexing and disfiguring the lexical surface. But in forcing the eye to move drastically out of direction, Joyce makes puzzling and problematic the most ancient of reading dynamics, those in space and time. These are the dimensions of the reader's world, not only because the reader is mortal but particularly because the act of reading of the text in hand takes place in real time and space. As a material object itself, a book is always read in space (the reader's place and also the place of the book in the line of sight); the pages are encountered in spatial order. Yet a book is read over time as well, particularly the real time of the reader's experience and also the time engaged in reading the pages in sequence. A dis-lexic text disrupts this essential pattern by moving the eye in the reading process to different sites and to different times, to different places in the book and to different times in the act of seeing, thus jumbling and altering the traditionally continuous dynamic. Disoriented in time and space, the reader is affected in his being as reader, infected with a visual illness; the real time existence is destabilized as was Joyce's experience of the world.

It was remarked before that Stephen, walking on the beach, closes his eyes to the world (eyes that saw it imperfectly and myopically anyway), and he is to be reassured that, on opening them, the world is there all the time "without you . . . without end." He seems comfortable with the classical existence of the universe. Yet that world is unstable because the letters that make it are unstable, a status sanctioned by the reading of Martha Clifford's typing error of "world" for "word," demonstrating that the world without *l* was the word. The instability of letters makes suspect (it was noted) Stephen's claim that the world without you or end could be the word without *u* or *n*. Correspondingly, the material world is destabilized for the reader. It is important that in Stephen's destabilization by sign or by shutting his eyes, he considers the necessary dimensions of time and space: "You are walking through it howsomever. . . . A very short space of time through very short times of space" (3.11–12). The distinctions he draws are from Lessing, but they can be applied to the reader's impeded "walk" through the words of the text, where the dimensions are the ones challenged in the reader's world, leading to destabilization and disorientation. As Stephen's world is challenged by sight, even with the dimensions of time and space, so too the reader's world is challenged by reading, as that activity takes place in time and space.

While walking to the Ormond Hotel, Bloom is said to spot Boylan a distance away as he too approaches the bar: "He eyed and saw afar . . . a gay hat riding on a jauntingcar" (11.302). Bloom's eyesight would have to be sharp enough to see so small a part of Boylan's person to recognize his rival over such a span; distance is added to perception here ("eyed and saw afar"). In Boylan's subsequent trip in this car, the reader encounters the puzzling phrase "gallantbuttocked mare," which requires that he too eye things from far away in the text, some before and some after the sight on the page. The activity of reading and converting the sign into thought takes place afar, over large distances in the dimension of space, making a disruption in the pages of a book.

Yet, as the eye searches for meaning, traversing several pages and consequently creating a distance in space, it engages the other dimension of time as well: it creates a site of meaning that reflects in thought what was seen in sight elsewhere earlier or projects what will appear later. This too is a function of what is on the page and what is on a later page, the flat surface that is interpreted by thinking as near and far, in the space between appearances in different pages; but that space is additionally measured by the passage of reading time, not in chronology but in the physics of Joyce's jumbled letters: a text must be read backward and forward, the eye jumping ahead or behind, in a disturbed physical motion. The movement considered here is the movement of the reader's eye across the page and its consequent movement over the turned pages progressing through the text.[15] Those motions are twisted, inverted, and crossed—they re-create the symptoms of eye troubles.

In one scale, what is on the page adumbrates (literally, shadows) what is not immediately there, suggesting an absence in space of the material of language; it also involves conversely missing what is there on the page. These both are the equivalent of the blind spot, the opaque eye's limitation. The other scale of the eye's movement is one in which what is on the page projects what will appear and be present proleptically on a later page in the passage of time. This is a sort of unclear mirroring or ghosting of what is seen unsurely. This scale has a complementary opposite in which something seen at an earlier time, but not recognized, is made evident and material at a later space in the text, requiring an unclear image to be later brought into focus and clarified, a visual form of a "retrospective arrangement" (as Bloom remembers Kernan saying) that literally involves looking backward to reorder reading. The distinction between these two scales of movement is between what is there or not there on the page in space and what was elsewhere or will be elsewhere in the space of the text to be encountered in time. Thus *Ulysses* is a text in many dimensions, one that must be seen by the eye carefully first as it is on the page and then later as it is in the mind's eye.

Here too the disruption of time and space of reading in a dis-lexic text resembles the symptoms of Joyce's eye disease. Thus, as the symptoms of his pathology resulted in opacity, blind spots, and obscurity, Joyce employs two scales of movement here, similarly disrupting the eye in reading. The tricks of the eye make the reader see things that are not there, the letters present on the page tricking him into seeing absence; there is a blind spot or opaque area in the limited field. Other letters and words make the reader see things that are not on that page but are elsewhere in some lexical version before or after on other pages. The notions of such "afterimage" and "foreshadowing" (this last not meant as a commonplace critical term) call up by way of metaphor the idea of a ghostly image on the page, blurred but glimpsed, that hovers around the material aspect of language printed as text and adumbrates as well the recurring images of the eye chart and the pathology of glaucoma that Joyce experienced. Absence and presence, a visible premonition of things to come, what Bloom calls in another context "coming events cast their shadows before"—all are created by what is seen on the page; all are part of the ineluctable modalitites of the visible surface, disrupted and disfunctionally seen by an eye that is puzzled by the poet.

In the first of these distinctions, absence in space, the reader's eye is tricked in two different ways, into seeing what is not there or missing what is, all within the space of the immediate page (or on the page in the immediate space). One example of each blind spot, seeing and missing, might suffice. In "Circe," Edy Boardman, clearly talking in a diction vastly different from the one employed in "Nausicaa," talks about another whore's fancy man: "Stag that one is! Stubborn as a mule" (15.94). The reader, expecting animal imagery in such a chapter, as a competent reader might, would note the feral references. Yet he would be wrong, not only because the second phrase is merely a cliché but also because the first term, "stag," does not refer to an animal at all but is rather argot for a police informer; the eye has spotted no quarry in this hunt. Later in the same chapter, the soldiers urge one another on into hitting Stephen—"give him a kick in the knackers. Stick one into Jerry" (15.4483)—with the last two terms slang for testicles and penis, respectively. Distance and delay play a role here; if the reader did not glimpse the diction, the text a few lines later has Bloom addressing "the privates"—the soldiers, surely, but also the definition for the terms "knackers" and "Jerry" if the eye has failed to see them. In the first instance, what is thought to be seen there is absent; in the second, what is there (only partly) will be revealed in print in a slightly different spot.

While the confusion of words spoken by the characters is a disfunction in their discourse, those errors are made materially present through alphabetical letters that are always shifting. Bloom originally misspeaks a telling mistake: "—Well, that's a point . . . for the wife's admirers.—Whose admirers? says Joe.—The wife's advisers, I mean, says Bloom" (12.767–69). This mistake betrays Bloom's thinking (it is the Piggot's forgery of *Ulysses*), and it recurs in "Circe" with a vengeance to suggest how much Bloom wishes to hide and evade its meaning: when Mrs. Breen comments on Bloom's criticism of her clothing, she remarks, "Nice adviser!" and he disparages Molly by saying, "Frankly, though she had her advisers or admirers, I never cared much for her style" (15.554, 565–66). Bloom wishes to elide the difference and the meaning of the two terms, not willing to see the meaning behind; he has a blind spot at that point. Yet the lexicality of the words makes evident what Bloom wishes to repress. Strengthened by the common prefix *ad*, the roots of the words indicate a common action, and that, not coincidentally, is the very act of seeing: *visum* (the past participle of *videre*) and *mirare*, "to look and stare."

Sometimes the text can make palpable what is present but not depicted in it. Bloom reads "Matcham's Masterstroke" from *Titbits* (and it is no surprise that so many of these examples involve a character's reading); and, although he is otherwise engaged, he thinks, "Something new and easy. No great hurry. Keep it a bit. Our prize titbit" (4.501). His attention is equally divided between the story and the stool—so much so, in fact, that the reader cannot determine whether "our prize titbit" refers to the fruit of Beaufoy's literary labors or that of Bloom's digestion. Of course the unitalicized "titbit" is Bloom's connection of the story with the title he sees printed in the tabloid, but the reader's eye ought to catch the lexical repetition of "it a bit" and "titbit," so that not only are Bloom's thoughts associative and repetitive, but so are the letters on the page. Moreover, the actual repetition of "bit" leaves the other part of the word, "tit," unbalanced as an association in Bloom's mind. Surely the other references to the pronoun "it" in the rest of Bloom's thoughts (as in "Hope it's not too big bring on the piles again," l.509) suggest another word to balance with "tit," as "bit" (from "it a bit") repeats "bit" (from "titbit"): the word "s-it"—something material and conspicuously present but not seen during the scene. When, while still seated, Bloom thinks of Molly dressing and of her "full wagging bub," the text presents another word to balance with and mean the same thing as "tit." Thus the reader's eye has been presented with a number of physical things that are not "there" depicted in the events but that appear in the text through the modality of letters, as words come in puzzling focus after halted reading and close scrutiny.

Even such an apparently crucial concept for the novel as the word "metempsychosis" is subject to being displaced yet made present by the text when not actually seen: it is not there but is shadowed in another form. So vague a presence for so critical a term seems fitting; "metempsychosis" is, after all, a notion of represence, the appearance, in another guise and form and in another time, of that impalpable shadow the soul. Kenner has shown quite well how the exchange of Bloom and Molly in "Calypso" contains less than a reader remembers having seen, notably the fact that Bloom is not told there when Boylan is due to arrive. The reader thinks to have read ("heard") Molly say "at four," but the time is not mentioned in the text of the fourth chapter. Similarly, there is a confusion about Molly's inquiry about the word "metempsychosis." As Kenner has noted, the text does not present Molly's attempt to pronounce the word as "met him pike hoses";[16] what actually appears on the page is Bloom's question in response to what is not seen (her answer) and to what Bloom does not completely hear: "Met him what? he asked" (4.336). The text goes on to have Bloom repeat the actual word twice. The reader may think he has seen "met him pike hoses" in the exchange in the bedroom, but he has not. Later, in "Lestrygonians," the text reads that Bloom thinks, "Met him pike hoses she called it . . ." (8.112).

Yet missing things in *Ulysses* are often to be found in sight at the very site where they are lacking; the reader just suffers a temporary blind spot for the various letters present. It is not only the narrative information in disorder that provides answers but also the letters of the picture puzzle. One of the two absent parts of the word, "pike hoses," is present in the passage in another form, itself transmigrating through permutations of language; the active reader's eye may see what is not really there, as he has read something else that should make him pause. When Molly asks for the book in order to find the word to ask Bloom, she points: "Following . . . he took up a leg of her soiled drawers from the bed. No? Then, a twisted grey garter looped around a stocking. . . . Other stocking. Her petticoat" (4.321–25). "Drawers" (soiled, of course), "garter" and "stocking," "petticoat"— what else is Bloom picking up, as well as clothing of various descriptions that Molly has left off, but all examples of articles of clothing for the leg, women's *hose?* Articles of clothing may have their own grammar, but the materiality of fashion is exceeded by that materiality of language that catches the eye to show that what was not there may yet be there. Much like the first sentence of the novel, where the missing *x* was to be found in the other letters that make up the word "cross-ed," the modalities of the letters here depicting Molly's undergarments fill in part of the blank in the picture puzzle: "met him what?"—"met him [blank] hose." (In her own right, Molly remembers of the two missing parts of the word just the one that pertains to clothing; she forgets the other, phallically suggestive one, "met something with hoses in it" [18.565].)

Sometimes what the eye glimpses stands in for what is present but ought not to be seen and thought about, much like the hidden but revealed connection of "adviser"/"admirer"; obscurity might be a helpful sort of repression. Late in the novel, his eye wandering aimlessly, Bloom falls victim again to a misperception that fools both his mind and his eye; as a reader he sees what he fears but what is not there. The eye missees precisely what it does not want to glimpse; the magnification of letters brings some unwanted things forward, as magnification is likely to do. Bloom is haunted by thoughts of Boylan and does not want to see him ("Not see. Get on" [8.1172]). In the cabman's shelter, as he glances over the respective captions of the *Telegraph,* "First he got a bit of a start but it turned out to be only something about somebody named H. du Boyes, agent for typewriters or something like that" (16.1238–40). Molly's tryst and Bloom's attempts to avoid her lover are both made material, combined in more than coincidence to flash a dis-lexic message before Bloom's anxious eyes. Equally reinforcing this context is the next caption but one given in the text: "Lovemaking in Irish, £200 damages." "Lovemaking in Irish" did appear in the actual paper;[17] but Joyce saw in the reality the modalities of the visible and has Bloom and the reader see them. The newsprint seems to conspire with context to play false with Bloom's eye, to make present what he has wished all day to keep absent. Yet there is more than the context of the paper and that of Bloom's personal predicament that reinforces this trick; the particular letters and signs that make up the text—"H. du Boyes . . . like . . . Lovemaking"—produce the effect. *H. du* appears to the aimless (or rather avoiding) eye like "Hugh," and the *l* in the words following (as well as in the pound sign) add to push the "Boyes" toward "Boylan." The letters of the text conspire to publish (as it were) to Bloom and the reader a comic misreading of the sad circumstances of Bloom's life that he has sought to banish from his thoughts. What is not there *is* there, the absent Boylan only too present in the magnified letters in the newspaper for Bloom and on the page for the reader. Bloom's superficial glance deepens the text in several registers, even in the areas where it seeks by repression to omit or overlook.

If the mind is thus engaged in thinking by seeing, so often is the heart engaged in feeling what is seen; and for Joyce, as for Bloom, emotion must be put away, made distant and absent. There is something particular in Joyce's art that needs to be well hidden, less apparent than humor and more deeply set back and made absent in the text than meaning itself: the considerable sentimentality of which Joyce was capable and which runs as an undercurrent through much of the novel.[18] So when the text blurs perception, it hides emotion as well as understanding. The tricks of the eye serve the additional function of hiding and distancing certain elements of the text that have a high potential for emotion, even bathos; thus the reader is further disengaged from the world of the text (in an area where traditional reader engagement was most prevalent). As Bloom reads the newspaper and sees what he wishes to avoid, the reader is shown the depiction of emotion only then to have it obscured by the puzzling magnification of letters. This blurring of feeling by the difficulties of sight is one Joyce experienced: he missed seeing Nora at their first planned rendezvous on June 15, 1904, staring in vain at a head of reddish hair ("I may be blind"). The date of the novel, it should be remembered, a date that centers the depiction of a world, is one created by absence, postponed from a day earlier because of absence and poor vision.

Emotion in *Ulysses* is always rendered as absence: loss of a mother for Stephen or a son for Bloom; the loss of opportunity in Irish history. The tricks of the modalities of language are a way of making present what is lost, the mourning for which Joyce wished to obscure. These puzzles of the eye on the page serve Joyce well; they reveal as they conceal meaning and emotion both. Readers are removed from the text because, as Zoe says to Bloom in "Circe," "What the eye can't see the heart can't grieve for" (15.1998). The cynical narrator of "Cyclops" endorses such distancing of emotion by occluding sight while parodying the pathos of a song by Moore, "The tear is bloody near your eye" (12.397).

Thus the indirection of the possibilities of letters, diverting the eye, leads to the submerging and obscuring of emotion, putting any depiction of it into a blind spot. Much effort needs to be expended to glimpse its presence, much staring at the page as Joyce stared after Nora. In "Proteus" Stephen observes the two women out to pick cockles; he assumes that they are midwives.[19] The reader does not know if they are; in "Wandering Rocks" they are called "old women" and "sanded women," and their bag, containing cockles, is twice mentioned, once as a "midwife's bag." Perhaps this is an example of parallax incompletely seen, but certainly it involves an instability of identity when such identity depends on sight. Stephen's inference leads him, naturally, to an image of childbirth and, inevitably, to a consideration of his own parentage. He speculates: "What has she in the bag? A misbirth with a trailing navelcord, hushed in ruddy wool. The cords of all link back.... Gaze in your *omphalos*" (3.36–38). The umbilicus provides him with the connecting idea of generations from belly button–less Eve down to his own begetting, and his imagination is vivid: a dead fetus—the word that shocked him in Cork's medical theater[20]—wrapped in a bloody cloth. Yet his own vivid imagination is the equal of the reader's active mind: the dead newborn certainly has its parallel with what the reader knows (or will come to know) about Bloom's child, who was also, and not incidentally, buried wrapped in a little woolen shawl. Any good reader can make that connection, without any umbilicus, through the threads of plot. Yet the dis-lexic reader will see more; additionally, and more unconventionally, the print on the page reinforces the parallel to sight: not only does "ruddy" resemble "Rudy," but the child's full name seems to leap off the page: "*rud*dy . . . om*ph*al*os*." By way of reinforcement and reiteration of the infrequent morpheme *ph,* Stephen muses two paragraphs later on Arius and his bishop's *omphorion.* The two words reinforce themselves in Stephen's mind because they are Greek to him; to the reader they reflect and deflect a different language, that of the poignancy of Bloom's, not Stephen's, personal history, hidden from obvious sight in the text as Stephen imagines the stillborn hidden in the bag.

The fact that Stephen's self-absorbed monologue hides but reveals Bloom's emotions through a trick of the eye demonstrates the displacement of the sentimental. Additionally, it strongly suggests another way in which the characters, who live in a world of words and are themselves words, are precariously associated in the novel, not by events of plot but by the very material of the text. Here too tricks of the eye work by their diversion to question an emotional presence: through a displacement of the words on the page, the characters are obliquely brought together in confusion by the disruption of the letters. It is no surprise to find, therefore, a passage in which Bloom's thoughts reveal a trick that brings Stephen's heartfelt emotions before the eye on the page.

After Stephen declines Bloom's invitation and departs from the house in "Ithaca," the "lonechill" Bloom returns to the front room. As a ritual as well as a hygienic measure, he lights incense, applying the burning flyer of the Agendath Netaim company to the "apex of the cone till the latter reached the stage of rutilance" (17.1327). In the Latinate vocabulary of the chapter,[21] the classical glowing of the incense might go unremarked, but the eye catches something. Bloom's "rutilant" resembles not a little the *rutilantium* in the *"liliata rutilantium . . . confessorum"* of Stephen's oft-remembered memory of his mother's deathbed, a phrase highlighted by italics. Most immediately, these words were seen in the "Ithaca" text in the passage in which Stephen takes his leave of Bloom; he hears the words in the sounds of the bells of St. George (17.1230–31). The words in the text, both the Latin and the Anglicized, tie Stephen's private thoughts and Bloom's action; and that action evokes not only a memorial for Bloom's own loss (of Stephen that evening and of the "companions now . . . defunct" in his recent thoughts [17.1252]) but the pain of Stephen's loss as well.

Rutilantius, both in the radiance of the confessors of Stephen's prayer and in the glowing of the incense, hides but points to the etymological provenance of the word "ruddy." So Bloom's action links Stephen's loss of his mother to Stephen's thought of a misbirth and the eye trick of "ruddy" to "Rudy"; the tricks of the eye make a strand, a loop, tying much of the text over time and space, beginning and ending, together. Bloom has the spirit of Rudy lurking behind many of his actions, especially those regarding kindness toward Stephen. One such is in the last scene of "Circe," where, as a reward for helping Stephen, he sees the figure of Rudy. That figure, the eye will remember, is wearing, not coincidentally, "ruby buttons" and a "white lambkin" (15.4965–66)—Rudy's wool, ruddy wool. Moreover, "Rudy" and "ruby" connect through the modalities and dislexicalities of letters, just turning one over, from *d* to *b,* an easy trick to solve on the last page of "Circe" but one that also has another turn as a chromatic connection between "ruby" and "ruddy." (And it might also give an additional gloss to Bloom's interest in a book called *Ruby, Pride of the Ring,* with *b* and *d* being mirror images.) So Bloom can be said to be tricked into reading Rudy in all of his losses, at the end of "Circe" with the fallen Stephen or in "Ithaca" at his departure.

Other vexing puzzles in *Ulysses* are solved by the act of reading in time, deriving their meaning for the reader by distance measured in space of pages. This is the second of the ways in which the material of the visible works to question the meaning of a text seen by making present what is absent. The process works by means of prolepsis, of the anticipatory quality of all language, which operates by accreted meaning and is read in sequential order, or by means of retrospection, in which an earlier word missed is later made evident; in both the eye must jump out of order, as in clinical dyslexia or as in the textual error of haplography, which results in dropped lines.[22] The reader's eye is challenged to move backward and forward in time, to peer ahead even when myopically seeing the magnified text immediately before the nose or to look backward at some distance to what was obscure even at first, close sight.

The very nature of art as devolving in time is considered by Stephen when he drunkenly mentions the anticipatory quality of his riddle of the fox and the grandmother: "Proparoxyton. Moment before the next Lessing says" (15.3609). This moment in time is movement in space as well as anticipation in mind, and the moment of art for Lessing (and for Joyce) consists of a glimpse of the eye, "Augenblick";[23] this is a relation that brings several issues into focus. It should be remembered that Stephen contemplates Lessing's dimensions of aesthetic space and time in "Proteus" when he shuts his eye to see. Later in the same discussion of the "moment," Stephen considers the weakness of his own eyesight. That scene speaks to the reader's experience of a text and plays out the very issues of items "seen" in space, as next to one another, and disparate items apprehended over time, after one another.

Stephen makes reference to his eyesight and notes that he has lost his glasses: "My sight is somewhat troubled." "Lynx eye. Must get glasses. Broke them, yesterday. . . . Distance. The eye sees all flat. . . . Brain thinks. Near: far. Ineluctable modality of the visible" (15.3628–31).[24] Besides repeating the issue raised in "Proteus" of the existence of the universe by means of the inescapable possibilities of sight, Stephen glosses some of his theorizing about aesthetics from his earlier life (and earlier texts); and he does this at the very time he cannot see. Most particularly in the word "distance" Stephen refers to the difference between "seeing" and "thinking" over time. The page in space is what the eye sees flat; distance (like the brain thinking) is a function of time of the reading process.

It is the mind that supplies the sense of space for what is observed even by weak eyes that try vainly to see distance: Stephen cannot even light his cigarette. The reader's mind can see accurately, too: the "lynx" will allow a reading as if it were German (underscored by the earlier phrase from Lessing in italics), *links;* it is the left eye to which Stephen refers as weak, as was Joyce's.[25] A reader must, for the sake of brevity, pass over the obvious doubled image of "lynx" and "Lynch" with their similar if infrequent combination of letters and the squinting etymological echo of the lynx to the wolf and the similar biological relation of the lynx to the fox of Stephen's riddle that is repeated during this exchange. It is worth remarking that "Lynx eye" attributes acute powers of sight to the animal kingdom and makes the reader connect obliquely Bloom's comment about his domestic cat ("Wonder what I look like to her" [4.28]) and another about his freezing a tiger by means of "my eagle eye." (This last line has occasioned much debate in the synoptic edition.) So while Stephen cannot see as far as the tip of his nose, the reader still can make some sense by seeing the letters over several chapters.

Such disjunctive materiality in the text, because it is present on the page and thus has substance, casts a sort of shadow on what is to come; the visible letters figure forth words that will be seen elsewhere in the text, or they reflect what was seen earlier. The materiality of letters projects an image much the way optical patterns cause the eye to see afterimages; the reader is compromised again into illness, the eye moving rapidly in a frenzied state. The term "afterimage" contains within it a measure not only of consequence but of time. The shadows that are cast before are also products of eye illness, spots that precede the visual field.

Such tricks take several pages to be played, requiring the reader to have either a retrospective eye for the earlier context or a prophetic, proleptic eye to anticipate a future one. Several lexical images must be held in sight at one time. This is where the eye and the brain read and think, "near: far." The act of reading is a process of looking ahead, a process of anticipating what is to come; reading is also a backward glance and rearrangement in the sense of a second reading. Thus any word or sequence of words projects into the void of the pages to come. If words and letters can trick the eye into seeing what is not there on the page, their material presence suggesting something that is absent, they certainly can trick the eye into seeing what is not yet there but will later be present in the material of the text; or the words and letters certainly can show the eye what it had earlier missed. The eye, reading, sees the image of the letters, and that image reappears at some later point, hovering around the page as the afterimage hovers around the edge of the visual field. A word that was not initially a puzzle becomes one after the fact of reading; what was stable becomes unstable, blurred by retrospection. What is actually on one page suggests what will appear on another page, and, when that other page arrives in the process of reading, the earlier word flits just on the margins of the text, an insubstantial lexical presence of what has come before, present on one page, suggestively present but not actually on another. The reader is conned and confused. Aware of having missed something, he is aware of his limitation, his inability (and thus reminded by replication of Joyce's sense of his own limitation). To be aware of missing something is to be cognizant of the instability both of the surface of the text seen and of the experience of being a fallible reader.

Here is a seemingly unpuzzling word that appears in the text twice to signal to the eye that something is up, that its future is to come. Twice Bloom is described in the text: "A darkbacked figure under Merchant's arch scanned books on the hawker's cart" (10.315, and similarly, "A darkbacked figure scanned books on the hawker's cart" [10.520]). As it describes the act of reading quickly and superficially, with the eye moving simply and conventionally across space as it might do with the example above, "scanned" should exhort the reader to more careful myopic scrutiny. The unremarked word "hawker," twice mentioned, is the trick. Several pages further on, Bloom is presented as reading and then renting *Sweets of Sin;* the narrative describes the "shopman" with some realistic, tubercular exactness, as "coughing. He raked his throat rudely, puked phlegm on the floor. He put his boot on what he had spat" (10.634). This attention to the old man's productive cough is more than naturalism rampant; it is the place, that blank in the puzzle, where something is not present but which harkens back to its own future presence. A "hawker" is not only one who sells; it is also one who "hawks" (or the product of such an action), which according to the *Oxford English Dictionary* is "to make an effort to clear the throat of phlegm, to clear the throat noisily." When the twice-mentioned "hawker" at whose cart Bloom browses is later depicted as a "shopman . . . coughing," having "raked" phlegm, the future of the absent word is suggested by the very letters on the page; the definition of the word not present is all provided by the various words earlier in the text. The other word, not seen but present, is waiting to be caught by the eye, waiting in its lexical possibilities to cast its presence out of the reading sequence into the material that is to come. The reader sees what was missed in the apparently stable word seen earlier.

Such straining in the reader's activity and experience comes on top of and adds to the irritation and vexation of seeing what is on the page by itself, the magnified letters; the reader is not only limited by the deceptive quality of letters foregrounded and oblique but is also handicapped further by not seeing what is there and is exhausted by needing to see over long stretches of time and space. Simple phrases begin to limit the meaning and depiction of the novelistic world as they become puzzling and opaque only in retrospect; they require increasingly major efforts on the reader's part to process the novel by the physical act of seeing through it. Here exhaustion looms as the cause of the fundamental unreadability of *Ulysses;* the density and opacity of letters long after they were initially read as unpuzzling fatigue the reader's eye and patience.

Thus in "Circe," where so much from the earlier parts of the book and day is transmogrified, the directions appear to read in the sort of detailed naturalism expected in a novel's depiction: "*In a room lit by a candle stuck in a bottleneck a slut combs out the tatts from the hair of a scrofulous child*" (15.39–41). The phrase "*a slut combs,*" however, is a trick to the eye of the retentive but disruptable mind of Joyce's ideal reader (a dis-lexic in *Ulysses,* an insomniac in the *Wake*); it was seen in the descriptions of particular whores in Bloom's thoughts in "Lestrygonians," matching this anonymous one: "Those two sluts that night in the Coombe" singing the song about Mary's lost drawers pin (5.279). One page later Bloom thinks of Jesus preaching, "Also the two sluts in the Coombe would listen" (5.291). The single whore is not the only avatar to appear in "Circe"; well into the chapter, "*two sluts of the Coombe dance rainily by*" (15.3442; the adverb attests to the transformations wrought in this chapter). The highlighting trick of the change from italics to roman, which has been observed before, adds another fatiguing element to the eye. It is the ability, despite the visual challenges, to retain an earlier context in visual memory and to think about it that allows the reader to see the word as an afterimage.

When Stephen creates his story of the two Dublin women for the newspapermen—based, it should be noted, on what he has seen during his walk on the beach—his description of one of them seems to be replete with local color: "Anne Kearns has the lumbago for which she rubs on Lourdes water, given her by a lady who got a bottleful from a passionist father" (7.948). The reader, however, has gotten this detail before in another form, encapsuled in the first description of the figure of the woman seen on the beach. When Stephen reacts to the sight of her, he describes her thus: "Number one swung lourdily her midwife's bag" (3.32). The essence of the later, apparently realistic detail ("Lourdes") is captured in the scholastic adverb "lourdily." What seems to be learning is only letters; what appears to be depiction is only puzzle; the reader's attempt at understanding is undermined by disruption. What Stephen had bottled up in his musings on the beach is released into a fictional account, but that account is in turn made unstable in the very same letters. Stephen needs some time before he can convert his observation into art; the text needs several pages to undo the representation, and at a cost to the reader's eye, which must hold the word in some lexical form to see how and where Stephen's inspiration is to be diminished.

One joke that takes place over several hundred pages involves the slow-witted, if otherwise graced, Boylan and another bottle. Buying a gift for Molly, he hands the shop girl in Thornton's "the bottle swathed in pink tissue paper" and, a few moments later (a few lines in the text), asks, "Send it at once, will you? . . . It's for an invalid" (10.322). His rendezvous at four prompts Boylan's wish to have his gift delivered promptly, and a slow reader might marvel at his providing the shop girl with the compelling excuse of a fading recipient for the gift. Yet Boylan has no imagination—or poetry either—to inspire him to his excuse: he has only read the label on the bottle. The perceptive reader will anticipate and the experienced reader will remember that he too will see the bottle and its label in "Ithaca": "a halfempty bottle of William Gilbey and Co's white invalid port, half disrobed of its swathe of coralpink tissue paper" (17.306). The "disrobed" is an obvious touch of a heavy hand; "swathed," the diction of a romance novel (and the color changes from "pink" to "coralpink" probably because we are at Calypso's island). But the abbreviation "Co" of "Gilbey and Co's" reminds us visually that we are seeing the label; more than a naturalistic detail about alcohol, we are given a recreation of the material object. Reading that label in the mind's eye, with its designation of a kind of port ("Invalid Port" like "Partner's Port"), a reader realizes that Boylan had seen the same, and it had provided him with his excuse. (Had Boylan bought a bottle of Partner's Port, he most likely would have told the shop girl it was to be sent to his partner.) His is no trick of the mind but rather one of the eye.[26] (Note as well Bloom's gazing at the bottle of Bass in "Oxen," where he too glimpses the entire label as written: "bottled by Messrs Bass and Co at Burton-on-Trent"[14.1182].)

This joke is not restricted to Boylan; it is also played by a character who resembles the "toff" and even notices him. Master Dignam, who talks like Boylan and who has the same sporting interests, thinks about the depressing scene of his mother in mourning: "and they at all their sniffles and sipping sups of the superior tawny sherry Uncle Barney brought from Tunney's" (10.1126–28). His "superior tawny" detail of the alcohol shows his preoccupation, like Boylan's, with the labels of bottles. Bottles are slang for thick glasses such as Joyce wore and such as marked and measured Joyce's disability. The reader's eye is continually disabled by these sorts of bottle-lenses. The eye of the reader becomes exhausted, as well as his patience (much as Joyce was by his eye examinations), as the examples of phrases reflecting each other become denser and more opaque. Greater effort is needed to peer at the irritating words, to find the puzzling parts spread out so far in distance over earlier and later parts of the text. Indeed the odder the word, the more likely it is that its irritation is achieved by much disruption and disjunction, as is certainly the case for words of immediately apparent density from *Finnegans Wake*.

In "Sirens," in the passage discussed earlier describing Boylan's journey to Molly in the hackney car, the striking word cluster "gallantbuttocked" caught the eye. It embedded a variety of words of similar letters from distant places. The intriguing sentence contains more in its middle unnoticed earlier, as if part of it were obscured: "By Dlugacz' porkshop bright tubes of Agendath trotted a gallantbuttocked mare" (11.884). The oddity of this last phrase was noted, but not the strange appearance first of the proper name Dlugacz nor of its possessive. Aside from the ethnic connection to Bloom by the Magyar name, there are the lone apostrophe and a concatenation of letters lexically impossible in English yet possible in another linguistic register—or in an eye chart. (The cryptogram of "Martha," it was remarked, frequently used the *z,* and the related Hungarian word for ox, *marha,* appeared in "Cyclops.") More striking still is the appearance of the phrase in apposition to "Dlugacz' porkshop": "bright tubes of Agendath," which is a combination arresting enough to suggest some meaning in its puzzling disfunctionality. The words that it poetically offers in its metonymy stand in stark contrast to the exactitude and realistic details of the hackney car, "number three hundred and twentyfour, driver Barton James of number one Harmony avenue, Donnybrook" and so on. Yet what it stands in for in its metonymic function is not apparent; its signified is absent. The depiction of the text is always compromised; the puzzling aspect of letters requires further scrutiny. When polysemy offers no meaning, look to polylexy. The poetic and puzzling solution to this phrase "bright tubes of Agendath" can be found in what remains in the mind's eye long after the eye has seen earlier pages (in the distance that is measured by time). The reader is required to think back to and see again the specifics of the scene from "Calypso" in which Bloom visits Dlugacz's to buy his breakfast. "He halted before [the] window, staring at the hanks of sausages, polonies, black and white. . . . The shiny links, packed with forcemeat, fed his gaze" (4.140–43). Aside from the necessary interest in food ("fed"), given the parameters of the chapter, the reader should note that Bloom is looking at something, "staring," engaging his vision with something that, like a text, is "black and white." As Bloom waits to be served, he actually does read, taking a page from the counter that he reads more carefully while walking home "back along Dorset street, reading gravely. Agendath Netaim: planters' company" (4.190–91). And that object and this text are further paralleled: the sausages are designated as forcemeat, referring to how the pieces are forced into a casing, and the Agendath circular wraps the kidney. Thus the whole experience of the reader as reader, as well as that of Bloom, in the world of the shop that morning from start to finish (three pages of text) is telescoped by the possibilities of letters into the phrase used in the eleventh chapter, as the "shiny links" that Bloom sees before he enters the shop are changed by equivalence to "bright tubes" to go along with a phrase in the circular he reads on leaving: "bright tubes of Agendath." The text reflects in afterimage its own not-present past.

So far, so good, but this is neither far enough nor good enough for Joyce because, while disruptive of reading over several hundred pages, it is not dis-lexic enough. The idea of Bloom's reading the circular and his "staring" with a "gaze" at the black and white objects of the sausages surely is an embedded paradigm of the act of reading. The critical mind and eye should be alert to the fact that there is another connection to be made here, one beyond even that imposed by the contiguity of events narrated over several pages of text and the equivalent semiotic substitution of "shiny"/"bright" and "links"/"tubes." To trace the etymon of "bright tubes of Agendath": the black and white sausages, those shiny links, are, the text shows the reader on the same page they are first seen, "polonies" (4.141). Hence, when the reader sees "shiny tubes" later he reads, in the mind's eye if not on the page, an afterimage of what was seen before: "brightlinks" as "polonies." The "Agendath," from the name of the planters' company, is an agricultural and political means to settle the Holy Land, as Bloom realizes when he considers the idea; but the reader can easily supply a synonym for those sorts of mercantile endeavors: "colonies." So the arresting phrase "bright tubes of Agendath," as well as encapsulating part of a chapter read earlier, deciphers as a puzzle in the mind's eye to present a meaning absent from the page but present in lexemes elsewhere and earlier: "polonies of colonies." Something is made present out of what was, in effect, retrospectively arranged from the past—back—of the novel.

There is another connection that links these sausages to a later part of the text, where the appearance of the "polonies" in the fourth chapter is strung together with something from several hundred pages further on in the sixteenth; sausages can contain rather odd bits in them. The term "polonies" in "Calypso" is a colloquial name whose probable origin derives from a corruption of Polish sausage (much like the meat bologna). Hence a foreign name (and from Middle Europe, at that) combines with the Magyar strangeness of the name Dlugacz to widen the borders of the page. As the polonies are described as made of "cooked spicy pigs' blood," they are recognizable as blood sausage; thus hidden between the black and the white text of these forcemeats is another national reference, as with Poland, the French word for blood sausage, "boudin." This word not present in the butcher shop or in "Sirens" is linked in "Eumaeus" by being the name of the addressee "*Señor A Boudin*" (16.489) on the postcard of the cannibals offered by the questionable sailor and far-flung traveler Murphy.

The reader's eye must be far-traveled, and the result is exhaustion and a halting, impeded progress of reading; the reader limps along in irritation.

There is constant jumping back and forth in the reading time, ahead to the "future" of the text, backward to its "past." In "Nausicaa" the reader knows how to read the two different discourses of Gerty and Bloom, but the words too appear differently over the pages of the chapter. Gerty MacDowell takes her leave of Bloom: "She slipped a hand into her kerchief pocket and took out the wadding and waved in reply of course without letting him and then slipped it back. Wonder if he's too far to. She rose" (13.757–60). Her elliptical thought concerns whether Bloom is too far away to smell the scent on her handkerchief. Several pages later, and in his own style, Bloom responds: "Wait. Hm. Hm. Yes. That's her perfume. Why she waved her hand. . . . What is it? Heliotrope? No. Hyacinth? Hm. Roses, I think" (13.1007–9). Bloom has to make an olfactory guess; the reader ought to know. In the first context the reader is not told what the perfume is, only Gerty's action ("she rose"). The second context tells him the fact, but the earlier verb and later noun both read the same, so that the eye has seen the prospective answer in the text in the first quotation. Bloom thinks while sniffing; the reader thinks over several pages when seeing and reading, the earlier word foreshadowing the later. Insofar as the term "roses" is a euphemism for "monthlies," as Bloom thinks about Martha in connection with her errors in typing (5.285) and as the term is true as regards Gerty, polysemy is added to the complex and disjunctive polylexy. As well, Bloom recognizes Gerty's handicap—"She's lame"—with repeated references to her "limping away" or as a "little limping devil" (13.852) when he himself, immediately after his orgasm, is equally limp. The reader's eye by now limps too, through the page, with the same impeded motion as Gerty's "halting" step.

Gerty's physical impairment seems to echo the visual one that the irritated text causes in the reader. The puzzle of her slow, dignified walk is solved by Bloom in the observation "Tight boots? No. She's lame! O!" (13.771). Yet while the solution has been anticipated earlier in "Nausicaa" by her evasion and silence, there is a material, lexical sign of her disability to be read in Gerty's first appearance in the novel, when she is seen during the viceregal procession at the end of "Wandering Rocks." The reader has probably missed it, despite the slow pace of reading. She is described as carrying for her father the "Catesby's cork lino letters." (What's in a [brand] name? More "letters" and a clue to read letters carefully.) And, after she has been depicted as failing to observe the fashion of Her Excellency, the text immediately jumps on to another character at another, seemingly unrelated, location: John Wyse Nolan standing "beyond Lundy Foot's" (10.1211). A competent reader knows that the shifts in "Wandering Rocks" are never abrupt,[27] but what is striking in the sequence here becomes clear after the fact: the afterimage is due to the letters that depict Nolan under the sign of the tobacconist. The location of Nolan surely is an ironic comment on Gerty's handicap, and the sign of the tobacconist inscribing the actual name is here compressed from Lundy, Foot and Co.; but surely it is so elided to form an apparent and visual sign of Gerty's condition as revealed chapters later: "Lundy Foot's."

So a handicap within the text is signaled and presented by the letters of the text, magnified and highlighted, missed at first but seen in afterimage. The reader is similarly handicapped, puzzled by the poet's pictures repeatedly into a limited status as reader: blind to parts of words or recognizing them only much later, disoriented in time and space, losing sight of the narrative depiction. The reader is made fully complicit with Joyce's illness by the irritated text: as the artist is limited, so is the reader. Moreover, the text has many readers, some contemporary with Joyce, some his printers and editors.

CHAPTER 5

Identity, Intertextuality, and Infection

In *Ulysses,* the identity, and hence meaning, of words depends upon the reader's recognition of the shapes of letters (in contrast to *Finnegans Wake,* in which any number of meanings is possible within and between words). "Rudy," "Ruby," "ruddy," "*rutilantium,*" "rutilant"—all share and change letters, are italicized or capitalized, over the space of the text within a narrow range of meaning, making the reader uncertain and handicapped in seeing whatever might be understood to be represented by the words. Identification requires that objects be stable, that they be, literally, the same—*idem*—at every appearance. Identity, however, operates only in a fixed context, one in which characteristics are stable. But when in the text the shapes of letters are deceptively similar to the eye, as in *b* and *d,* their own identity is questioned, and also thus questioned is the identity of the words they constitute. The foggy shapes and blurs Joyce saw with his iritis had no clear identity, and the words he made of them were as deceptive and difficult to identify as the letters of the eye chart.

If the letter is questionable in identity, then all other items that are made up of letters are also questionable, not only the words and the "world" of the novel but also the characters, the text, and ultimately the reader. As Joyce makes letters unstable by magnifying them in size, they also have, as noted, a corresponding magnification in their consequences outward to the text and to the reader. One consequence of uncertainty is the status of the characters in the text whose own existence within the novel is constantly set up and set in play by their expression in and by words. The world depicted for the reader is unclear and opaque, and so too must the characters be. Any empathy or association is withheld from the reader, who is puzzled and distanced from the world depicted. A character is assaulted thus by being obscure; loss of the subject is caused by the unclear identity of the object seen, the letter.

The other consequence of the foregrounding in importance of letters hard to identify is that their shapes and particular combinations are impressed by opacity and repetition in the mind so that they challenge the identity of all texts—the text they are in, disrupted in space over many pages, and even other texts that the reader might have read and seen over time. The distance in reading time and space brought on by Joycean dis-lexia, which causes the reader to becomes disoriented in *Ulysses* in complicity with Joyce's illness, reaches yet another level, where the reader cannot be sure of the identity of the text in which a word appears, cannot tell whether the text read is not indeed some other text previously seen. The text can become, through its visual disruption, the intertext, as opacity and questionable identity lead to a particular Joycean intertextuality.

In both these cases, the reader's role and thus identity as reader is further called into question, not only disoriented but destabilized, limited and separated from the text and its context by the opacity and deceptive similarity of not-identical letters. The reader never fully empathizes with the characters or fully identifies what the text is. There is an example of this double confusion of character identity and textual identity in a particular reader of Joyce—a case study of the sort of infection, so to speak, that can be caught from Joyce's dis-lexia, in which the reader is so affected that his own identity and memory of texts is incapacitated and changed by visual exposure to *Ulysses*.

Before examining that case study, however, it is necessary to discuss the unstable identities of both character and text. One consequence of the magnification of letters is the resultant diminution of character. Characters within the text are created, quite obviously, of written characters (indeed written characters constitute their entire existence for the reader), and as the letter looms large in puzzlement and uncertainty, so the presence of the character is dematerialized. Nowhere is the challenge of the opacity of the letter to the material representation, the depiction of the novel, better and more clearly seen than in the uncertainty of character identity undermined through unstable letters. As the stability of the epistolary letter is disrupted by that uncertainty of the alphabetical letter, so the identity of the fictional character is made indistinct by the opacity of the written characters.

In this regard, the status of M'Intosh is worth a glance. When so much critical concern is given to his identity, what is obscured is the fact that simple letters play an important role in his devolution and increasing indeterminacy: first by the name M'Intosh, derived by abscission of letters from the textured-coat "Macintosh" (6.894–95) and then even from the fact that the name that appears in the text has further cut off a letter from the actual name in the lexicon, "mackintosh." Letters are the issue in the obscuring of identity; those missing from the lexicon induce dis-lexia as the figure of M'Intosh becomes more and more indistinct by erasure.

If letters missing obscure a character, their presence can build one up. One letter can make a great deal of difference: would there be any comedy, or memorable quality, to a woman Molly remembers from Gibraltar if her name were Mrs. Opiso instead of being much increased by the additional *s?* Letters create characters in ways that are hard to credit with real existence. Stephen, as example of all his writerliness and myopia, tries to imagine an identity and a life for one of the women he sees on the beach. Creating a "poet's picture puzzle" of his own, he thinks, "Mrs Florence MacCabe, relict of the late Patk MacCabe" (3.34)—thinking, that is, an unspeakable abbreviation for someone, a form that would appear in an obituary notice in print. (It does, not incidentally, as the reader should know, in that evening's *Telegraph,* including an appropriate period in the abbreviation: "*The mourners included: Patk. Dignam (son)*" [16. 1255].) Even the narrator-manipulator-arranger writespeaks in such abbreviations and signs, which signal identity. In "Wandering Rocks" Mr. Denis Maginni is described as "professor of dancing, &c" (10.56) so that first, the ampersand stands in for the usual pejorative attributes of dancing masters (the Citizen, for example, speaks of the French "dancing masters, not worth a roasted fart"); and second, the abbreviation reproduces the printed qualities of advertisements or business cards of this most garishly dressed self-advertiser. Maginni's identity is a construct of forms. On the same page, a character apparently speaks such an abbreviation (or is heard to speak one) improbably regarding a proper name. When Father Conmee somewhat patronizingly asks three schoolboys to mail a letter, he inquires of their names: "And what was his name? Jack Sohan. And his name? Ger. Gallaher" (10.42). Hearing or speaking, the text presents an abbreviation for the reader to see and thus confuses and makes complex the act of reading to identify character.

The similarity of Milly and Molly, Bloom notes, is caused by biology, genetics, and gender: "Same thing watered down" (6.87). (What waters Molly down into Milly is Bloom's genetic contribution, but that is a point that he does not contemplate.) Yet the similarities of Molly and Milly are reinforced perhaps to Bloom but certainly to a reader by the change of the letter *o* to *i,* a vowel change that represents all the others. It is a change in sound, *o* being larger and deeper than *i;* these are also the same letters and sound changes to be found in Milly's tomboy oaths that Bloom uses to express her identity: "Ye gods and little fishes."

So individual written characters seem to be a mark of questionable character. When Bloom questions the identity of "A.E. . . . Initials perhaps" (8.528), his inquiry is also a question of the presentation of a self in letters, somehow prolonged and extended by the use of the diphthong (and, below, Joyce's first published work has recourse to a similar diphthong). Stephen can make a full statement about his indebtedness to Russell merely by using select letters of the alphabet in a fortuitous modality of the five vowels, "A.E.I.O.U" (9.213). There are characters in *Ulysses* presented solely in letters, such as the choric Kelly, "Kay ee double ell why" (6.374, 900), as well as Mickey Hanlon, whom Bloom imagines trying to write his own name: "Moooikill A Aitcha Ha" (8.894). All these are what is read of them; the characters of the text make up these letters, yet unstably and indistinctly so.

Any unstable and insubstantial character in the novel is subject to some further obscurity. As M'Intosh was diminished and made indistinct by the loss of letters, letters make a difference in the figure of the possibly pseudonymous Murphy, "a sailor probably" (16.338). He presents himself and his credentials so as to make them visible to everyone's sight, including that of the reader: "There's my discharge. See? D.B. Murphy. A.B.S" (16.452). The very common name of Murphy is bracketed by the presence of various letters magnified by capitals, as if by way of adding weight to his claim. Likewise, when Murphy's boast of having seen man-eaters in Peru meets with a lack of interest, he offers another text, a postcard sent to him depicting the cannibals; Bloom notes skeptically that it is addressed to a *Señor A Boudin*. And however much is questionable about Murphy and his postcard, there is another identity here created by the lexical material of the text: the same letters appear on both the certificate and the card, "A.B.S." (Ablebodied Seaman) and *S*(enor) *A B*(oudin). With the shifting foreground of the letter, identity may be more than meets the eye. (The reader has seen how the word *boudin* is already complicated, being screened into exhausting opacity by the word "polonies.")

Even so firmly substantial a character as Bloom has his identity put into question by various letters in disruption. It is a small and often remarked point that the *l* additional to Martha's letter is subtracted from Bloom's name as it appears in the *Evening Telegraph:* "L. Boom," this identity obscured by the loss of a letter. Bloom, of course, is "nettled" by the error, and the nettle is just such a small but troublesome irritation as the letter (and its synonym, the thorn, is also an Anglo-Saxon letter). The *m* from Bloom goes missing when Bloom misreads the handout from the Y.M.C.A. man—"Bloo. . . . Me? No. Blood of the Lamb" (8.8–9)—although the reader sees what is missing both in the word *me* and even in the abbreviation Y.M.C.A. One way to speculate on what Joyce means by dropping from Bloom's name the letters *l* and *m* (which are, not coincidentally, the initial letters of his major characters Leopold and Molly) has to do with a recognition of the fragility of their existence by the modalities and instabilities of all letters.

Yet when Bloom writes clandestinely to Martha in "Sirens," he wishes to hide his identity and signature by writing "Greek ees" (11.860). As is often the case with the lexical, Bloom is wrong: a true Greek long *e,* in lexical form similar to that of our *e,* is called not "ee" but *epsilon,* and the name of the letter makes an altogether different sound. Moreover the term "Greek ee," opening the field of unstable lexicality, suggests another language and another name for the identity of yet another letter altogether: the French *y* (pronounced "ee") *grecque,* which represents the *y.* This "greek ee" appears in Bloom's nickname Poldy, pronounced as "ee." Yet in Bloom's error of "Greek ees" and "y grecque" lie the fortuitous visible modalities of dis-lexia: the other Greek *e,* the *eta,* resembles the latin *h* in form, so when Bloom writes a hidden message to Martha, he signs his name "Henry," framed by versions of what he has mistaken for "greek ees" (H *eta* and Y *upsilon,* "y grecque"; his hidden identity in letters shows his Homeric materiality).

Bloom's unstable self is a common concern. In that exchange about the identity of Murphy, Stephen notes, "Sounds are impostures, . . . like names. Cicero, Podmore. Napoleon, Mr Goodbody. Jesus, Mr Doyle. . . . What's in a name?" In response, "Yes, to be sure, Mr Bloom unaffectedly concurred. Of course. Our name was changed too, he added, pushing the socalled roll across" (16.362–66). The change in the family name strikes right at the issue of identity in the novel, as it also embraces the issues of ethnicity and the law; and it, like the throwaway, addresses something essential and fundamental to the existence of Bloom within the novel, the questionable status of a name or of any word as the reader unclearly sees it. (Stephen, of course, glosses over the falsity of sound, a problem of letters and letter names that will be discussed in the next chapter.)

Such a change of name is a fact that says something about the process of nomination and the issue of identity, if only to indicate that both are mutable. It is substantiated specifically by two other references in the novel. One of them is made by Martin Cunningham in "Cyclops": "His name was Virag, the father's name that poisoned himself. He changed it by deedpoll, the father did" (12.1639–41). The second is in "Ithaca": "a local press cutting concerning change of name by deedpoll" (17.1867). The name change is an attempt, but with limited success, to obscure Bloom's ethnicity and his foreignness. It is achieved through the imposition of the power of the law, but the public, through gossip, resists subservience to that law.

The name change itself, like Stephen's ludic list of names, is only a metaphoric substitution of one language for another (Virag/flower/Bloom); it is a polysemy of one very limited signified. Stephen's free play in transforming names indicates that not only is language malleable; so too are different language registers. By mixing historical figures with unknowns whose names mean the same thing in other languages (such as Cicero/chickpea/peapod/Podmore),[1] he obliquely (or not so obliquely) glances at the change in language from Virag in Hungarian to Bloom in English, both glossing, of course, the unstated Flower of Bloom's written endeavors. Thus Stephen suggests the imposture both of history and of language, in which meaning is the same although there is an apparent difference in the words: the signified can easily slip into signifiers of various letters, challenging identity over time.

Thus when the family name is changed, Virag to Bloom, it is done by means of a simple alteration in the letters of the alphabet. While the meaning of the name is the same, as is true of the names on Stephen's list, the letters that constitute the old and the new are completely different, none repeating from the first to the second (as would be the case with a change from, say, Braun to Brown); and yet precisely because the "meaning" of the name is the same, the fact that the letters are changed constitutes a significant difference that challenges the stability of the similarity and thus of the identity itself. The smallest units of language, the letters of the alphabet, are most fundamentally subject to malleability, slippage, and the questioning of identity. A character is never more stable than the letters of his name.

The other two passages in the novel about the name change are in various discourses, each underscoring the diverse and changing nature of language. The quotation from Cunningham is gossip, a Dublin tradition of hearsay and innuendo, and it removes the ruse of the name change to reveal the foreignness it sought to mask ("His name was Virag, the father's name that poisoned himself. He changed it by deedpoll"). The other passage, from "Ithaca's" studied style, emphasizes the written nature of the legal proceeding, the deed, by reinscribing it into the language of journalism with the publication of a public notice ("a local press cutting concerning the change of name by deedpoll"). It is the very public nature of Cunningham's comment, of course, that by hearsay undoes what has been printed. The exchange in "Eumaeus" between Stephen and Bloom is a failed dialogue, a sort of conversation of disfunction, wherein Stephen first remarks on the deceptive quality of sound of the Italian that Bloom earlier misheard (and misunderstood) and then, probably unintentionally, comments on the deceptive mutability of names. Bloom, not "unaffected," thinks that Stephen alludes to his own name change.

The challenge to Bloom's name for the reader of the text is further put into question by a disruption in the reader's seeing these three different passages about his chosen identity from different and distanced parts of the text. (Here is the sort of challenge to reading space and time discussed in the preceding chapter.) The first disruption is grammatical. If a name is changeable, so too is the system of grammar. All three quotations of the change in name are consistent and mean the same thing, but each is a different grammatical structure: "He changed it [the name] by deedpoll"; "change of name by deedpoll"; "our name was changed." Active verb, noun, passive verb are all the possibilities inherent in the grammatical system. Moreover, that two of these references carefully use appropriate legalistic terminology by referring to the "deedpoll" is an indication that established conventions of law are being followed as well as those conventions of grammar.

The second and most fundamental disruption is visual, relying on the similarities of words. In the two similar phrases, with their constellations of letters "he changed the name" and "change of name," the legal phrase "deedpoll" is a constant. In the accretive way *Ulysses* is read, the reader becomes accustomed to seeing all these together; a more conventional reader might expect such a configuration every time. Yet when the Joycean reader comes to the conversation with Stephen in "Eumaeus," the third reference to the issue, he reads that Bloom says, "Our name was changed" but omits the phrase "by deedpoll," making a pregnant sort of absence, a blind spot of opacity, that would not be anticipated in an easy dynamic of reading. Yet when there is a blind spot, the irritated text presents something else that is similar to the omitted phrase but materially and deceptively changed from it: in full, the pertinent text is as follows: "Our name was changed too, he added, pushing the socalled roll across." Where there was "deedpoll," there is now "socalled roll." This comestible roll has its own questionable identity, so that it too is nominally uncertain—"socalled." It also questions what's in a name. (Earlier in the same chapter, Bloom offers Stephen this roll "of some description" [16.333].) Moreover, the "roll" in this sentence substitutes for the "deedpoll" in the other usages by semantics, the fact of diction that "roll" is also a term for a list of names.

Such similarity in meaning, however, is reinforced by the deceptive similarity of letters, as there is more change of identity even within this smallest compass of "poll" and "roll"; it is a change that challenges the act of reading the text, as the text itself seems to change. The elusive similarity of "roll" to "poll" is established by the repetition of the configuration of the letters *oll* and the partial resemblance of *r* and *p;* thus the changed letters visually supply the connections already established by the semantics. Indeed the two phrases side by side repeat letters in fragmentation to reinforce the resemblance to the first that the mind's eye has anticipated: "de*ed* p*oll*" "so-call*ed* r*oll.*" This is a similar figure in different letters, a resemblance of one word to another by some letters that are the same and some not the same but deceptively similar. There is a tension here of words, meaning, and names: in the name change similar meanings slide under different word names (Virag to Bloom); in the "poll/roll" pair similar letters make differing words.² In all, identity is destabilized. So the change from Virag to Bloom is a material expression of identity within the text, yet it is achieved through the changing of letters that questions any materiality; and the text that presents the facts of the name change dematerializes and unsubstantiates the identity sought by that change for the reader through a lexicality that conflates "deed poll" and "socalled roll." A character is made and unmade by dis-lexic characters, which the reader reads uncertainly.

Identity and the reflections of letters in texts seen unclearly are not only a concern for the characters and the reader; they are the essential identity of the writer as well. He appears to the world in the print of a text and is recalled through the presence of texts read and remembered but not present. His identity too depends on how his texts are seen. As Joyce was at pains in *Ulysses* to present his text in a particular way, correct and corrected so that it could irritate, he was also particular about the presentation of his own identity in characters and letters.

The experience of the young author at seeing his work in print is a major one, even for the posturing, hyperborean Joyce: he never forgot that impression, down to its most physical, visual sense. His first public fictional work, "The Sisters," appeared in Russell's *Homestead* under the nom de plume Stephen Daedalus.³ The diphthong is classical, pedantic, pretentious. It elongates the space occupied by the author; it seems material, foregrounded, ponderous; it was meant to arrest the eye by being large and long, even then, when Joyce's eyesight was only myopic. (It also may be a sly echo of Russell's own pseudonym AE, which has led Bloom to question what that meant.) Joyce's contribution was placed, as was the custom of Russell's publication of "Our Weekly Story," toward the end of the periodical, carrying over to the last page, which also contained advertisements with pictures of such items of interest to the readership as milk separators, pumps, and machines that resemble dynamos. In fact, Joyce's first story was bracketed by an ad for Cochrane and Cantrell's nonalcoholic beverages, among them ginger ale, and a "double effectiv" mammary milk pump (with an intentional error, as the ad copy has it).⁴ Joyce was framed, as it were, by other visual forms. (And it has already been noted that an ad for "Cantrell" has been enshrined in disruptive modality with "Cantwell" within

Ulysses.) The irony of the nonalcoholic beverages, given the crucial incident with the sacramental wine in the story, was not likely lost on Joyce at the time, and that the dairy ads rankled him is attested to by the "dreamery creamery butter" (15.2275), digs at AE in *Ulysses*. The next story published, "After the Race," appropriately for its plot about the mechanics of auto racing, is placed alongside an ad for the "Little Sampson" oil engine and power plant, described as "wonderfully cheap."

So the first editions of Joyce, the first expression of his identity as a writer, he had to be aware, appeared in print along with ads, those other visual impressions of print; and the young author had to feel that his works were even competing with them. The first view of himself in print was compromised by diversion and diffused density of visual forms. Thus perhaps when Bloom briefly refers in passing to a hoarding promoting "Cantrell and Cochrane's ginger ale (aromatic)" (5.389), Joyce is making an oblique reference, a cross-glance at the equally cursory glances his name and stories must have received in the *Homestead* sandwiched between the ads for the identical product. Later in the same chapter ("Lotos-Eaters"), when Bloom thinks about the wine of the mass (again a very distanced glimpse of issues from "The Sisters") as more "aristocratic" than "Guinness's porter or some temperance beverage. . . . Cantrell and Cochrane's ginger ale (aromatic)," he is clearly reproducing in his thoughts the visual ways in which the drinks are advertised and, in the specific case of the "ginger ale (aromatic)," the way the ad appeared to him in the printed hording a few moments and pages back. The ad in the *Homestead* of 1906 appeared in print to Joyce and to any other reader as nearly identical to the one that appears in *Ulysses:* "Ginger ale 'aromatic.'" Identity is established by the same sight of something read again across time and space. Ads appear in print, stories appear in print, and the novel reproduces what appears before the eyes of a character as print and what appeared beside the author's first story in print. This is a circularity of crossed and recrossed reading, of advertised text and what is seen by character and reader both as print, made dense and difficult. A further reference to Joyce's first appearance in print is made into a seamless whole when the "text" of the name "Cantrell and Cochrane" appears gilded on the mirror of the Ormond Bar; Miss Douce "with grace of alacrity towards the mirror gilt Cantrell and Cochrane's . . . turned herself" (11.214). It was remarked earlier how the "Cantrell" here reflects the similar but different word "Cantwell" a few pages earlier in "Sirens." Here the reversed word order gives a "mirror image," itself crossed as reversed, to a character viewing herself and her actions, and the mirroring reflects other texts seen before in the novel. Likewise, art may hold a mirror up to nature, or the cracked looking-glass of a servant, or the magnifying glass of the sufferer of iritis, but one of its reflections gives back another work of art, Joyce's first story mirrored in his later fiction in words, the name of a commercial product inscribing his first written product, "The Sisters," by an author identified as "Stephen Daedalus."

The ginger ale ad that competed with Joyce's first story for space is not the only one to be materially inscribed and enshrined in the text of *Ulysses*. There was also the ad that bracketed another of Joyce's stories, an ad for those geared and belted machines. When Stephen in "Wandering Rocks" sees "the whirr of flapping leathern bands and hum of dynamos" and thinks, "I between them" (10.821–24), he may not so much be thinking of a suicide of a modern kind as placing himself amid machinery just as "Stephen Daedelus" of "After the Race" is placed in the *Homestead* between power plants like the "wonderfully cheap" "Little Sampson."[5] A fictional character and an autobiographical author each exist in print struggling for expression and space. Identity is suspect because it must be presented through print, which lingers on after the appearance in the mind's eye.

If the author himself is identified only obliquely by unclear and uncertain letters that linger on pages through time, what of the identity of the text itself made up of letters? That is, if deceptive identity of letters destabilizes those identities of character and author, how can the identity of a text be certain? It is Stephen who actually speaks the title of the book during the day, appropriately while in his discussion in the library of another author who put his identity into his works—Shakespeare—"like another Ulysses" (9.403). (The name is also mentioned by Eglinton, in his reference to the anachronism in *Troilus* of having Ulysses cite Aristotle; the only other uses of the words "Ulysses" are two, both as parts of proper names: Ulysses Brown and Ulysses Grant. These last two figures are a sort of diversionary eye trick to take the glance away from the text's awareness of its created identity.) While this mention alone of the superficial cover of the novel—the outer envelope, as it were, of its material universe of letters—seems slim, the effect is reproduced in the Gerty MacDowell episode, the one referred to but never headed "Nausicaa." There, as Gerty/Nausicaa encounters Bloom/Odysseus, the reader's eye will find shadowy references to both unlisted titles and unstated epic characters: first "Nausea" (13.1187) and then "Useless" (13.1259).

Stephen elsewhere displays an interest in what letters make up the titles of books. On the Strand, he self-referentially characterizes his future as an artist with "Books you were going to write with letters for titles. Have you read his F? O yes, but I prefer Q" (3.139–40). He was planning perhaps an apparently large output of works, possibly as many as twenty-six, all to be designated by the most basic and essential elements of language. (Yet is that first "O" a title, easily confused visually with "Q," or is it merely an interjection, a sound without sense?) This comic titling of his works is a demonstration that Stephen is himself aware, as is his creator, of the lexical materiality of language to make a text, even the one he is in. His idea of giving his *opera* letters as titles is not so extreme: all titles, after all, are nothing but letters. *Ulysses* has just seven. Only five are different, and one is used three times; that one is Stephen's initial letter in a trinity. As he gives material letter-titles to his future books, Stephen can also name the title of the book he is in and can be said to initial himself on the cover through a recognition of the jumbling of identity through dis-lexia.

As a text for Joyce is seen, defined, and remembered foremost in letters magnified and disparate, the identity of such a text will be questioned by just those highlighted letters in any portion of it. Words and letters are deceptively malleable, if finite; separated from context and made disjunctive, they can exist in various texts by the same author. All letters are enlarged in size and magnified for the handicapped Joyce, so that he could read them in parts. Any and all texts, his own and others, seen so myopically and disjointedly, would begin to resemble each other, their identities blurring; that is, when peered at closely, the small fragments of one text may resemble those in other texts. If the identity of the letter is in question, the identity of a text is also in question; if the reader remembers only a portion of a text, can he remember what text it is in? Among the host of modal possibilities of the alphabet, certain odd configurations of letters might repeat from text to text.

The dynamic of reading and the challenge to a word's meaning and identity lead to the sense that Joyce's self-referentiality to his own texts and his intertextuality with other texts may well be a form of interlexicality, whereby magnified letters in one text, foregrounded, opaque, and puzzling, may also resemble similar letters and words present in others. Such a confusion would challenge identity of a reading by complicating identification of sources. An awareness of a Joycean intertextual allusion, the crossing over into another text, depends less for recognition on the traditional registers of context or associated meaning (two registers of meaning that are always destabilized by puzzling letters in the disrupted text); Joycean allusion relies rather on a recognition by the reading eye of a constellation of similar letters from one book to another. Joycean intertextuality starts from (and may even end with) the letter.

As letters magnified and disrupted blur their context, their depiction of the "real world," so context is not absolutely a determining part of the identification of Joycean allusion. The similarity of letters and the shapes of several letters together are enough to establish the connection of two texts. That is to say, intertextuality for Joyce is based, as is his type of misreading, on the smallest and most irreducible part of literature, the letters: it is an interlexicality, a cited transposition of letters from one site to another, a sort of trans-lexic reading by the reader—distanced, unclear, disruptive. Moreover, this sort of intertextuality as a lexical feature contains all the disruptions with which Joyce complicates the reading process. It produces a disfunction of reading because, when it alludes, it is ludic and puzzling, engaging the free play that disrupts the surface of the text. It is also disruptive as it disengages the reader from the text and distances the depicted world within it. Last, because many of the visual tricks of the novel expand in ever widening circles of disruptive textual materiality, an even greater bridging of time and space through the visible page is achieved in the way exhausting to the reader discussed in the previous chapter: by reference to other places in *other* texts read at different times and by the recurrence of other letters. This intertextuality crosses sites and sights to other, not present, texts; it requires a kind of dittolection similar to dittography, in which the eye rather than the hand repeats letters.

Thus Joyce can make the reader often look no further than his own earlier texts, the language of the past in the space of his earlier books, as a way of challenging the identity of his current text. It was remarked in chapter 2 that the "boustrophedonic" cryptogram of Martha's letter recalled the Bous Stephanoumenos of *A Portrait* by the odd configuration of *bous, st,* and *ph.* Context was not an issue in identifying the self-allusion, but rather the similar and odd letters foregrounded by italics to the reader's puzzlement and to the connection of Joyce's own texts.

The particular sentence in "Lestrygonians" on which Joyce told Budgen he had worked the better part of a day is itself highlighted by commentary but made opaque by its own density: "With hungered flesh obscurely, he mutely craved to adore" (8.638–39).[6] Yet this sentence probably took him less effort than he let on. He possibly had in the mind's eye, or could have spent his time looking up—and backward—a similar sentence from his *Portrait:* "in utter abjection of spirit he craved forgiveness mutely of the boyish hearts around him" (126). They are similar in syntax and in diction and identical in particular letters—"mutely craved" and "craved . . . mutely." The two sentences make a chiasmus that reinforces the dynamic of crossed readings. The two sites, as citation, produce the same lexical sights; the contexts are disparate, but that is of no matter, as the letters are the same. When Virag in a "Circe" hallucination lectures to his grandson about sexuality, he ends with a simple, nonsensical exclamation: "Chase me, Charley! . . . Buzz" (15.2426). However silly and seemingly empty of meaning, the phrase has a familiar appearance that valorizes it as a "cited" text. At another lecture in a hall at University College with a bored Stephen in attendance, a fellow student, Moynihan, jests about the figure of the ellipsoid: "What price ellipsoidal balls? Chase me ladies, I'm in the cavalry" (*Portrait* 192). Pseudoscience, the lecture, and the appeal to ladies all seem to make the scenes parallel, but the eye makes the connection that lets the mind see the different texts together. Not only are the imperatives the same ("chase me"), but "Charley" and "cavalry," sharing several letters, appear similarly enough in the mind's eye to establish trans-lexia. The phrase "chase me ladies" comes from a real incident in Joyce's life;[7] but for Joyce, what transpired in his life was only a shadow to be challenged in the deceptive possibilities of letters in print both early and late.

The presence of transferred letters as trans-lexia requires a puzzling series of words from *Ulysses* to be seen yet again: the much impacted phrase *deline the mare* (3.24) from Stephen's musing on the beach about rhythm and poetry. The phrase is already dense with visual confusion to the reader: "mare" reflecting the odd cluster "gallantbuttocked mare" and *mare* as an italicized foreign glance at Latin for sea. These are vexing possibilities. With the disruption opened by the chance that the last word may be seen as Latin, the entire phrase looks as if it is an imperative to perform a grammatical exercise: "de(c)line the (word) *mare.*" (The missing *c* is found just beyond Stephen in the Irish Sea.) The phrase seems familiar, and not only because it is reflected in *Ulysses* but also because the reader has likely seen the very words before elsewhere: the phrase is trans-lexic because it alludes to another text with just those constellated letters in it. In *Portrait,* on the fatal day in which Stephen is pandied, his fellow student Fleming, like the rest of the class, was not able to do what the teacher asked—"decline the noun *mare*" (47)—and thus he suffered pandying as well. It is the scene in which Stephen cannot read without his glasses, seeing no context, only the curves of the capital in the title of the essay he is to write. As the scene is emblematic of Joyce's (and Stephen's) myopic condition as a reader and thus his limitation as a writer, it has a memorable aspect. The memorable quality also adheres to the phrase "decline the noun *mare,*" set off by its being in dialogue, so that it might be recalled as an allusion in *Ulysses*. It was a lesson that stuck in Stephen's memory, and perhaps by trans-lexia in the mind's eye of the reader.

Joyce increases the range and distance of this intertextuality, referring not only to his other texts but to other languages and the letters of their texts. And when the depth of field so increases, so do the complexity and confusion of crossed vision. The reader must peer through various depths of obscurity, as foreign languages add to the alien quality of language magnified. Moreover, the reader might be aware that what is so carefully distanced most certainly must involve a passage in reading time and memory to an earlier text. The effort is always disproportionate to the result, just as Joyce had to stare hard and long merely to see. As distance involves disengagement from the text, reducing immediacy and empathy, the passage most likely will de-emphasize sentimentality and emotion. In "Lestrygonians" we are told that Bloom remembers the night Boylan and Molly walked together in his company: "He went on by la maison Claire. Wait. The full moon was the night we were Sunday fortnight exactly. . . . Walking down by the Tolka. . . . She was humming. The young May moon she's beaming, love. He the other side of her. Elbow, arm. He." Bloom does not want to dwell on the memory: "Stop. If it was it was" (8.586–92). The French phrase (the name of a dressmaker on Grafton Street) intrudes in the sentence, making it present to the eye, and the repetition of "moon" in fact and in song ought to trigger ("wait") a halting flash of recognition in the dullest of retinas: a sort of *clair[e] de* "moon." Moonlight is itself a reflection, and reflection on the submerged text by Verlaine shows how the immediate context here substantiates the crossing of the eye to other texts by Joycean intertextuality.[8] Bloom's sad memory, concerning the beginning of what will be that day Boylan's success in love, is similar to the poem's "triste" aura, its reference to music in a "minor key," and its subject of "amour vainqueur." (The good reader ought to anticipate visually that Boylan will be called the "conquering hero" [11.340]—the words equal in the mind and analogous to the eye.) That the memory Bloom has is similar to the tone of Verlaine's poem is reinforced by the reference to the moon and the waters, either the River Tolka or the poem's fountains. Additionally, part of the remembered Moore song (itself an embedded text by simple conventional and contextual allusion), a part tantalizingly not given in the text, concerns dreaming: "When the drowsy world is dreaming." This notion of dream corresponds to the symbolist poem: "clair de lune . . . qui fait rêver les oiseaux." (It is certainly not beyond Joyce to have infinitely regressive allusions mirrored within allusions to the effect of crossing a reader's eyes.) To round off the particular connections that lie before the eye in this moonlit trick, Molly remembers this very scene by the Tolka, "singing the young May moon," and notes that that night was "the last time he [Bloom] came on my bottom" (18.78), making yet another visual joke about the "moon."

Lest even a patient and willing reader think that this connection of "maison Claire" and "moon" to a text by Verlaine seems improbable, or lest a duller eye not see the trick at all, it is repeated in "Wandering Rocks," this time with Boylan, the conqueror-lover himself and another character, not the lunar body: "Outside la maison Claire Blazes Boylan waylaid Jack Mooney's brother-in-law" (10.984). Allowing for a change in the phases of the "moon[ey]," a sort of lunar modality, the connection is unmistakable and immediate on the page: "Claire," "Mooney." With repetition, the eye catches on. The exfoliation necessary to see these tricks suggests that considerable pains are taken to distance something, and what is hidden so deeply is that potentially sentimental tone that lies at the heart of the novel and must be masked. The allusion revealed allows the reader to be removed from the text and the events of Bloom's grief. Yet to see even that absence is to wrench greatly the reading process in a crossed vision, as it involves seeing quite far, the distance in space and that in time remembering texts of "past" reading, seen earlier; the reader can be excused a visual exhaustion of trans-lexia.

Thus a tired eye begins to peer mistrustfully beyond the immediate text to the past and space of other texts. An innocuous and fatuous remark of Bloom to Stephen in "Eumaeus" can be a poser whose answer has to do with another text: "My belief is, to tell you the candid truth, that those bits were genuine forgeries all of them put in by monks most probably or it's the big question of our national poet again, who precisely wrote them like *Hamlet* and Bacon . . ." (16.780–83). Bloom's contribution to the authorial controversy, the question of the identity of the writer, is limited to the conventional: Bacon as author of Shakespeare. And even the text, reproducing what he says on the page, is itself a sort of genuine forgery: *Hamlet* and Bacon, the redundancy of two pork products. Yet the eye, cross-trained to allusion regarding the identity of other texts, can read more into what Bloom says. Through the title the reader is obliged to "see" across, as if in strabismus, to another part of the text: "omelet on the belly *pièce de Shakespeare*" (15.3909). Consequently in on the game, he "resees" or transposes *Hamlet* and Bacon into breakfast, omelette and bacon, solving the question of authorship on the way. Eggs will be on Bloom's mind as he retires to bed in several hours; they are in the reader's mind if he has been alert.

As this last puzzle concerns texts and authorship, it brings back the essential question of authority and the identity of the text itself. When the eye is being drawn in *Ulysses* to other texts, thereby reinforcing the materiality of all texts while simultaneously disrupting the reading process, the identity of a text, its integrity, is in question. In particular, the disruptive trans-lexia alludes not merely to other works but to spaces and gaps recognized as cruxes within those other texts. The opaqueness of Joyce's vision, making blind spots, is reproduced by gaps that undermine the status of a text.

A crux is a challenge to context and meaning, of course, but it is a challenge to reading and to the identity of the words and letters. The challenge results in a confusion of different "readings" and of what is the text. Textual cruxes in other works come about, Joyce understood, because of the modalities of the visible, the possibilities of letters to convey disparate meanings with similar signs, and because of the fragility of the lexical surface when it is mechanically produced (à la Darantière's typesetters or Martha Clifford). This disposition of Joyce's to play with textual problems from other works must certainly have some implied connection with the fallible status of his own text, rife with the "mechanical" printers' errors he sought to eliminate but could not because of yet another eye attack. (He would, no doubt, have enjoyed the debates about the synoptic edition that have spawned new and potentially mistaken texts—books, symposia, and a flurry of letters exchanged in periodicals.) All textual cruxes are some reader's sometime dis-lexia.

The parable that Stephen tells, "A Pisgah Sight" (the parable itself always an example of a problematic text), derives from the newspapermen's discussion of Moses and the promised land, Professor MacHugh notes. Yet Stephen's description of the statue of Nelson standing on his monument as the "one-handled adulterer" (7.1018) repeatedly refers not only to Nelson's amputation and his reputation; it too is derivative because it is allusive. It arises from his having taught Milton's "Lycidas" that morning. Stephen's teaching technique was little more than an elementary glance at the poem, and likely his eye has seen the much-puzzled phrase "the two-handed engine." Indeed, it is a text glimpsed by afterimage and shadow. Stephen's students, bored with their lesson in history, ask him for a ghost story, and he gives them, not wholly ironically, "Lycidas," which is, in its own way, a ghost story; but it is a ghost story for Stephen in that it is also a text reflecting other texts and remembered by the textual crux of the "two-handed engine." "One-handed" or "two-handed" would make some sense, but in crossing sights in trans-lexia, Stephen creates another error: "onehandled." It makes little sense, but Stephen tries to make some meaning of "Lycidas" in retrospect. Adding complexity to this lexical node, on hearing this phrase "onehandled" in the anecdote, Professor MacHugh remarks, "I see the idea. I see what you mean" (7.1019; later, "I see" occurs twice, in lines 1059 and 1061), as if he also saw in afterimage the text that inspires Stephen.

The identity of this same poem seen in trans-lexic allusion appears to the reader at another site in *Ulysses*. In "Circe" Bloom, speaking his politics against the Dutch merchants on their golden poop, says, "What reck they?" This odd phrase is an afterimage of the passage in "Lycidas" that culminates in the crux of the "two-handed engine": "What recks it them? What need they?" Although this is but a shadowy glance in reflection glimpsed through the lexia, "Lycidas" is a central text within *Ulysses:* it has a drowned man too. The reader confronts *Ulysses* through its resurfacing opaque and oblique visual similarities to other texts.

Hamlet provides two other such tricks as textual cruxes in addition to part of the joke of "Hamlet"/"omelet" and "Bacon" seen above; its importance to Stephen and to the text of *Ulysses* almost requires that it be a source of allusive word puzzles. One appears in the comical list of names of those attending the hanging in "Cyclops"; among the delegation, which includes the Countess Marha (the Hungarian cow), is to be found "Pan Poleaxe Paddyrisky" (12.565). Aside from an embedded joke at the Irish in "Paddy," the figure of the Pan-Polish nationalist Paderewski hovers behind the name, obliquely suggesting the riskiness of Irish Nationalism, and thus the middle name is easily converted by the eye to read "Pollacks." Yet in doing so, the eye has repeated one of the famous cruxes of the play, the textual question as to whether, in his description of the ghost as he was in life, Horatio refers to the time the elder Hamlet, in act 1, scene 1 of the play, "smote the sledded Pollacks" or the "leaded poleaxe on the ice." Much lies frozen in the name "Pan Poleaxe," which the peering, puzzling, myopic eye can just make out; what is evident is the puzzling quality of how words of similar signs can call all texts into question. Modalities of the visible and the dislection of the text question identity and authority.[9]

Even so unlikely a literary critic as the prostitute Zoe in "Circe" alludes to Shakespeare's play. When she says to Bloom, "Hamlet, I am thy father's gimlet" (15.3655), she clearly associates a great writer with rhyming. So does Bloom; when himself thinking of Shakespeare, "that's how poets write, the similar sounds" (8.64), he too next thinks about *Hamlet*. Yet Zoe also compounds the density of her misstatement with the sort of depicted elusive materiality associated with these deceptions. "Gimlet" looks like "Hamlet." Additionally, "gimlet" is a hand tool, much like an awl, and surely somewhere the text is playing off another crux in the play, Hamlet's knowing a "hawk from a hand-saw" (hernshaw, or heron) in act 2, scene 2, conflating nature and utensils in disruptive letters.

Because disruption is always present in the act of reading any text, even Bloom's brief acquaintance with *Hamlet* is subject to error in allusion. Bloom misremembers the passage describing Hamlet's ghost as "*Doomed for a certain time to walk the earth*" (8.68) when the limit of the ghost's purgatorial bondage is *term*. These words are similar in meaning, and perhaps Bloom remembers seeing another part of the text in which the ghost says, "My hour is almost come / When I . . . must render up myself"; yet it is also possible that he is confused by the trans-lexic modalities of the visible, as "time" and "term" share three letters; such is the fallibility of reading in establishing intertextual allusion.

When a reader of *Ulysses* is so challenged and affected by the text into irritation and exhaustion, and now, as in the above examples, into uncertainty as regards the identity of which text he is seeing, the reader's own identity in turn comes into question as a reader and as a person. And if any reader is so challenged, one might well wonder how much more challenged and influenced someone would be who knew Joyce and appeared in one of his texts. There is a case in point.

Oliver St. John Gogarty was such an acquaintance. Joyce spent much of his late youth with him (and he spent some of his life avoiding Gogarty). Gogarty's study of medicine gave him an identity useful to Joyce, and Joyce relied on Gogarty early for medical advice, particularly in 1904, writing to Gogarty at Oxford before their residence in the Martello regarding a bout of syphilis. If this bout was inadequately (or tardily) treated, it is possible that it was one of the causes of Joyce's iritis.[10] When Gogarty saw Joyce in 1909, after his several years in exile, he thought to have diagnosed him on sight: "Jaysus, man, you're in phthisis." Yet finally it was not Joyce who was ill but rather Gogarty who was infected, having caught that particular irritation of Joycean dis-lexia. The "infection" occurred precisely and clinically in ways discussed in this chapter: through an uncertainty about Gogarty's identity in *Ulysses* and his role (in actual life) as a reader of it. The text vexed Gogarty not by what it said about him but by what it made him do. What it made him do was write a text that obsessively redoes *Ulysses*.

Uniquely "real" in Joyce's actual, physical world, Gogarty was nonetheless a "character" of self-created identity, and that creation was by and through words. Gogarty saw his actual living identity as caught up in words; he lived in words, in his poems, puns, anecdotes. All of his autobiographical novels are about his feats of language, quips, or poems. He presented his life and marked it by the poems and puns he produced; he wrote many memoirs. These writings purport to be autobiographies, descriptions of his life as he actually lived it, but they all are mummeries of the sort that he practiced all the time; they are fictions of his own created self, a "character" that was all language. Much of Gogarty's early renown in the years Joyce knew him well was due to his poems and anecdotes: he wished to go to Oxford not primarily for the instruction there (as he preferred Trinity) but for the chance to win the Newdigate poetry prize.¹¹ As the last Irishman to have done so was Oscar Wilde, what must have inspired his emulation were writers and things written down; he imitated Wilde's own created identity.

Thus Oliver Gogarty provides a provocative example because of his amateur interest in writing literature and in his self-expression (one might say self-representation) in many autobiographical texts. Joyce lived with and knew Gogarty, but for Joyce, none of his acquaintances were people to be remembered but rather occasions to be written down, to become objects not of his past but of his art. If they were types for him, they were so less because of their "characters" than because they spoke, and what they said would appear printed in characters. Indeed, one might argue that Joyce picked his friends for what they would do for his art rather than chose his art because of what he had experienced with his friends. The identity of experience is suspect, as well as that of individuals; what is lived may only be a confirmation of what is already written down and read, as true of the living as of the fictional. Joyce was right about this, and his contemporaries were wrong. When Dr. Richard Best was approached by a man from the BBC who wanted to interview him for a radio show about Joyce just after the author's death, he inquired why he was chosen. When told that he was identified as a character in *Ulysses,* Best retorted, "I am not a character in fiction. I am a living being."¹² But both are subject to the same unstable ontology of identity as characters in the letters on the page. The way in which Joyce's language constructs identity of letters may reverse the traditional order of the transformation of life into art; and in this Gogarty was uniquely qualified to be his subject, the object seen as letters on the page.

Gogarty was not to Joyce a person so memorable as to be enshrined in literature; rather, like all of the characters in Joyce's fiction, he was of words, wordy; he was a talking text. What Joyce saw in Gogarty, aside from the occasion to revenge real or imagined scores, was his own sense of the use of language. Early on in his Trieste notebooks, Joyce noted down ideas about Gogarty, as he did about others of his fellows; these notations are not aide-mémoire or reference works alone, they are also the places where persons change into personalities as they become characters substantiated in words. Joyce recognized that Gogarty was aware of the importance of language and the fact that it has malleability; he saw that Gogarty was presciently aware of Bakhtinian heteroglossia. In those notebooks Joyce writes of Gogarty, "He speaks fluently in two jargons, that of the paddock and that of the science of medicine."¹³ It was Gogarty's verbal tics that commended him to the writer of fiction. Stanislaus Joyce notes in his own writing down of experience in the Dublin diary that Gogarty had certain favorite words that were rather droll, one being the term *bonzes,* the name for Japanese priests, which he used for the Catholic ones in Ireland.¹⁴ Joyce appropriated Gogarty's diction in "Oxen" (14.674) where that term appears, appropriately attributed to Mulligan. This is not the least example of where the actual physicality of Gogarty appears as the material of letters in print, when and as the word once spoken is made into the text seen. This exchange was drawn to the point of breaking.

When Joyce goes to create a character in *Ulysses* that resembles Gogarty, it is mostly by means of a particularly lexical quality, his diction filtered through allusion and unstable letters. Mulligan's first expressions in the novel are invocations, in Latin to the Mass, in English to Stephen; his last spoken words are part of the maelstrom at the end of "Oxen" or the imagined apocalypse of "Circe." The reader has seen how these phrases are the very opaqueness of Joyce's art, foreign, reversed, dis-lexic with confused letters: "*Introibo,*" "Dog Drol Eht." That he gives them to Mulligan is quite telling. Indeed, the very variety of Gogarty's language, its mercurial shifting from high to low that Joyce noted down in Trieste, the contrast of the paddock and medicine, is encapsulated in deceptive letters in the opening by his alternately talking about the majesty of the Greeks—"I must teach you [Dedalus]" (1.79)—and by the appropriate fit of his trousers, cast off on Stephen, the "secondhand breeks" (1.113). From Oxford's classicism to Dublin slang, "Greeks"/"breeks" serves as the ends of a lexical spectrum of spoken discourse inscribed in the text that characterizes the mercurial Malachi. That the two words spoken in conversation are rhymes only enforces their oral dimension, but the fact that they are written down in the text (albeit as dialogue) as visually paired with five identical letters out of six again figures forth the necessary modal, visible nature both of spoken language and of character as made up of that which is written down disjunctively. As an additional signal of the insistence on the disruptive lexical materiality that the text itself has and then confers on its objects, this first chapter has Mulligan shaving with particular attention to and emphasis on his "cheek," mentioned two times on the page before either "Greeks" or "breeks" makes an appearance as spoken ("cheek" or "cheeks" appear five times in all in "Telemachus," perhaps as a sign of Mulligan's talkativeness); thus the text seems to gloss in dis-lexia Mulligan's inscribed language with the materiality of his own physical being, itself created through the materiality of the text's own letters (and see below, on the importance of cheeks). So Joyce creates a character out of whole cloth. While Mulligan is drawn by the sartorial and semiotic quality of the model Gogarty (and dress obviously has its unstable semiotic function in *Ulysses*—Mulligan's dressing the part), that detail has its source in trans-lexia: to blur fact and fiction in strabismus, Stanislaus notes in his diary that Gogarty's "Punch-built waistcoat" was a feature of his character, corresponding to the primrose waistcoat in the novel.[15] While Mulligan's physical gestures are important—his hands, his hat, his rolling eyes—*Ulysses* reminds a reader, they too are "language" made up of letters, so that identity is questioned.

Thus the actual Gogarty (and the adjective is used advisedly) of Joyce's past appears bodily in and by print, confirming the fact that all existence is down on the page to be seen. Yet in a way of holding the mirror up to Nature, the text allows Gogarty to "see" himself in the print of *Ulysses,* see his part as a "character." This portrait in words, the lexical depiction of his material body, must have impressed him, because the visible text of *Ulysses* lives in Gogarty's mind's eye. It infects him. Seeing his own unstable character in a text of unstable letter characters makes him, as it makes all readers, misread *Ulysses.* When he comes to recount his version of the past in an autobiography, Gogarty does not remember the actual experience of living in the Tower so briefly with the young Joyce; he does not plumb the depths of what one would think was his personal and unique memory; rather, what he remembers is a textual version of the past as written down graphically in *Ulysses.* His vision of the past is a revision of a text seen earlier; his sense of his past is trans-lexic. That Gogarty wrote several autobiographical pieces covering many of the same early years of his life attests to his tendency to create several versions of his past identity out of words rather than deeds. What is surprising is that, in the last of these autobiographies, the text that Gogarty had seen and used to make his past present is not even one of his own earlier works, not the text of his life (such as the famous *As I Was Walking down Sackville Street*) or the life of his texts. Rather he used the very one that is more famous than anything he wrote and one that puts him in a less favorable light, *Ulysses*. He has, like all readers, caught the disruptive visual contagion of reading *Ulysses*.

From the subtitle of *It Isn't That Time of Year at All* one finds the evasiveness that was the hallmark of Gogarty's changeableness: "An Unpremeditated Biography" is a suspect claim, as nothing Gogarty describes himself as doing in life, least of all in writing his autobiographies, was without forethought and purpose. When Gogarty comes to write a late memoir of his youth, in 1954, he confronts the fiction of his own past, that which is no longer present. Thus the subtitle points up the tension between the past and the recent present that seeks to remember it, a tension in all autobiographies, surely, but a fact that undercuts this one's "unpremeditatedness"; the tension makes disjunctive the entire status of his text. A portion of the text displays this tension by a rather unsubtle—and probably intentional—tense shift. Passing judgment on the Joyce of their youthful years, Gogarty writes, "He is planning some sort of novel that will show us all up and the country as well." In the next paragraph, he goes on: "Little did I think that *Ulysses* would be a masterpiece of despair. And all the worse because it represented the *disjecti membra poetae*. . . . Joyce was the most damned soul I ever met."[16] Not a smooth transition from "He is planning" to "Joyce was . . . damned," it is rather one that betrays the air of spontaneous composition and slips to show the reminiscence as premeditative rather than merely meditative; in the shift can be read the disruption between the absent past of the completed past action and the ongoing presence of the present tense of print. It is the tension between living and reading. The passage glosses something else even less hidden, something the wish for mutilation of the artist, the castration of his pen, seems to seek to prevent: Gogarty's fear of reprisal from Joyce's art, a wariness of Joyce's own premeditation. In that fear he would feel himself substantiated by the presence of *Ulysses*.

Thus Gogarty remembered reading that text and wrote another text in response to it as a kind of counterwriting; his account is a response to what he has seen and misread, and so it is trans-lexic and dis-lexic at the same time, a case study of how he had been affected by Joyce's irritated text. And when the reader reads *his* version of the "Telemachus" scene in *Ulysses*, in which he creates another written version of a person named Joyce and—turnabout being fair play—a version of a person named Gogarty, he is very much aware of the insubstantial nature of identity, writing, and reading that is behind all these things (persons, events, physical facts of the past) and much less aware of or sure of there having been any life at all. If it is true that the identity of characters within *Ulysses* is suspect and that of the reader is questionable, it is finally no less true of the real people who lived in Joyce's world. Gogarty's last "life," what he writes as what he was, is based on his having misread the text of *Ulysses*.

As the letters seen as print on the page are of concern here as well as the issues of character and identity as being made visible in that foregrounded, dense materiality of print (and here applying both text and character to the identity of a person who has indeed lived), lengthy quotation from Gogarty may be excused. If the two texts *That Time* and *Ulysses* were put side by side, as if on a Hinman collator to read across, or as if in an eye examination, it would become apparent that Gogarty's text is an afterimage of the novel, a trans-lexic reflection of its materiality, but also a misread counterimage. He has caught the symptoms of the original; his text is itself a modal possibility using similar letters. Gogarty has Joyce's novel floating in his mind's eye (and may even have had the novel before his eyes when he wrote). The text of *Ulysses* is like an afterimage of the eyes or a ghost to the living, even as the actual Joyce was a ghost for Gogarty by 1954. His account is a crossed misreading that causes the doubled image of strabismus. The persistence of text precedes that of memory, as the material in the years he purports to chronicle takes place before the publication of *Ulysses* or the writing of his own text. Yet its possibilities envisioned are those that are present in the printed novel, visible since 1922. Gogarty's account of the past is a possibility, of course, like Stephen's musings on Pyrrhus, an actualization of the possible as possible. It is a speculation that cannot happen in history (as Stephen notes); yet it can and does happen within the dislexic modality of the possible in print.

> One morning back in Sandycove I was shaving on the roof of the Tower, because of the better light—it is a good idea to shave before going into salt water—when up comes Joyce.
> "Fine morning, Dante. Feeling transcendental this morning?" I asked.
> "Would you be so merry and bright if you had to go out at this hour to teach a lot of scrawny-necked brats?"
> *Touché!* He had me there: not a doubt about it. Why don't I think

of other people's problems? I must develop a little sympathy: suffer with them; realize their difficulties. I am glad that he has a job, though it is only that of a teacher.

The golden down that would be a beard on a more robust man shone in the morning light. Joyce did not need a shave.

"Yes," I said, "that is enough to obscure the Divine Idea that underlies all life. But why be atrabilious about it?" He gave me a sour look. He turned and stooped under the low door.

"I suppose you will bear that in mind and attach it to me when you come to write your *Inferno?*" I said.

He turned and made a grave announcement: "I will treat you with fairness."

"Put a pint or two in the fairness and I won't complain."

He was gone.

What would be the use of sympathy with a character like that? He would resent sympathy.

Gogarty continues:

His mother was a naked nerve; and Joyce himself was torn between a miserable background and a sumptuous education. My cavalier treatment did nothing to help, nor did the attitude of his friend, the lighthearted "Citizen," who insisted on seeing in Joyce "a great artist": a droll.

Presently I heard him climbing down the ladder. I went into the overhanging balcony and called down, "Don't stop at the Arch on your way back." He never looked up but he raised his stick in a grave salute and loped off.[17]

In the fragmented, episodic style that characterizes all of his anecdotal reminiscences, Gogarty briefly covers a great deal of ground that takes the course of several pages of *Ulysses*. The disjointed nature of his narrative clearly indicates that he is not recreating a past but rather adopting such different literary modalities as those in the original. He too writes his past as *disjecti membra poetae*.

The opening of the scene is consciously literary, suggesting not merely a story but a fairy tale, as a way of undercutting the "original" text of the novel: "One morning . . . I was shaving." The prominent first action in

Ulysses is glimpsed here as irrefutable proof of the connection by texts, not life (one shaves nearly every day if not every day; why should the act hold any prominence in a memoir?). Moreover, the word "shaving" logically suggests the site in the other text of the "cheek" repeatedly mentioned in "Telemachus," and it thus calls to the mind's eye by intertextuality the visual, lexical transposition and repetition of "cheek"/"Greek"/"breek." Not incidentally, that "shaving" is a term for cheating or prevarication puts into question the accuracy of either account, Gogarty's or Joyce's. There are subtle, modal changes of words here that show just the proximity of the two authors and the instability of a text when it is read by a reader handicapped by Joycean dis-lexia. "Golden down" in this passage does not evoke Chrysostomos, a flattering comparison (one would think) to Gogarty in "Telemachus," but rather is here turned on Joyce's cheek. Who is being shaved or shaving? In the fact that it is morning, Gogarty's word "golden" is easily associated with sunlight and thus with the sight of the elaborately poetic passage of Bloom on the same morning, the "girl with the golden hair" in "Calypso." This association is probably made as an oblique criticism of the particularly overwritten nature of that passage in *Ulysses* (which suggests that Gogarty probably misread the purpose and effect of Bloom's musing as a set composition). An aside on the "Golden Dawn" and theosophists who excluded Joyce is probably also intended by Gogarty, especially in light of the fact that the society is mentioned two pages further on in his chapter's account: he too can write dis-lexically of "golden down"/"dawn." And particularly, although least subtly, the "golden" is a dig at Joyce's masculinity. He describes Gogarty as shaving in his novel; Gogarty counterwrites that Joyce didn't have to. Stephen might think that Mulligan fears him, but Gogarty tries to show that the razor is mightier than either the lancet or the pen.

There is an implied struggle of the two authors to recreate the absent past in words, a dynamic interchange from life to art and from art back to life (a dynamic affirming less the life lived than the text written and seen). This interchange can be seen in the fact that alternately Gogarty makes language spoken in dialogue in *Ulysses* into text in his work or takes what was the written word in the novel and turns it back into spoken language. This inversion, similar to Joyce's shifts of italics and roman type, creates a depth of field, changing background and foreground to make the reader uncertain and disoriented. The paradoxical nature of Gogarty's enterprise is due to the chronological fact that he is rewriting the text of *Ulysses* thirty years after its publication in 1922, yet he seeks to describe events that happened nearly twenty years before that, in 1904. But both disruptive alternations reflect the nature of the misreading of Gogarty's view of *Ulysses* and the counterwriting of his own version; additionally, they challenge the substance of what each text aims to recreate.

Thus the narrative tag line "up comes Joyce" recreates in the third person what Mulligan says in the novel, "Come up Kinch"; it illustrates foremost that Gogarty had to have the other text in mind (and perhaps in sight) to write this, his text, as it is so minor a detail as to be hardly necessary for an autobiographical account. This switch in person reflects the issue that Gogarty is reacting to the identity of the literary character—that is, reacting as a living person as if he were a character. This transfer of what Mulligan says to what Gogarty writes only brings together the connection of living person as character, where the living copy the written, in the face of the normal assumption that the life comes first and then the textual creation. Mulligan the character "speaks" what is only written down; Gogarty has himself write with similar letters. Foreground and background shift abruptly, and the reader may be made ill.

Gogarty's presentation of himself in terms of Joyce's text, as here most notably in the word choice, recreates the materiality of language seen in *Ulysses* yet subverts it enough to his own ends; it is as if Gogarty seems to recognize in Joyce what Joyce saw in him, a talent and a particular way with words. There is, for example, the use of the word "merry"; it is attributed to Joyce in this section, forming a sort of joke, as it is the character Mulligan who says it in the first chapter of the novel in the song "On Coronation Day." Yet the repetition here not only draws the parallel to the text but also puts into question the notion of text by the very nature of these two interlocking works. What is identity in a world where everything must be translated into twenty-six letters, common to everyone, and how easy is dislection? (And if there is reason to suspect experience, why trust memories or memoires? These last two nouns, after all, are anagrams, dislexically similar.) Gogarty is cleverly correct in his attribution of the word: while Mulligan "speaks" this word in *Ulysses,* it is Joyce as author who actually "says" "merry" as a modality of the visible in print.

Similarly, the term "scrawny-necked brats" is attributed by Gogarty to Joyce (a level of diction not usually associated with the scholastic Stephen) because of Joyce's unwillingness to teach; and the choice fits with Stephen's account in "Nestor" of the student Sargent with his "lean neck" and unkempt appearance (2.139). This parallel is less in the service of corroborating the truth; perhaps it is rather the case that Gogarty wants to show that he has read beyond the opening of the text he is writing against, to present a "true," unflattering picture.

The anecdote of the morning in the Tower seems to end on a positive note, one favorable to both Gogarty's generosity and Joyce's intent. His account seems to have an innocuous, even just, purpose, a sense of balance in the fictional representation of the shared past of Gogarty and Joyce. Indeed, the exit of Stephen, so fraught with the heavy notion of "usurpation" in *Ulysses,* is here turned into Mulligan's Parthian shot in favor of "fairness." This, his retelling of the past, is to be equitable, with the underlying suggestion that Joyce's retelling tells tales. Gogarty tries by this evasion to suggest he is correct, his version being the law (*lex*) and Joyce's therefore being illegal (dis-lexic). The last part of the episode, however, creates another tension. Gogarty suggests by jocular negation that Joyce meet him later at the Arch on the day described: "Don't stop . . . on your way back." In *Ulysses* Joyce has the place as "The Ship, Buck Mulligan cried. Half twelve" (1.733). This disparity might suggest Gogarty's better memory setting the record straight, or more convincingly a statement of the fact that Joyce literally accepted Gogarty's invitation in 1904 not to go to the Arch and instead went to the Ship. While the name of the latter pub seems to evoke shadows of an Odyssean past, the actual pub and the truth are irrelevant as long as there are possibilities of the visible.

Moreover, the confessional comments about Gogarty's lack of sufficient "sympathy" seem to answer a charge of Joyce's: Stephen's sense of Mulligan's slighting not his mother but himself. In his account, Gogarty briefly encapsulates Stephen's mourning in *Ulysses* in a terse physical and oddly inappropriate phrase, "His mother was a naked nerve." The clinical and grotesque diction, given Mulligan's statement of how professionally he views death, runs roughshod over an emotional spot in Joyce's text and life. The "impossible person" of *Ulysses* ought, Gogarty suggests, to be given his due; the fault lies with Gogarty in being unable to provide sufficient quantities of compassion. Yet Gogarty's account is done more in the spirit of criticism than fairness; it does not aim to set the record straight but to replace one version with another, to set up one record rather than another, the earlier and more widely broadcast and published one. Instead of sympathy with Joyce, Gogarty has the symptoms of Joyce, indicated by Gogarty's dis-lexic reading of irritated letters. The Joyces, both Stanislaus and James, were skeptical of Gogarty; while Stephen may console himself with the sense that Mulligan "fears the lancet of my art," Stanislaus recognized a corresponding threat from Gogarty. In the *Dublin Diary* he notes that "Gogarty is generally regarded as a dangerous companion. He is scarcely this until he is intimate, but he is certainly a most demoralizing person intellectually."[18] This comment is followed by an editorial notice in the edition of the diary that "a leaf is lacking in the manuscript": it is tantalizing to speculate on what has been removed from this critical version, what was mutilated as a sort of revenge on Gogarty's *disjecti membra poetae,* with the one text castrating or mutilating the other. The gap in the diary seems to replicate the various irritations of the texts of both Joyce and Gogarty.

What would come as a surprise to both brothers was not Gogarty's vindictiveness but rather that the vindication would appear not in the social world or in conversation but in their chosen medium of print. Gogarty's late account contains further a series of digs by the worldly doctor at the expense of the world-famous author. Joyce struck first in *Ulysses* and was dead by the time Gogarty wrote his account, but Gogarty was published later and has the last word. He tries to supplant the larger, more famous text with his own counterversion: indeed he tries to supplant Joyce himself. Stephen may have only been slightly wrong in calling Mulligan a "usurper": what is supplanted is not the physical being who used to occupy (and materially paid the rent for) the Tower; what is supplanted is the physical presence and materiality of texts. Gogarty's dis-lexia as regards *Ulysses* tries to replace the novel in which all this reality takes place. Yet, because he is infected, Gogarty loses the battle to Joyce, who had (and has) the most lasting effect.

The episodic nature of the account in *It Isn't That Time of Year at All* continues with a description of the physical Joyce and clearly purposes an aside at the artist's hygiene.

> Joyce very rarely bathed and never in the Forty Foot, which was below the Tower. Once, when we took a tram to Howth on the other side of Dublin Bay, he did get into the swimming bath at the north side of the Hill. I forget if I saw him in the water, but I remember

seeing him naked on the side of the bath, carrying a sweeping brush over his shoulder and deliberately staggering along. I was about eight feet up the rock at the side of the tank trying to get a foothold for a dive.

"Jesus wept; and when he walked, he waddled," Joyce announced.

I studied the naked figure. "So that's what his uncle wants to make a half miler out of," I said to myself. "He'll never do it with that physique. Why, his knees are wider than his legs. He has lost his faith. Now what is to become of his form?"[19]

Oddly, given the associative, anecdotal nature of his narrative, Gogarty's digs at the past here in this ostensibly biographical account are chronological. While the incident of the bathing comes from *Ulysses,* it turns on notions from *Portrait,* when Joyce is younger than he is said to be here; this order is clearly established by Gogarty's reference to knees, which relates to Stephen's running with lifted knees (*Portrait* 61). Thus it is that, while he seeks revenge on Joyce, Gogarty has been affected by Joyce's dis-lexia and has thus become trans-lexic, alluding to other texts of Joyce. The comments about the authorly physique are clearly done to aggrandize Gogarty's actual and bemedaled physical prowess as an athlete in track and cycling. As an act of revenge for his being consigned to the novel, Gogarty restores the absent ghost of the dead Joyce to the material presence of texts, both Joyce's and his own; in his chronological reference to the two Joyce texts, Gogarty plots the genealogy of Joyce's autobiographical art. So Gogarty easily and readily turns life into text by making the physical figure of the living Joyce—many years after the fact and when the body is no longer present but in the grave—correspond to the textual Dedalus from the novel earlier than *Ulysses,* the Dedalus from whom the one in *Ulysses* is derived. He also moves from getting his digs *in* print, what he writes, to getting digs *at* print, what Joyce wrote; and that is a particularly pernicious attack. The printed text is the legacy by which the artist, faded into impalpability, has his identity remembered by the material he leaves behind on his written pages. And here again the fact that what Gogarty has on his mind is not memory of life lived but rather memory of texts read is evident as dis-lexia; he is writing against the written account that he has seen. His "unpremeditated autobiography" is not only not unpremeditated; it is also no autobiography. His own "character" in the pages of this work is formed from what he has read about his "fictional character" in the letters of Joyce's pages; and conversely, his "biographical" Joyce is made up from the "fictional" counterpart. In this, Gogarty becomes literary and a man of words, as he always envisioned himself, but in a way that only confirms the truth about what Joyce does with all the characters in *Ulysses* and all the readers of it: the sight of it leads to a disruption of identity and a contagious dislexia.

The dead Joyce is given a corporeality, a delusive presence in insubstantial letters on the page, like a ghost hovering in Gogarty's text. Ghosts are shadows dimly seen of identities faded into obscurity, and they give the names to the occluding opacity of the glaucomatous eye.

CHAPTER 6

Ghosts, Sounds, and Errors

The spectral Joyce resuscitated through Gogarty's account hovers in the eye and on the page, represented in unstable material depiction, of uncertain identity, with malleable presence and language changed and inverted; he is a product much like his own text, unclear and insubstantial as a ghost. There is some justice in this representation: Joyce's iritis, the cause of his handicap and of the reader's dis-lection of *Ulysses* that affects Gogarty, creates opaque spots and blank areas. The essential consequence of his illness was a blurring of the eye, making the lens opaque and resulting in a restricted, clouded field of vision. The resultant "unwanted secondary images" are called in ophthalmology—by fortuitous coincidence—"ghosts."[1] Joyce must have seen many of these ghosts, more even than the number of ophthalmologists he saw. Considering that Joyce's eyesight worsened during the writing of the polyglottal *Finnegans Wake,* and considering that he saw eye specialists in Zurich in 1917 at the start of *Ulysses* and in France at its end (as well as being operated on in the American Hospital in Paris after the publication of *Ulysses*), it is informative to see that the same term appears in German and French: *Geisteserscheinung* and *spectre secondaire, image blanche.*[2] The ghostly apparition and its appearance in several foreign languages are pertinent to further consequences in the irritation of the text and the resultant dis-lexia.

Impalpable, shadowy forms of things seen are not only the traditional stuff of literature, as Keats notes in his "Ode on Indolence" and as Shakespeare was aware in all his drama; they are also something that was appearing in a very modern art form, the cinema. Surely Joyce's interest in starting up the ill-fated venture of Dublin's first commercial theater, the Volta, was whetted not only by the chimerical prospect of financial gain and the opportunity to get a paid trip back to Ireland in 1909 but also by his sense of the visual quality of this new form. The movies, so modern and so potentially powerful as a popular art form, appealed to those concerns of Joyce for a new art that was based, if deceptively, on the "actual" seen world and that was itself a popular cultural artifact, much like the ads and songs within the novel. (It is due to the symbolic of history that Joyce had the second of his attacks of iritis on this trip.)[3] The visual aspect of a film, even when Joyce's eyes were so poor as to keep him from seeing it, would be a quality that he would present increasingly when he began to work on his new art form of *Ulysses* some years later. Joyce's visualizing a text and then jumping about in it, referring to its forms and shapes (those of the letters),[4] projecting parts of the text into later spaces and pages are all aspects of a visual motion.[5] The Russian filmmaker Eisenstein was approached to produce a film of *Ulysses;* there is also the story, perhaps apocryphal, that Eisenstein claimed to have learned montage from the "Circe" episode. In an eerie coincidence, Ellmann notes that Eisenstein described his visit to Joyce as "'a ghost experience' because the room in which they met was so dark that they both seemed shadows."[6] The insubstantial voice, coming from this void, itself a nearly immaterial presence—much like the ghost of Hamlet senior under the stage—would be for Joyce part of the shadowy material within a text to be presented by words. Ghosts are often more easily heard than seen.

    The ghosts of Joyce's vision indeed function the way the ghosts of superstitious belief do: they represent a sense of limit, of things lost by being poorly glimpsed or not seen, of absence. When Joyce punningly refers to his novel in *Finnegans Wake* as his "usylessly unreadable Blue Book of Eccles," he is not only commenting on its effect; he also calls it "*édition des ténèbres,*" a book of shadows and spectral sights. It was the first complete work of his illness, as the *Wake* was to be the last. *Ulysses* is unreadable precisely because it is filled with letters disoriented and irritated, such as those seen in the word "usylessly," puzzled, disordered, inchoate. All *Ulysses* is a ghost story foremost because of the magnified irritation of its letters, because of its resulting blind spots and opacities; the glimpse of letters unclear and deceptive adds possibilities of mistake, of not seeing, of nonmeaning (and of missing or lost meaning). "Useless" is nearly contained in "Ul(y)sses," straining the eye by disorder and excess. That extra *y* in "usylessly" is to be glossed with the French "*édition des ténèbres*" so that it is *y grecque,* the foreign glance that makes the Homeric parallel, evoking the ghost of the classical (and the foreignness adds further to the alien aspect of letters). Moreover, the two *l*s in this word reflect the added *l* of Martha's other "world" and the one omitted from "L. Boom." Letters are always the cause of useless error and loss of meaning in shadowy obscurity.

Ghosts appear in spectral thematization frequently in the text.[7] They do so first because the novel is about the past of the writer, and, as with Gogarty's account, the past is only elusively recreated. Ghosts also appear in part because their appearance plays to the dematerializing quality of the picture puzzle text; that is, they undercut the depiction of reality in the novel in ways analogous to the magnified opacity of letters blurred and indistinctly creating meaning and puzzle. And pertinently, ghosts often appear obscurely to talk unclearly, to speak in mystery.

One particular appearance of a ghost introduces issues wherein the ghost within the text aligns the spectral sights of the text, bringing into focus issues of loss, of the voice of the unclear message, and of error. Stephen sees the ghost of his lost mother, the object of his memory and mourning. When she appears, she is described with the elements that have made up his elusive memories, elements that have become the fabric of the text, as "breathing wetted ashes"—breath and ashes things ephemeral too, so that she is herself a sort of unclear text. As she appears, he interrogates her; the immaterial ghost must express itself in the equal ephemerality of spoken language: "Tell me the word, mother. . . . The word known to all men" (15.4191). He asks for a word, the Logos of a message that she should know. He believes she does because of a simple syllogism for him: in the beginning the word was with God; May Dedalus is with God; she should know the word. What he wants is to be told something in language by the immaterial voice of the missing, and the absence of his mother resembles what he seeks to know: the word is something he has already seen and should remember but does not. It appeared in an unclear sight of a text seen in allusive crossed reading, some word he has presumably seen in trans-lexia and imperfectly. The word is from a text from Aquinas he remembered in the library: "*Amor vero aliquid alicui bonum vult unde et ea quae concupiscimus*" (9.430). That true love is to be connected to what he has thought as both noun and adjective in "Nestor," *amor matris.* Italics in both passages visually highlight a connection so that the similarity will be evident despite the alien quality of the language. Stephen's memory is of crossed texts, one from school, one from the Library. Sight is necessary to connect these in memory, and, because sight is subject to the blind spot of forgetting, it is also necessary to prompt the shade to speak. (The reader may also have been haunted by the connection discussed earlier wherein the "liquid" in Dublin bay and its association with the deathbed bowl are reinforced by the Latin *amor vero aliquid.*)

Stephen must imperfectly remember a glimpse of those words from the library at 2:00 P.M. or the classroom at 9:00 A.M. if he is unable to recall them, despite much emotion, at midnight at the brothel. The gap in his memory, his blind spot, needs to be filled appropriately by being told what he seems to have missed. A word imperfectly seen must be evoked by being spoken by a specter of a lost mother, and it is to be presented with unclarity, incompleteness, confusion, and error.

Yet the words that Stephen would have the ghost of his mother speak have themselves been subject to absence, loss, and error. As Stephen notes in the same conversation in "Scylla" in which he thinks of Aquinas, a ghost is "one who has faded into impalpability . . . through absence" (9.148). So too has the text he wishes to have told by a ghost: it has been subjected to fading and impalpability, absent since the first appearance of the novel in print and in all subsequent editions until Gabler. The passage of love, *amor vero,* by being lost in the text, is an emblem of the unintentional error Joyce sought to avoid with his careful proofreading and scrutiny (that is, he wanted Stephen to miss thinking of this passage, but not the reader). Yet Joyce himself missed it in his own corrections, as he rarely read from typescript to proof. Moreover, its loss was caused by the very features that thread through the irritated text; it is an error of a particularly spectral kind, one in which the typesetter has become infected by blind spots and unclarity.

The whole sentence from Aquinas, "*Amor vero aliquid alicui bonum vult unde et ea quae concupiscimus*" (9.430), had faded into absence as another text, that of *Ulysses* itself, eclipsed it. Gabler notes that this omission was no doubt caused by the typist's eye jumping from one set of italics to another when the typist transcribed the manuscript of "Scylla" (from the line of French "*L'art d'être grandp . . .*" [9.426]);[8] this is an example of haplography, which conflates two appearances into one. The visual foreignness and otherness of italics (remarked on earlier) as standing out from the surrounding words on the page are here confirmed in their effect on the typist, as the deceptive similarity of the phrases caused the eye to jump. Joyce would no doubt have to assent to the irony that what was absent from his original text was caused by a slip in the eye's seeing the modality of print; his irritating the text in a disruption of lines materially similar in form on the page creates an immateriality in which misreading and crossed reading lead to loss, absence, and unclarity. The error occurs despite the fact that the two passages are in two separate languages. That the voice of the ghost is to "tell" the phrase only adds to the resonant difficulty, where two parts of the text are reduced to one.[9]

That the ghost is asked to *tell* the word, lost and obscured from the text by the typist disruptively missing letters, is another index of confusion and loss. It is a confusion of the material with the immaterial, the impalpable ghost asked to speak a sound. Sound itself, like the ghost, is elusive, insubstantial, and easily faded. Sound is a fleeting entity in life, and it is particularly insubstantial in a text; difficult to represent, it is something grasped only imperfectly in meaning through reading, as reading conflates sound with sight. As all the irritation of letters in the text leads to confusion and blurring, so those letters used to create sound imperfectly add a further disruptive dimension to Joyce's dis-lexia. Moreover, with the synaesthesia of sound in visible letters the reader is more and more confused, and this furthers the likelihood of error in what is read and "heard."

The ghosts and spectral sights of lost letters and absent texts are another part of Joyce's enterprise and will be discussed further in this chapter, but first some myopic scrutiny needs to be given to the elusive sounds presented by letters. Thus if all of *Ulysses* resides in the ineluctable modality of the deceptive and irritated visible, a good portion of it is found in the modality of the audible. Especially evident among those oralities of story, gossip, and the like are the songs within the novel whose very presence entangles sound with sight (an issue too large to entertain here in detail). One blending of a song with the text makes an important connection to the visual dynamic of reading that Joyce disrupts. In "Sirens," appropriately enough, a song is reproduced and melded into the text to have Simon Dedalus "coo" a "nightcall, clear from anear, a call from afar" (11.855). The rhythmical and echoic quality of the song is indicated by the assonance and consonance, but the text first and foremost represents that similarity through the simple letter configuration of the words "clear" and "anear." Earlier, Bloom is described through the modalities of just such letters as having "eyed and saw afar" (11.302). The "call," in its nominative "a call from afar," and the eye, as the verb "eyed," are connected despite the separation in space by the text in the parallel distance of space, "afar." (The word "afar" has its own immediate parallel in distance and diction within "Sirens" with "anear.") Yet when it is subject to disruptive lexicality, a chiastic connection like a strabismus forces the reader to combine the phrases "eyed from afar" and "a call from afar" with "clear from anear" into seeing an "eye" and "an/ear" to suggest the conflation of two sensory acts. To the primacy of sight—which even alone always complicates the reading process—is added another complication of sound, and the two are conveyed through the disruption of words seen on the page.[10]

What can be made of the eye and ear being put so near together, but only so far apart ("afar") on the page as they are on a human head, is that the two are set off by their contiguity to be interrelated but unequal. The reading line has been broken, in a Joycean first heave that corresponds in prose to Pound's break in the metric line in poetry, to open a space where sound might enter. Yet the sound that resonates in that open gap is contingent on and not equal to the sight because it exists only at the power of and as a function of the sign.[11] Dis-lexia, as visual, is a deconstructive challenge to phonetic writing, hence its confusion of signs and letters; the phonemic possibilities of writing are merely one among many modal possibilities for the letter as a preponderantly graphic visual form of irritation.

Thus even the sound of music must be lexically represented. Molly, the chanteuse and siren of the novel, sings to herself in the last chapter, but the reader must see the song and in seeing have the reading disrupted. In her consideration of the elision of words sung lies just this tension of eye and ear. As she plays up the enunciation of words along with the melodic phrasing, the disjunction of the sounds sometimes makes for low comedy: "on the brow and part which is my brown part" (18.276). In another instance she extends a word to fit the sustaining of a note, blending her "song" with the sound of the distant train: "sweeeee theres that train far away pianissimo eeeee one more tsong" (18.908). The reader must span the chiastic break in the words to recover the lexical from the musical: "sweeeee . . .

eeeeee . . . tsong."[12] In a similar but inverted process, Molly "speaks" words in her monologue that are written out as if they were phonetically pronounced, again combining eye and ear into halting confusion: "neumonia" (18.727). (The missing *p* is to be found, presumably, later in the chapter when Molly urinates or found earlier in excess in Bloom's phrase "Do ptake of some ptarmigan" [8.886–87].) And in a confused blend of the orthographical and the audible, commingling a comestible vegetable and a visual cipher, Molly thinks/speaks about a ring that is "pure 18 carrot gold" (18.870), a mistake available only to the eye. Reading is halted when sound is reproduced by sign.

(The musical notations in *Ulysses* add just this density of sound to sight. While the figures printed on the page represent sounds, their notation is the same sort of symbolic system of substitution as is writing, again privileging the visible. The forms are historical: both archaic, in "Scylla's" plainsong, and modern, in "Ithaca's" folk song. It is intriguing to realize that these musical texts in "Sirens" and "Ithaca" were written out by Joyce for the printers, and thus the page gives a reader the hand[writing] of the artist to be glimpsed in the sign system materialized in print.)

The letter underwrites, as it were, everything that the text is as a visual object. In recognition of this dominance, when Stephen contemplates metrics, he notes that rhythm may be heard, but it is also to be seen: "Rhythm begins, you see. I hear." The text obligingly scans the phrase before the reader's eye: "Acatalectic tetrameter of iambs . . . *deline the mare*" (3.23). To this already dense phrase, discussed before, is added an additional tension in the secondary dimension of sound.

Within this primacy of the visible, then, phonemic possibilities exist to complicate and strain the text as object seen on the page. That text is already freighted with difficulties to sight, and the adding of the dimension of sound to that essential process is further discomfiting.[13] Sound is a lexical feature because it is used to disrupt further the act of reading, causing a confusion of the eye and ear, of the graphemic and the phonemic. It is an additional disfunction of dis-lexia, which is itself already a complication in the processing of visual information, to the confusion of sight and sound.

Everything that is both aural and oral in *Ulysses* exists only as it appears on the page; all sounds in the text devolve into what must ineluctably be visible in order to be heard: all signs may have sound, but all sounds must sign. As paradoxical as this tension may be, it is routinely understood by the denizens of Dublin in the world cum text. When Big Ben Dollard, in conversation with Dedalus and Cowley, makes the strange motion of wiping "away the heavy shraums that clogged his eyes to hear aright" (10.941), the reader is not surprised (or ought not to be), accustomed to a disjunctive and handicapped reading enterprise: Ben is doing the correct thing; he is, for all his failings at solving the picture puzzles, a competent character of Dublin discourse. The synaesthesia of his act, clearing the eye to hear better, only reinforces the connection for Joyce and for the reader of *Ulysses* that to hear what is going on one had better look sharp and be wary. Any act must privilege sight. (That what Dollard hears after clearing his eyes ends up as the joke about Jacko and the nuts reminds readers that all the visual—or at least much of it—in the novel is in the service of the ludic.) As aural as Joyce's work is (especially in "Sirens," Joyce's voices, and the polyphonic *Wake*), it is all there on the page to be seen. To hear in *Ulysses* is to read the text as it writes its sounds; all voice or sound is text and visible.

To see through hearing is the necessary option of the sight-impaired, yet Joyce seemed convinced that the audible was secondary to the visual. He planned a coup de théâtre, literally, to that effect. To support the Irish singer Sullivan, during a performance at the Paris Opera, Joyce, rising from his box, "removed his heavy dark glasses from his eyes and said, 'Praise God for the miracle. . . . I see the light once more.'"[14] While this act was calculated to boost Sullivan's appeal to the public, the wish Joyce implied was that sound would heal and rectify sight.

In this dominance of sight over sound on the page, *Ulysses* further distinguishes itself from *Finnegans Wake* despite their similar deceptive lexical surfaces. Thematically, ghosts cannot "exist" within the text of the *Wake*, where all identity and time are codeterminate; it is only *Ulysses*, with its "depicted" if disrupted material of representation, that can sustain the immaterial subversion of the spectral. The *Wake* is all voice; *Ulysses* has its puzzling picture of the world depicted by the poet. While Joyce may have commented to Budgen or written to Weaver about *Ulysses*, he wrote it alone and proofread it largely by himself. The *Wake* existed for Joyce in many ways in a realm in which hearing and speech were a greater part of its construction. He claimed pertinently in its defense that, "in a word, it is pleasing to the ear."[15] The *Wake* was sometimes dictated (an activity that caused the humorous anecdote of Beckett and Joyce's "come in"), and its proofreading was done in conversation with others.[16] Joyce frequently had recourse to foreign dictionaries or to native speakers for words and phrases that embroider the diction. The disruptive letters in *Ulysses* have no meaning or particular sound behind them other than their function as deceptive shapes that challenge reading; no symbolics adhere to them. In *Finnegans Wake* certain letters are backed up by meaning, as the sigla, and all are crucially and constantly important for their sound. Only part of the phoneme is useful or necessary in *Ulysses*. Indeed the difference between the two texts as regards sound is most evident in their titles, that of the *Wake* deriving from a song, that of *Ulysses* from a written tradition. The Ruby/Rudy transfer in *Ulysses* is a function exclusively of sight; in the *Wake* a split such as *l* to *r* might be visual, but that of *p* and *q*, if tantalizingly an inversion that effects a dis-lexia, has a particular and necessary function of sound. (Joyce sought out those splits of graphic expressions, as *l* and *r*, precisely because their aural component is an essential tension.) *Ulysses* is meant to be seen, ineluctably visible; it is, as Stephen says, "what you damn well have to see." Although there are parts of it that read well aloud (as Joyce himself did with "Sirens"),[17] to understand it takes the magnified snail's pace of the visual act of reading—hence Joyce gave Budgen the magnifying glass. This dynamic is reversed in the *Wake:* for it, Joyce commented to Claud Sykes, "If anyone doesn't understand a passage, all he need do is read it aloud."[18] Thus the *Wake* has a much greater dimension of meaning resident in sound than *Ulysses;* indeed its ideal reader must also be a speaker (as well as an insomniac). The ideal reader of *Ulysses,* by contrast, is challenged and limited but still and always a reader with his eyes myopically close to the page. (Thus the example of "neumonia" from Molly's soliloquy, a spoken form, makes sense only when seen.)

While the different ways to reach meaning in the two texts are telling, in both the act of reading must involve sight. In the *Wake* Joyce refers to "aural eyeness" (623.18), a phrase that captures just this dual-dimensioned paradox and its valorization of sight over sound. What is aural in his work, especially the studied aurality of the last (understood by reading aloud), is created of the stuff of the eye, the material*ness* of what the handicapped eye sees in print. Yet the "eyeness" is dominant, the royalty of the graphic dimension (this from a man with a much keener ear than eye), and it is additionally "high" by being the essential expression of what the dis-lexicality of the visible can achieve in print on the page, the empowerment of the letter.[19]

As an example of how the aural connection is less pertinent to *Ulysses*—that is, how the graphemic aspect of letters on the page to be read is dominant over the phonemic—consider certain riddles in *Ulysses* that devolve around homonymy. A pun in *Finnegans Wake* such as "nepogreasymost" (156.17) is first more than a pun; it is a nexus of various words, to be unpacked partially by the eye but also by the pronunciation, by the expression of being said aloud. It has something to do with nepotism, with St. John Nepomuc, with the greasy anointing by chrismation; yet, pronouncing it with a knowledge of Russian elicits the word for "infallibility." Both activities of reading and speaking are necessary for the reader to derive a meaning—indeed here is an example of how the reader must be a speaker in order to understand (and additionally a speaker of various languages). Yet a riddle in *Ulysses* is first of all spoken by a character, a factor that already limits the origin and audience within the text on the page. A riddle from Lenehan will have a limited effect comically, and any such "riddle" told and answered is written out, so that it is limited in function to the page. As an example there is the one posed, not coincidentally, in "Aeolus"; the fact that the aural puzzle appears in a chapter in which a newspaper is turned out reconfirms the status and primacy of print. It is necessary to see how the joke's limited substance as oral is made evident through the foregrounding of letters: both the posed riddle and the answer are immediately present on the page in similar letters so that meaning is irrelevant. That the pun is solved so quickly attests to its poor quality: "What opera is like a railway line? . . . *The Rose of Castille.* See the wheeze? Rows of cast steel" (7.591). Lenehan's insistent inquiry—"See the wheeze?"—is not only a sign of the poor comedian; it marks two facts about this as all such posers. First, the "wheeze," while a colloquialism for a weak joke, is a reminder of insubstantial breath, the air that produces the play of sounds; second, the "see" is a reminder that in order to understand the riddle one must read the signs of those sounds.[20] The signs have the deceptive similarity of irritated vision: "*Rose*"/"Rows"; "*Castille*"/"cast steel." An additional fillip of the foregrounding of the letter is provided by the italics, that constant sign of Joyce for the unusual, alien quality of print. Printed letters create and solve this puzzle simultaneously (much as the cryptogram of Martha's name and address is posed and solved). There is no need to speak this puzzle aloud after reading it; the sound is secondary, as meaning is fleeting and elusive, because of the letters.

The end of "Oxen" makes the case for letters over sounds most strongly. There language, which has predominated in its written form from the earliest Latinate section of the chapter, begins to be a wholly oral enterprise, although it still appears on the page written in letters the same as those in, for example, a parody of Macaulay. The irony of the "British Beatitudes" (14.1453) is enumerated out loud in alliteration—"Beer, beef, business...." (14.1459)—yet all eight are headed by the word "atitudes," a mistaken stance whose orthographical error is rectified by the repeated presences of the letter *b* (thus *b*-atitude). The verbal deconstruction of the homophonic riddle and answer of Lenehan appears again on the page to confuse sight and sound ("Rose of Castile. Rows of cast" [14.1510]). Yet the speakers are difficult to identify; they are, as one critic notes, "invisible—although of course highly audible."[21] Indeed they are like ghosts, difficult to see but not to hear. Amid the polyphony (or is it polylalia?) of "Oxen," one character speaks a phrase that is rendered phonetically: "help ... frend [who] tuk ... kee tu find plais whear to lay ... his hed" (14.1540). This is a rare transcription of the sounds in an otherwise simple declarative sentence in normal diction referring to the major incident in the opening of the novel; it is only somewhat complicated by the unnecessary addition of the visual feature of the *l* in "help" (where the word would likely be pronounced with it diminished) and the telling signal effect of rendering "where" more complex by embedding an "ear" in it. Indeed, "friend" is a word clearer seen as "frend." The sentence is not difficult to understand; the sounds are there only as a transcription of speech that is exaggerated because it is drunken. What is difficult is the lection of the sentence, seeing the scripted part of the transcription. The "plais" looks odd; given the tendency of the only twenty-six letters derived from the Latin alphabet to make words in different languages, it could look like the second-person singular of the French verb *plaire*. French appears in "Oxen" clearly italicized on the previous page as *Bonsoir la compagnie* (14.1536) but compromised in sight in an earlier line as "au reservoir mosso" (14.1506); it is not surprising to find such inconsistency in the irritated text. Language is always correct and incorrect when languages that sound different from each other use the same letters. The different languages, pidgin dialect, argot, and slang—all spoken forms—

make a farrago reproduced exclusively by the same letters on the page. While the reader cannot identify the speakers or understand the words "spoken," they are both represented by language.

Thus the depiction of speech is just as threatened by letters as is any other depiction. All such illusions and tricks of the eye (as noted in chapter 4) were to be "seen in black and white through the eyetrompit" (*Wake* 247.32). This last word was considered earlier as a prosthetic device much like Joyce's magnifying glass, to enable the user to see what was in black and white, the letters on the page, greatly enhanced, and thus largely to increase the possibility of deception, trompe l'oeil. Yet in that the ear trumpet is a device to augment sound for the deaf, it also suggests that the dimension of the phonemic has too a handicapped quality, that errors are possible in seeing what is to be "heard." As the letter in *Ulysses* is magnified in prominence, it has a predominant function as a graphemic, visual feature; but as all that is visual for Joyce and his readers is subject to unclarity, blurring and imprecision, so too the sound of letters represented through sight will be unclear and imperfect, subject to confusion and error of a spectral kind in sound as well as sight because of the shadowy quality of signs. Unclear people speak in "Oxen," impalpable ghosts "tell" words of unclear texts in "Circe," and all speech is itself unsubstantial sound spectrally presented in a text of letters.

Some of the puzzles posed by letters in *Ulysses* also partake of such confusion and error of sound. Not only do puzzles cause the text, but the text causes further puzzles by echoing in sound; the consternation of the reader goes to further dimensions: not only in seeing, nor in reading through time and space, but then further in hearing, and these levels play off one another. At one context, that of the process of reading in two dimensions, such vexations represent both the disruptive visible quality of the text and its puzzling dis-lexic gaps and absences in space and time (as occurs in Lenehan's riddle solved on the page in "Aeolus" but repeated several times). Yet going back to the "poet's picture puzzle," there are sounds too in the rebuses Bloom offers: "tee blank ar courageous mariner" and "see blank tee domestic animal." More than their semantic problem, these puzzles present another issue to the astute reader; they are present not only as letters *t* and *r* but depicted and written out as words themselves—"tee" and "ar"—to be read as words rather than as the constituent parts of words. That they are additionally read as sounds confuses the activities of reading and hearing. They also have gaps and absences in them in the aural dimension of sound.

One other verbal puzzle that appeared in "Aeolus" along with Lenehan's riddle is pertinent here, that of the "spellingbee conundrum" (although it is neither) of Cunningham that "he forgot to give" and that Bloom remembers in "Aeolus" (placed under the heading "ORTHOGRAPHICAL" and followed shortly after by the reversed name of Dignam): "It is amusing to view the unpar one ar alleled embarra two ars is it? double ess ment of a harassed pedlar while gauging au the symmetry with a y of a peeled pear under a cemetery wall" (7.164–69). While the number of *r*s in "embarrassment" is a question, the *l*s in "parallel," oddly, present Bloom no trouble, perhaps because he has thought of "parallax." (Does Bloom misremember this puzzle? Shouldn't "pear" be "medlar" for the symmetry and "gauge" echoic of "gage" as a plum? Shouldn't dis-lexia pertain here?) The aim of these two sorts of word puzzles is different: the first, "tee blank ar," is a crossword whose blanks are to be filled and whose answer is a word; the second is an aural puzzle whose homonymic quality is precisely at issue in its orthographical answer; and neither puzzle is particularly filled with meaning. Nothing is hidden in them to be revealed. Such puzzles are merely exercises with the possible letters of words, much like the letter from Milly and the cryptogram of Martha Clifford's name hidden in Bloom's drawer. This spelling out of letters meant to be seen distinguishes them, of course, in their identity *as* letters, those constitutive parts of words, thus fragmenting reading. Yet what is worth notice in both these different sorts of puzzles is what they have in common; they also all involve an aural dimension within the text that presents them, in which the letters are written out as they sound (as Bloom thinks/speaks both puzzles interiorly to himself). But because doing that on the page of the novel requires that they appear as signs, something as visual as words themselves, they are subject to limit and error.

Here, then, is the other purpose to these writings beyond making evident the lexical status of all letters: the sound of the letters is being represented; their identity in an aural/oral form is represented by their identity as a visible one, as Joyce consistently represents sounds graphically, thus asserting the predominance of the visual sign.[22] Because the sound of a letter is a rare phenomenon in spoken discourse (where there is little call to speak a letter, and within the monologue the thinking about letters is a form of internal vocalization), what is indicated by their presence in the text is a conundrum in itself: their status as objects outside spoken discourse of single letters must perforce be reproduced as sound and also in print. They stand as the farthest modality of the visible, as impalpable, elusive sound rendered into sight. There are two complementary effects here (as there are always two difficulties to be found at any juncture of Joyce's text): sights are given sound, but sounds are reproduced as sights. This doubling effect further disrupts the conventional reading dynamic, if reading prose is considered simply the scanning of small elements; here Joyce has added the additional impediment of engaging the ear by the text, "eyed from afar, a call from anear." This involvement of one dimension of sense in terms of another occurs precisely because of the disruption by the dynamic of dis-lexia. The resulting disfunction in the act of reading is caused by letters changed and manipulated to cause the reader to stop reading, to think, and, moreover, to try to hear. Thus all the disruptions to which the reading act is subject are here transferred to another dimension, making for mishearing and misunderstanding (because sights and sounds both are letters). Misreading of the visual is repeated by the mispronunciation and misapprehension of both the oral and aural; the errors of impeded hearing are a sort of dis-phonia and dis-audia.

Sound, within the confines of the page, is an immaterial presence, somewhat like a ghost. To give a name and a sound to a letter—which is a visible representation of various possible sounds depending on the configuration of the letters chosen to represent them—is to translate the immaterial of sound into one particularly recognizable and delimited form of a sign. Yet it is more than a translation; because of the fact that a character in a novel "says" the sound (either outright or in the sense of "thinking" it in the monologue), that sound must, through the ineluctable materiality of the page, be transcribed back into various other letters that comprise the sound that is made by the vocalized letter: *t* "spoken" on the page requires three letters, "tee." Into this seemingly infinite regression of sight into sound and sound into sign, with its omnipresent gap between word and sound, between the material of print and the immaterial of air, Joyce again asserts the primacy of the visible aspect of language's materiality. Even in the density and form of print on the page, Joyce offers an insubstantial and empty place where ghostly air is broken.

It is interesting to see what the editors of the *Oxford English Dictionary* have to say about the intriguing problem of reproducing sound into sign (the statement is reprinted from the introduction to the earlier *New English Dictionary*, which Joyce would have seen): "But the living word is *sound* cognizable by the ear, and must therefore be itself symbolized in order to reach the understanding through the eye." With this last phrase, the editors seem to have gone to the same school of Aquinas as Stephen did, where intellection is a function of the visual, and they seem to agree with Joyce on the domination of the sign. Thus in the spelling conundrum Bloom thinks of in "Aeolus," in order to reproduce the pronunciation of the letter *r* when thinking of the spelling of *embarrassment* ("two ars is it?"), Joyce by necessity must present the sound by means of visible letters. The approximation Joyce provides, "ar," resembles the rendering of *är* by simple signs and is close enough to the phonetic one, [r], by the conventions of the International Phonetic Association (the *Oxford English Dictionary* has this last, more exact rendering). Yet Joyce's is not an attempt at a transcription of sound. It has the additional benefits of appearing more like a word someone would say than does the phonetic equivalent and of being more easily rendered by a machine with conventional type. Not that Joyce was moved by practicality; if he did not tax Darantière with the backward setting of mangiD. kcirtaP., he did ask him to reproduce the long final *s* of eighteenth-century printing. Yet in all cases what interested him was the constellation of more letters that most resemble the usual single ones encountered in unencumbered reading, but used disruptively to unusual effect so that the sign disrupts the sight.

Joyce is at pains in the course of the novel to develop his own system of the phonetic representation of letters. This endeavor is by no measure consistent; the modality of it is part of the playful supplementarity dis-lexia makes possible, as malleable and prone to error. As with the letters Joyce writes and sees, the sound is no less susceptible to confusion than is the sign that represents it. This system first appears in a reproduction of the alphabet as recited, quite appropriately in that the alphabet originally was a symbolic graphic system intended to represent sound; Bloom imagines overhearing this recitation as he passes under the window of the schoolroom near his house early in the day: "Ahbeesee defeegee kelomen opeecue rustyouvee doubleyou" (4.137). This is a reasonably witty mimicking of a child's pronunciation by rote; yet it establishes early in the text the conventions Joyce will adapt when he has recourse to writing out how letters are spoken. These are his particular notations; and where he diverges from them are important places where the materiality of letters and their missed meaning are present, as therein is the tension between sound and sight to be found. For example, here the *u* and the *w* are internally consistent (if semantically confusing), their shared sound reproduced lexically as "you." Yet there are confusions: "rust" (for *r, s,* and *t*) looks like the word "rust," and it is unclear how "defeegee" is to be broken up ("de" or "ef," and what is "fee"?). Then again there is consistency: some consonants that contain the long *e* sound are reproduced alike: "bee" "gee" "vee." The "pee" rendering the *p* sound is found again later when the text describes the letter from Milly to Bloom, with its salutation "capital pee Papli" (17.1792). That letter encoded much; it showed its status as an opaque material object hidden yet revealed in alphabetic letters. It is obviously additionally a site where something else is encoded, the letter reproducing its sound: the name of a "letter" is a sound as well as a sight. ("Pee" and "bee" are also, of course, nouns, and appear elsewhere in *Ulysses* as objects.) Interestingly, in the recited alphabet there are to be noted the spaces of absence and silence, the blind spot that makes no noise: Bloom does not hear spoken the letters *h, i,* and *j. H* is elsewhere rendered as "aitch," again in Milly's letter ("capital aitch How are you" [17.1792]) and in Bloom's thinking of Micky Hanlon's attempt at writing out his own signature (8.894)—both examples of substantial if oral form, encrypted and written down. *J* doubled, of course, yields that ever-absent presence, the author; it was also missing, obscured, from the possibilities of the letters in the opening sentence. (For the *i,* see below.)

Yet there are further inconsistencies here in which the tension between sound and sight emerges in disruptions that are the playful supplementarity of Joyce's enterprise. Some of the letters given in this alphabet are not the reproduction of sound, only that of sight—for instance, the presence of the *m* as a sign, although it is followed immediately by the phonetic rendering of *n* as "en." Elsewhere the novel presents the *m* phonetically as "em," again from the same example of Milly's letter ("dated, small *em* monday" [17.1792]). Likewise *d, r, s,* and *t* are transcribed as to their sight, not sound. Yet the phonetic "ar" is used later by Bloom in the spelling conundrum; both it and "tee" are used in the picture puzzle "courageous mariner," "tee blank ar."

When the *t* is reproduced in the text as "tee" (or *p* as "pee" or, for that matter, the *e* itself as "ee" [6.374]), the double vowel serves in lieu of the long vowel sign in phonetics; Joyce is merely replicating, within the constraints of the letters available, the sound of the sign. Yet he has, within the visual matrix of his page, increased the extent of the word, magnifying its length to challenge the identity as letters, not sounds. It is coincidental but hardly immaterial that to reproduce the sound of the letter *e* Joyce must repeat the letter itself. Several letters given in the text to reproduce sounds, in either the alphabet or elsewhere, have additional letters in them, with (for Joyce of the magnifying glass) the desirable result of adding to the space and lexical presence of the sound on the page. They may be heard, but they are also easier to see. The opening *a* of the recited alphabet, for example, adds less a sound than a configuration, "Ah" (where the vowel sound would approximate "ay"). That "Ah" is also a spoken interjection or open-mouthed sound of no particular meaning only adds to the sense of the "stuffness" or density of language in print and its empty noises on the page.

There are more alphabetical examples that have the inconsistency of irritation. Joyce reproduces *l* as "el," following the dictionary's symbolic marking; yet elsewhere in the novel, the letter is reproduced as "ell," which, while it is an attempt to replicate the sound, has an additional letter added to it, one not necessary to limit the short sound of the initial open vowel.[23] The letter *s* in the alphabet is presented as visual, but elsewhere it is transcribed as pronounced, "ess" (in the conundrum and in Gerty's "Society with a big ess[13.666]"). It is no accident that these last two examples (as with *ee* for *e*) duplicate the very letter whose sound they are trying to produce, *l* and *s*; it is as if Joyce were additionally stressing the preponderance of the sign, piling on to the materiality of letters by adding to their length and appearance, as well as cannily scripting again the letter under transcription.

When the letter *y* is given as "why" (rather than as *wy* [6.374]), it represents the puzzle of all sounds put into words: it asks a question concerning the encrypting of sound by sight (encrypting a word that contains a *y* and suggests the ghostly). This changeable, dis-lexic *y* appears elsewhere in the text, described by form and by its place in the alphabet rather than by sound: "Ithaca's" "bifurcated penultimate alphabetical letter" (17.1194). This is another visible designation of *y* (other than the rote alphabet's *why*), yet it too stresses the ephemerality and changeability of sounds. Bloom urinates in this figure when he "pees"; and urination, Stephen discovered in the morning, makes its own noises: "a fourworded wavespeech: seesoo, hrss, rsseeiss, ooos" (3.456). Bloom makes this sign in all its transience because it is being writ in water with a changeable sign, heard in fleeting sound.

In that rote alphabet from "Calypso," the transcription of *c* and *i* is the final place where Joyce inserts the predominant weight of the visual aspect of letters onto their aural aspect to make the "aural eyeness" of dis-lexia, whereby what is heard is to be seen mistakenly. The recitation, while omitting *i*, reproduces *c* as "see" (as does the picture puzzle "See blank tee what domestic animal?"); the necessary presence of sight in this rote exercise is indeed ineluctable and essential. *I* appears elsewhere in the text as "eye" (again in Milly's letter). Surely these last tip the sight to the issue at stake, that the fact that all sound may be an echo to the sense, but that all sense and sound are the visible and disjunctive signs on the page, subject to confusion, to inconsistency, and to puzzle.

Thus sound is subject to error not merely because of its limitations as fleeting but particularly because it is conveyed through a text whose letters and their meaning are always unclear and unstable. Sound is immaterial because it is absent within a novel that exists as material printed on the page, and sound is even further immaterial because it is fleeting in the actual existence the novel seeks to depict. So where immaterial sound is heard to be made material on the page, the tension between these two dimensions of sound and sign produces a gap or blank in both form and meaning, as do the puzzles and conundrums. Thus error and mistake in "hearing signs" becomes nearly as prevalent as disrupted reading. As there is dis-lexia, there must be a corresponding mistake in hearing, a dis-audia: misreading causing mishearing. When Stephen asks his students the meaning of a name they have encountered in reading their history lesson, the answer he gets becomes a riddle and a joke because of just this confusion of sounds and signs. Students are poor readers; Stephen is irritated less by pedagogy than by the text he is holding in his hand: "—Do you know anything about Pyrrhus?—Pyrrhus, sir? Pyrrhus, a pier.—Tell me now, poking the boy's shoulder with the book, what is a pier?" (2.21–30). He asks the boy to "tell" as he asks his mother's ghost, and in both cases the answer is empty confusion.

What is clear from this exchange, aside from the fact that Stephen is not a good teacher, is that his student Armstrong has not read the assignment nor even cursorily glanced at the book for the faintest recognition; there could be no confusion of the name and the object if the text were seen. Thus the exchange between teacher and pupil has absence and error at its inception. Their conversation has no further substance, being only misheard, its confusion here coming from the sounds words make. It is possible, to compound this already chaotic classroom, that the boy hears the question "Do you know anything about Pyrrhus?" as "Do you know what a pier is?" and that his answer was thus a self-evident definition: "Pier is a pier." He could also be temporizing. Thus his reply was not "Pyrrhus, a pier," but rather, given the fact that if Armstrong were even distantly attentive to what was discussed in class, he would know that the interrogation was about famous events and men in history, and his temporizing answer was first "Pyrrhus, a peer." (And then, in honored schoolboy tradition, he goes on to waste time by extending his pun, answering Stephen's next question, which might appear in the text as "What is a peer?," with another homonym: "A pier, sir, . . . a thing out in the waves.") The text that confronts the vexed reader trying to hear may have a gap here—"Pyrrhus [peer is] pier." The page, as well as the student, would be playing tricks with both Stephen and the reader: Armstrong teasing out the various words that lie behind the way sounds are similarly pronounced; the text playing disruptively with the same sounds that lie behind the way words can be dislexically presented. Armstrong does not look at his book; Stephen points with his; but readers must try to read theirs. What is to be seen is an absence of pedagogy, a ghost of history, a gap in meaning, and a vacancy of sound.

No sound is more vacant than that of Bloom's digestion, yet it too is magnified and enlarged: "Pprrpffrrppffff" (11.1292). This is a material presentation of immaterial sound as broken air, an internal wheeze, made up of the repetition of letters to stress that pneumatic if empty materiality of noise. Moreover, as he passes air, Bloom's ever active gaze is caught by an object, "a gallant pictured" Robert Emmet, and he thinks of Emmet's last words interspersed with his own rumbles from within and from those of the passing tram. Last words are the way in which those of history, lost to death and absence, continue to speak, while immaterial as ghosts, their passing spoken words written down as epigram, as is true of Pyrrhus. So the broken air of sound, broken wind, and the last words of lost heroes ought to be combined: "*Let my epitaph be.* Kraaaaaa. *Written. I have.* Pprrpffrrppffff. *Done*" (11.1291). The italics are foregrounding and also a visual marker that Bloom is reading the last words; they are, presumably, written out beneath the picture (he is said to have "viewed the words"). As such, they provide an epigram to the picture and are a fitting connection by similar disruptive letters with Emmet's intended epitaph: both epitaph (mentioned in the text) and epigram (projected as afterimage) hover above the text like spectral presences, seen and not seen, coupling the text: writing and the tomb, *gram* and *taph* (and see below for their connection). Yet the similarity of the words is disruptive and asserts the absence of Emmet, as the epigram is substituted for the epitaph. Moreover, the impalpable of Bloom's passed gas is no more ephemeral than the quality of Emmet's patriotism. The empty—even stale—air of Emmet's rhetoric in those final words to the court is represented by the paradox that Emmet speaks his own epitaph, turning sign into sound by saying what is supposed to be written down; he is a speaker about to memorialize his own last words about lost causes. His heroism was in vain, his legacy only a memory with a captioned picture. What he wished to come about as a future is not even true in the present of Bloom's day; Ireland not yet a nation. Joyce knew that well in 1920, the date of "Sirens"; lost causes are things passed by, not glimpsed: history was for Joyce, like his eyesight, a record of missed opportunities.

Emmet is gone, absent, no longer to be heard, but identified by the letters of his epitaph. All characters' identities, as noted, are formed by letters and subject to disruption and loss in their instability, being seen and misseen. Yet letters also seek to present and represent the sound of the particular entity, the recognizable feature of an individual speaker, by reproducing the sound of the voice. But an identity is that much more fragile and unstable when presented by the impalpable voice reproduced in these fallible letters.[24]

Bloom, staying away from home all day, thinks of Molly's singing the duet from *Don Giovanni,* the lyrics of which have posed for him an aural problem of the pronunciation of the *g* in "voglio"; he responds to the effect of her voice: "Beautiful on that *tre* her voice is: weeping tone. A thrush. A throstle. There is a word throstle that expresses that" (6.239). All singers are identified and remembered by their ranges and timbres, as evidenced by the dinner-table conversation in "The Dead." In seeking to describe Molly's sound, indeed after already granting the sound a pathetic quality ("weeping tone"), Bloom strikes out into the lexical. And the word that Bloom hits upon, which occurs to him because of the similarity of its meaning to "thrush," is a the name of another bird, the throstle, itself alliteratively similar to "thrush"—similar letters producing similar sounds and ideas. The *New English Dictionary* notes, by way of underscoring Bloom's self-conscious diction, that "throstle" is now "as a word only literary." What Bloom comes up with in his attempt to find a way to describe Molly's identifiable and "enchanting" sound is something very literary and literate (as in letters), a sort of bird/word that in its flight (as in "Sirens") represents the winged words of literary art. But such winged words for identifiable sounds are not "viewless" wings of poetry nor only the soaring sound of voice but rather only very visible; in fiction, all sounds must be seen. Much as the "word" Stephen asks the ghost of his mother to speak, a ghost giving voice to what is an error in the text, the "word" Bloom speaks to describe the absent, ephemeral voice of Molly is empty and lost in error. The word "thrush" is a Gabler restoration. Previous editions had the word "thrust,"[25] typesetters enjambing the "t" in "throstle" into "thrust" by dittography. Such errors in reading create wraithlike words, of no substance, as spectral sights on the page. And these mistakes of the machine are often fortuitous as well as inevitable (if unintended by the author): the equivalent of the incorrect "thrust" of the projected voice (as Bloom thinks of Molly's singing) is the expression, the forcing out of diction, of word choice; as Bloom notes, there is "a word to express that," expression as a kind of thrust. The typesetters captured the meaning, a sense in the sound; yet in so doing, they chose the wrong letter to create a wrong word as a ghostly presence about sound.

Bloom is describing Molly's voice in the account above, thinking about Molly when he is away from her; voice expresses identity, both in its own resonance and in the fact that it is here constituted of the same sorts of letters in disruption that give all characters their only identity, however unstable. There are ghosts (like Stephen's mother) or those lost (like Emmet) and those absent (like Molly), speaking unclear, impalpable sounds in words often subject to error in hearing and reading or by reading alone. What complicates this chain of capture, fading, and memory is the attempt to remember what is the most fleeting, the greatest absence, the dark void of death. Bloom's account of the play of *Rachel,* entangled as it is with his memories of the dead father who left his last voice on the page in the letter, similarly focuses on the recognition of a voice: "Nathan's voice! His son's voice! . . . who left the house of his father and left the God of his father" (5.203). Bloom's father remarks about this filial apostasy and prodigality, "every word is so deep, Leopold." The words are not themselves profound, but, as they are aural, they have an "eyeness" in height and a depth, too, which comes from the fact that they are about absence and loss, about voices as fleeting as the weaver's shuttle, and as deep as the grave that holds not only the Nathan who dies in his father's arms but the senior Bloom who dies in his hotel bed. Death makes the most obvious emptiness, the most complete blind spot. It is the loss of losses, the one that creates the presence of ghosts and the need for memory to fill in the blanks.[26]

Most spelling conundrums and puns are themselves a sort of emptiness, drained of meaning. They have no context or sense, express no voice or person; their sense comes only from the placement of similar homophonic words in proximity. As Bloom notes of Cunningham's puzzle, "cemetery put in of course on account of the symmetry." Yet the fact that the spelling bee, because it concerns the transient sounds of words, "takes place" in a cemetery seems pertinent to the issue at stake, not only the conundrum's questioning of the reproduction of sounds but also the novel's recreation on its pages of all sounds, fading and unclear. Not only do sounds fade more quickly than material objects, but they seem themselves to enact the sense of absence and emptiness essential to the reading of *Ulysses*. Thus it is pertinent that Stephen's mother's ghost "tells" or Emmet speaks his last words as texts in print, as these are signal scenes to evoke the unclearly glimpsed, the lost, as printed constructs always subject to blindness and obscurity. The voice from the grave (especially when it appears in print) is the culmination of the void and the emptiness of all sight, which is why Joyce's text must be so close to ghosts and shadows. The text's being subject to error only empties it further. The blindness of vision, the impending darkness of loss of sight, and the persistence of fallibility are all emblems of death. And it is while Bloom himself is at the cemetery for the funeral of Dignam, looking at the various graves, that he thinks of just this issue: how to capture, to remember, what has passed.

Besides how could you remember everybody? Eyes, walk, voice. Well, the voice, yes: gramophone. Have a gramophone in every grave or keep it in the house.... Remind you of the voice like the photograph reminds you of the face....

He looked down intently into a stone crypt. (6.962–71)

He is trying to remember the physical aspects of the absent entities by peering into the emptiness of the grave to see features that can be observed, ones that can be depicted.

The walk is certainly the manifestation of the material body. So too are the eyes: they are the palpable connection between generations for both Stephen and Bloom. Stephen thinks of Simon as "the man with my voice and my eyes" (3.46), and Bloom thinks of Rudy, "Me in his eyes" (6.76). But the eyes are first mentioned because they are the necessary and primary precondition for limit and loss in Joyce's life and in the text; they peer and see only darkness and the grave. Of course in this very act of Bloom's trying to remember the past, lost by biology to the grave, the eye is an important adjunct, and it is for Bloom or for Joyce not only the poetic act of Hamlet's seeing his dead father in the mind's eye; it is the physical act of the eye's seeing unclearly and with error what is to be inscribed. A text is a physical object. Like it, the photograph is a visual object, one of the body that eventually will fade; and so, too, is the gramophone, which, aside from the materiality of its machinery, is an aural object of the sound that immediately fades. Yet Bloom recognizes the connection of all three: voice and picture appear to him in the "spoken" epitaph under the portrait of Emmet, which Bloom reads. Such texts are the sights of memory. And in the sighting of both Emmet's epitaph and the epigram is the connection of the tomb and the writing, the grave and the graven sign. Both the photograph and the gramophone are material objects, cardboard sheet and wax cylinder; yet beyond their ability at capturing the past, they are materially similar *as* words: each inscribes (*graphein*) the transience of light and sound—"photo" and "phono"—and thus they are etymologically parallel and arrestingly similar in their letters. Dis-lexia forces their similarity, and they both write graphically on that special paper or wax disk what is most fleeting and not present. As a neologism, "gramophone" had a synonym—"phonograph"—which would make the obvious etymological parallel of the two words even more visual; Joyce may just be twigging here in a disjunctive, chiastic move by using "gramophone." The word, however, connects with the empty word puzzle of Martha's name and address, the crypto*gram*, with gramma, the writing, as the essential and necessary connection. By way of reinforcing this connection to the reader's eye, Joyce has Bloom think disjunctively of the gramophone while looking into the *crypt*. If all *gramma* is *crypton,* as was noted of the letters unlocked in the drawer, it is so because writing encodes by means of the hidden and puzzling signs of letters. Similarly subject to the same lexical impulse, all *phone* is also encoded into the cryptic of the grammar of dis-lexia: crypt, cryptogram, gramophone, epigram, epitaph.[27] The writing is always essential to essence. *Graphe* is meant to be seen and is essential to all of Joyce's work.

In Bloom's pragmatic rumination, trying to accommodate to all mortal loss by the use of a machine, is a recognition of the visual and textual as the materiality of what is engraved; what is not present is always embodied, for Joyce with his vision, in print that can be disrupted to cause shadowy uncertainty. To the absence of death, Joyce places the presence of what is written down but unclearly seen, encrypted by gramma in the voice and lexical sign by the machinery of the printing press. As his text is a studious but disruptive re-creation of the past, a dubious depiction of Dublin nearly two decades earlier, it inevitably also engages in a dynamic of retrospection and nostalgia, but with these impulses grounded in letters fading and unclear. Here is where the traditional ghost in both of its forms—as the impalpable body and the disembodied voice come back from the past—meets with that other "ghost" seen always floating on the margin of the eye or the margin of the page: the spectral sight of what is written down, the unstable materiality of the words on the page that are not seen, or not yet seen, or once seen and now to be remembered through the text.[28] Such a text might be perhaps the paper of the photograph, perhaps the wax disk of the gramophone, both the epitaph and the picture of Robert Emmet, but the text is always the paper of the page on which the novel is printed. So when Bloom looks into a stone crypt he is not only looking for the obese rat; he is peering into the absent past that all memory seeks to make present by means of things enscribed and that a narrative particularly makes disruptively present, heard, and live again by means of letters seen and misseen on the page.

This funeral Bloom attends, with loss and its representation by the grave and the epitaph, is rendered in another material way by the text of *Ulysses* through the unstable, opaque voices in "Oxen" in the spoken question "Seen him today at a runefal?" (14.1554), where an act of observation much like Bloom's looking is highlighted ("seen"). "Runefal" suggests "ruin" and "fall" by portmanteau homophonics, but it is worked over anagrammatically to replace the loss and absence of the burial by the material of the graphemic, "rune" as glyphic visual form. The order of letters opens up this space without any recourse to sound. The word thus disarranged, the actual letters in it switched, evokes the mythic secret figures that seem to be as much a part of the cryptogram as of the crypt. And finally, runic writing is itself lost, fallen away in time, and a "rune" is subject, as are all graphemic figures, to the fall of error, *fal*libility. The importance of the word "funeral" to the economy of Joyce's making material what is absent or lost is indicated by its presence in *Finnegans Wake* by the self-alluding sort of translexia described earlier. There with slightly altered and additional letters and in italics is the famous "*funferal*" (120.10), where comedy has been added to everyone's pain, especially the pain of iritis. Yet even here the difference between *Ulysses* and the *Wake*, between aural and eyeness, re-emerges despite their similar disruptive lexical surfaces. The *Ulysses* "runefal" sounds neither like "funferal" nor "funeral," nor need it; it works by transposing letters seen. "*Funferal*" is similarly visual (with an extra *f*) yet works additionally as homophone: read aloud it is meant to sound like "funeral" and like everyone's comedy.

Both the death of Bloom's father, explained in a suicide note, and the death of Stephen's mother, conveyed in the telegram, are messages from the lost, texts from the dead that stand in for the void. Both bring loss, absence, and the past into the presence of the page through the agency of the material letters of those written forms and the disruption and error to which that material is prone. Both characters are never present to the text; they are absent before it begins. Both are emblematic as generators of the "life" of the text. The two deaths appear in the text as notices written, as ghosts substantiated in print (again asserting the primacy of the sign): in a tele*gram*, reproduced by a machine, and an epistolary letter, copied out in the hand of the dead man. The two objects of written language, telegram and letter, take the place of what is missing and are substantiated by being depicted within the text, but they are (and must be) subject to and part of the opaqueness of the irritated text: they are unclear in sight and in substance. The always very compromised reading of unstable texts suggests its own ephemerality, constantly sliding into immateriality and misunderstanding because of the intentional disruption. While letters make their own materiality out of what is immaterial, ghosts and the lost past, they are themselves always slipping in jumbled forms into the immateriality of unclarity, the emptiness of error, and missed meaning. Thus absence and emptiness are inherent in the reading experience and the transcription of a disruptive scripting.

Stephen calls his blue telegram "a curiosity," largely because it is foreign and informs him and the reader of the grievous loss. Yet the telegram itself has been a site of loss, a spectral and obscure text. Gabler does well to recover what Joyce intended to have visible in print, in that crucial correction of material meant to be error: the telegram Stephen remembers receiving while in Paris is restituted by Gabler in the text to read in print not "Mother" (as was seen for years) but "Nother dying come home father" (3.199). The intentional error is an example of the sort of mistake Joyce wished to have stand in the text: it is an essential figure of dis-lexia.[29] This startling change in the synoptic edition only reinforces an understanding of Joyce's sense of the modality of language, the potential confusion of similar letters, *m* and *n*. He wished his text to inscribe his own errors of intent, not those unintended. The telegram's "nother" makes the death a "curiosity to show" in that it portrays her death as if one in an endless series (as Claudius's remarking to Hamlet in Shakespeare's play, "your father lost a father").[30] The word mistake compounds the loss of the mother with that of meaning because the disrupted letter is disruptively similar to sight, and consequently itself produces immateriality, absence, erasure, and loss.

This example is particularly rich, as Joyce seems to suggest that the error within the telegram came from a mistranscription by a French telegraphist's getting the message to Stephen in Paris. The presence of such error in transcription indicates clearly that Joyce was aware of the similar errors to which his own text is prone without his intent, that he knew the possibilities of dis-lexia would extend from his text. The modalities of all letters are similar, even if they make no sense in other languages; all disruption, Joyce knew, occurs at the expense of meaning and results in a possible loss and an obscuring of all written work, even his own. (And see below about just such foreign-language mistranscriptions as this.)

Bloom hides his note from his father in the drawer below the one with the hidden letters in cryptogram; it too is secret and locked away in an even deeper layer. Bloom has merely to look at the envelope, the cover of the letter, in order to "see" the contents of it in memory; he never actually reads it. The text tells us that "the lecture," the act of reading, the address is enough to evoke "fractions of phrases" (17.1881). His reading itself is disjunctive, being fragmented and incomplete; and, as a consequence of this half-reading, Bloom is distanced from the emotions (see chapter 4). These "fractions" of the text obligingly present the opacity of words by their syncopic separation into incomplete parts, as if broken up by an unsure eye, and the message thus cannot be clear. What is materially presented in the text as Bloom's father's last words is a gap, cut off and abbreviated as if the letter itself were a symbol of the loss by death. Its brevity as well indicates a reticence that marks its closeness to Bloom's emotions. Its foregrounding as text, stressing its material nature while presenting the immaterial and absent, is indicated by the italicized address standing out from the envelope, "*To My Dear Son*"; by the German syntax of the message, "that is not more to stand"; and by its foreign words, again italicized in otherness, such as "*das Herz*" (17.1885). All these features are characteristic of Joyce's enterprise. Most pertinent is the final word, "*dein*," in which the loss is clearly indicated in the abscission of the missing word, "*Vater*"—the missing father, the generator and the maker of the law, that other lexical entity.

What is lost to the past and to death is partially recovered and substituted for by the materiality of print and also partially obscured by that lexicality: both the absent Stephen's "nother" and Bloom's *Vater* are presented and misrepresented. Yet just as signs only imperfectly recover the fleeting sounds, so they only incompletely recover the loss of the past. A voice from beyond the grave is text, all past is text, but text is unclear and spectral. The letters of the lost are represented by lost letters. Sound and sign are subject to the immateriality of the disrupted reading of letters; both telegram and suicide note are disrupted, broken, incorrect. Their messages are disjunctive; the identity of the subjects is questionable. Lexicality can make materiality, but dis-lexicality makes immateriality. Moreover, the text is how Joyce was himself to be remembered; it is his own epitaph standing in for him. The author who seeks to "speak" from beyond the grave through his text and be remembered by it will also suffer disruption, loss of meaning, and opacity.

If this emptiness is true of any text inscribed within and by *Ulysses,* it is also true of the text of the novel itself. Emptiness is always present in the material of letters presented as magnified; error is rife; and meaning is suspect, as the effects extend outward. Any word choice by the author might be misprinted in unintentional error. Thus for years readers read "thrust" for "thrush," a mistake creating an unwarranted ex-pression, a pressing out, of the author's voice and the loss of an object, a winged and fleeting bird. Much as Bloom says while looking into the crypt, so might the reader peering into the cryptic text say, "Besides how could [Joyce] remember" a text at once so dense and complex, materially enlarged and immaterially ephemeral?

The answer is that he often could not. To all his intentional errors, there were unintentional ones caused by the printer. Joyce's note to Weaver expressed his irritation at those "mechanical" errors, but the printers too became victims of Joyce's studied and infectious dis-lexia. The text is empty and flawed by its own logic, as Joyce is hoist by the petard of his own disruptive symptoms of letters; his own irritation infects as it affects the printing. The text is flawed by the unintentional confusion of those very sights and sounds, affecting not the mechanical work of the photograph or the gramophone but the press of the printer. While the effect of the text on the printer is similar to the effect it had on Gogarty, this disruption is additionally caused by the very missed meaning of sound and sign observed here within the text. The printing of *Ulysses* by Darantière's men is fraught in its own vexation with possibilities of errors of meaning in sound and sense and errors of sign and sight because there is a disjunction in its transmission. This disjunction is due first, of course, to the dense and unclear status of the text and galley proofs, scribbled over with Joyce's spidery hand; but it is due also to the additional complication that meaning must be conveyed to the printers in two registers of two languages, that of the writer and his text and that of the printers. It is a disruption that operates much as the foreign words within the text do, as other, alien. The same letters of the Latin alphabet make different sounds and different sense in another language. Here the repressed phonemic, coupled with the additional confusion imposed on the author and the printers having to work in two different languages, comes back to haunt the graphemic power and intent of the author.

In a scene that is pertinent to the confusions of the print of *Ulysses*, Bloom and Stephen speak and write other languages at cross-purposes with each other in "Ithaca," disjunctively misaligning the graphic and the phonic:

> What fragments of verse . . . were cited with modulations of voice and translation of texts by guest to host and by host to guest?
> By Stephen: *suil, suil, suil arun* . . . (walk, walk, walk your way . . .).
> By Bloom: *kifeloch, harimon rakatejch* . . . (thy temple amid thy hair . . .).
> How was a glyphic comparison of the phonic symbols of both languages made in substantiation of the oral comparison?
> . . . Stephen wrote the Irish characters for gee, eh, dee, em, simple and modified, and Bloom . . . wrote the Hebrew characters ghimel, aleph, daleth and (in the absence of mem) a substituted qoph. (17.724–39)

The confusion, inaccuracies or lack of meaning, and lacunae of this interrogation are paradigms of all the letters in the text; the foreignness of the sentences resembles the extraneous quality of language. Further, letters are capriciously substituted for others (*qoph* for *mem*); the lines quoted are incomplete, fragmented, and devoid of context because neither Bloom nor Stephen is a competent speaker or reader. The different sounds that these letters make (the modalities of sounds, so to speak) add to the density of that dis-lexia by presenting the glyphic aspect of the sounds. No meaning can arise here; the exchange is empty—a dialogue without a conversation, a recitation without an audience, what the French call "une dialogue des sourdes." The symptoms of this possible confusion that results from reading and hearing in different linguistic registers, the confusion as a return of the repressed phonemic amid the graphemic, are to be found most evidently in Darantière's shop.

In "Circe," as Bloom holds forth in a rhetorically calculated speech as Leopold the First, he is cheered, the text says, by "THE CHAPEL OF FREEMAN TYPESETTERS: 'Hear! Hear!'" (15.1531). Those typesetters are ones he sees in operation that morning, especially Monks, the dayfather, setting backward the lead type for the funeral announcement of Dignam's death. Bloom has seen the finality of print and its importance as chronicle as well as its potential for error. Print captures death in the notice or the obituary, yet both are fallible by their letters, fading and obscuring not only the dead but the living "Boom." None of Bloom's actual speeches in the course of the book receive any such commendation from his peers in

Dublin as does this imagined speech, but all of his words, spoken or unvoiced, thought or said, have the final approval, the literal imprimatur, of the typesetters at Darantière's shop in Dijon. It is they who make Bloom material, "remembering" him by publishing, make him a public figure as he here envisions himself to be, by enshrining him in letters. And that the typesetters in "Circe" say "Hear! Hear!" is a reminder of the tension in *Ulysses* between what is heard throughout the book and what is always read; but it refers foremost to the difficulties those French-speaking typesetters had with the perplexing English manuscript that Joyce provided them. (Indeed, poorly marked and unevenly typed, Joyce's notes must have seemed as backward to them as the lead of Dignam's name does to the reader.) They became dis-lexic, with the contagion of the irritated letter, and they were the first of those infected by the irritated creativity of Joyce, so that they were the ones who passed the illness on to the other readers by printing the intended errors and adding their own. It was they who often confused letters in Joyce's corrections, notations that involved his using a register of another language to attempt to convey meaning. Both he and they often fell victim to dis-lexia and dis-phonia by confusing sights of different languages; his corrections only added to their misapprehension and resulted in the ever threatening possibility of an unintentionally mistaken text.

Take two examples of compounded errors, ones that appear at a pertinent point in the production of the novel. Both of these appear in the page proofs, the last stages of Joyce's scrutiny, which continue to show his concern for the texture of his text in its lexical surface; his corrections are proof of his reading carefully despite his visual handicap. Both examples occurred during the same period, October 1921, while Joyce was writing "Penelope" and recovering from an attack of iritis he had suffered in September. Thus these errors fall at the juncture of writing, correcting, and reading, all hampered by illness, a juncture that indicates the unique place of *Ulysses* in the history of Joyce's works and the pathology of his eyesight.

The sentences in question are: "Catch them once with their pants down" (regarding Bloom's thought of visiting Milly unannounced; 6.484); and "Did I write Ballsbridge on the envelope I took to cover when she disturbed me writing to Martha?" (6.742). Both were additions to the last pages, increases that Darantière's men patiently added to the text in time for the next set of proofs. Yet they mistranscribed the additions because of

Joyce's handwriting, that manual sign of authority, and were finally corrected only through Joyce's careful and continued ministrations. Thus both potential mistakes proceeded from the vagaries of inscripting that led to encrypting; they enacted the very dynamic of dis-lexicality discussed here. Joyce's unclear hand, read by a foreign eye accustomed to a different language, created errors in the material of the text that finally were overborne by modalities of the visible, a combination of lexical and phonic restitution. That both these errors appeared in the "Hades" episode recalls the paradox of the absence and loss of the cryptic of meaning that Bloom wishes to recall by the mechanics of the gramophone but that Joyce knew had to be substantiated by the mechanics of language, the press, and the typesetters—however fallible each and all could be.

The first nexus of these literally scriptural confusions is the sentence "Catch them once with their pants down," which Joyce inserted on the page proofs on September 21.³¹ In his handwriting, the capital *C,* written with curled embellishments to top and bottom 𝒞 , seemed to the printers to be a lowercase *b,* which also has a loop at the top; hence they added the first words of the sentence, nonsensical in English, as "batch them once." Their unfamiliarity with English allowed them the sight of the sign as another letter that made a word of no sense. In the next set of proofs, ten days later, Joyce corrected this sentence by indicating a carat over the incorrect *b;* a crossed-through, corrected capital *C* above; and then in the upper-right margin an insertion mark and a capital *C*.³² Yet this letter was nearly identical in appearance to the one in the earlier addition, still resembling a lowercase *b* (Joyce's handwriting having its own poor consistency because of his eyesight); and the printers saw no sense in correcting a word that appeared to them as correct on the page, even if it had no sense as an English verb.

At the next proof, that of October 3, Joyce corrected the "batch" a third time to begin with a capital *C,* which still resembled (to this reader as well as the printers) the other two misseen as a lowercase *b;* but now, because of the press of time and the persistence of error, he resorted to elaboration of his markings: he defined his sign by its position in the alphabet but did so in the language of the printers, thus combining two registers of language with the recognition that there must be a phonic disability to explain the continued dis-lection: "*C* (le troisième lettre de l'alphabet)."³³ This time the printers got it right.

The other sentence concerns these issues of handwriting and the foreign language of the printers and adds to them one of absence. The second example was a marginal addition to the text in the proof of October 1, into which Joyce further inserted the phrase in question (graphically represented): "Did I write on the envelope ^I took to cover^ when she disturbed me writing to Martha?"[34] The second insertion appears in the lower-left margin, and the carat for the insertion melds with the capital *I* to obscure it, so the addition appeared on the next set of proofs (October 3) omitting the pronoun: "the envelope took to cover when she. . . ."[35] To this proof Joyce added the missing letter, although the correction in his hand looks more like a mark of insertion than a letter; but, perhaps made wiser by his experience of the misunderstood *C* of "catch," he had recourse to the same dual linguistic lexicality to avoid the dis-phonic confusion; he emended parenthetically and pedantically after the *I* further definition: "(la parole anglaise pour 'je')." The quotation marks around the French first-person pronoun add the dimension of hearing to this handwritten message; Joyce wanted to reach both the eye and ear of the printers. (In a French way of thinking, he wanted a text that was not only *lisible* and *scriptible* but also *audible*.) Hirschwald, Darantière's assistant, found Joyce's novel method of correction obscure in all senses and wrote in large grease pencil in the right margin an encircled "I took."

Joyce wished to take no chances with what should be correct and would allow no misunderstanding of eye or ear. Having written the dis-lexic text par excellence, he was fully aware of the modalities of the visible and the confusion that he could play in them—such was his purpose. He wanted his text right so that it could also be wrong, but he did not want those two states confused except as he intended. As he noted to Weaver, he was irritated with these errors in the printer's work, which he was too ill to correct; yet when he wished, he would irritate his own work into intended error.

Yet his text thus is always empty. Loss and emptiness are always present in it as a condition of its possibilities of the life depicted or the letters doing the depicting; all is obscured by the emptiness of the blurred, glaucomatous eye. Meaning is not fully possible, not only as a philosophical postmodernist condition but also as a physical one. The text is intentionally flawed and disrupted by confused letters—some intrusively present, some absent— and by phonemes. And the text is unintentionally flawed by the sorts of errors to which the printing process is prone, the very sorts of errors Joyce practiced in the text and sought to avoid in its correction. The intentionally error-prone text makes much emptiness of reading and hearing. Reading it is much like looking for the lost down in the crypt; lost letters and sounds are peered at down to the lowest level of the encrypted, the lexical. Thus there will never be a perfect text of *Ulysses,* not only because of complexity and confusion caused by the printers' unintentionally mistaking sound and sign and language and letter (although, heaven knows, these are causes enough) but because Joyce wanted the text always to be complex and confused at its very basis, its letters disfunctional and disruptive because they are always dis-lexic. The ghosts caused by his iritic glaucoma were to haunt the sight of his text, irritating it and causing loss and ephemeral obscurity, unclear sights and sounds, challenging reading and even compromising the text that would be his epitaph from beyond the grave by the very unstable book he sought to have correct and saw into print.

APPENDIX

What Joyce Saw in *Ulysses*

The actual publication that Joyce sought so eagerly with his comment "My book will never come out," and that Beach accomplished with difficulty, is now, of course, quite suspect. The edition of *Ulysses* Joyce wanted to have printed is the subject of too much critical debate to consider here. The current controversy revolves precisely around what did "come out" in 1922, what should have, and what ought to come out now as a definitive edition. The irony is that the original publication, the coming out, of *Ulysses* through the philosophical and legal agency of Shakespeare and Co. both superseded and submerged the hidden, lost, buried, and sold transcripts. Its first existence as a book made its meaning appear from the obscurity of private writing; yet the text that did come out has a questionable appearance, its "signs on a white field" subject to error verifiable only by those superseded drafts, typescripts, and proofs that themselves have "come out" only in recent years with the appearance of the "Archive." Joyce, concerned as he was in 1921 with the chance of seeing his work in print, would be amused now to see how much more of that work has come out.

It is not the purpose here to engage in the lists of the fight over the synoptic text of *Ulysses;* the debate continues, and it has already been the subject of much print.[1] Yet two issues regarding the edition are pertinent to the importance of the impeded visual quality in Joyce's work that has been the focus of this study. The first is the very appearance of that print—that is, what Joyce saw when his book came out—and how that visual form has been changed by the 1986 corrected text. The second is a modest suggestion as to whether, given Joyce's dis-lexic disruption, there can be a definitive edition at all.

What the new edition presents to the reader's eye is different from what Joyce saw in the first and subsequent editions. It must certainly be the case that Joyce, poring over the final page proofs of the first edition, indicating widow lines and bad fonts even at the last moment, saw the whole of his creation; and he must have been pleased—on the sixth day, as it were—with what he saw: *et vidit Deus quod esset bonum* . . . and it was good because what he saw was pleasing in its final form. (The above quotation is from the *Vulgate;* Joyce glosses the same phrase in "Proteus" as "*Et vidit Deus. Et erant valde bona*" [3.440]. As well as a change in number and meaning, one can account for this difference by the deceptive substitutability of letters.)

Putting aside crucial questions about what should be in the text, it can be said that what the synoptic edition does is radically change the visual aspect of *Ulysses* on the page, as a page and as a book: this is what Joyce saw in and on it. While the author's reading of a first edition is not privileged by the synoptic text, the important component of the author's view of his work as an object is undervalued. What Joyce saw come out in the first edition was replicated in part by the first and subsequent Random House editions in no small part because they were set from that first edition of Shakespeare and Co.; yet the form of what Joyce saw is drastically changed in its visual aspect by the recent synoptic edition. Most noticeable of all the features is the odd decision to put all the passages of dialogue flush left. This detail is the sort about which Joyce took particular pains from his earliest printed works (from the time when he was only myopic); it is a form that breaks the integrity of both line and page, seriously compromising the appearance of each. When it is remembered that, in the stages of contracting to have *Dubliners* finally published, Joyce requested of Grant Richards that the dialogue not be set with inverted commas, one sees that there is a reason for his fastidiousness with this issue. Joyce noted that he found such marks "an eyesore,"[2] a term that points to the crucial issues discussed throughout this study about the troubled and important act of seeing.

Moreover, there are other visual features whose effect is indeed part of the meaning of *Ulysses.* While the Random House editions (both 1934 and 1961) have their flaws (not only textual but also typographical, most evidently the unwarranted capitalized initial letters of the three sections S, M, and P), the one thing they do is preserve the proportions and balances of the harmonious text created by Darantière and supervised closely by Joyce himself (as noted, this condition is largely a result of the American press's having set its edition from the original). Most striking is the relative Pythagorean proportion of the text itself. In the original the page size is $9\frac{1}{2}$ by $7\frac{3}{4}$ inches (the width with a ragged edge); the Random House is 8 by $5\frac{1}{2}$ inches. Similarly, the margins of the text—side, top, and bottom—are proportional.[3] The Gabler edition page size is 6 by $9\frac{3}{8}$ inches; the text size is larger, as the margins are smaller and less balanced.[4] Thus while Gabler is a rectangular text, the original and the Random House editions are much closer to a square. As the journey of Bloom is a circle and his last appearance in the text is as a point, so the form of the novel does what Bloom sought to do one summer: to square the circle.

The typefaces of the original and the Random House editions have the same size, although they are different fonts.[5] The Gabler typeface is much more constricted, the margins are smaller, and hence the text is longer than the original. It is as if the editorial board and the publishers had no visual memory of the original they consulted in order to produce theirs. The visual impression is odd in that John Rider set the Gabler edition; he also designed the fine 1960 Bodley Head.

Such differences are not merely aesthetic; they are meaningful precisely as they engage the visual aspect of reading so crucial to Joyce. The headlines in the Random House's "Aeolus" stand in relation to their text in the same way that the originals do in typeface and size. The ones in Gabler are not in boldface and are smaller, surely no small matter given their importance in the genesis of the novel.[6] In "Ithaca" the original has no line break between question and answer, and the initial line of each question and answer is indented; so too in the Random House. In Gabler there is a line break between question and answer and no indentation, all lines being flush left with the text. In Darantière's "Wandering Rocks," each section is separated by a triangular configuration of stars, the apex higher than the two equally at the base. Random House has but one star; Gabler has three, all democratically level.

One feature of the text, visual but not made up of printed letters, is the system of musical notations. The interplay of symbolic systems of sight and sound was remarked on briefly in chapter 6. These notations mattered enough to Joyce to warrant his own care in writing them out by hand. In the Rosenbach manuscript, on page 16 of "Scylla,"[7] the *Gloria in excelsis* is written out by Joyce in the fair copy. He took pains to produce the notation himself; it is a place where he creates (like Sterne) another dimension of his page. The plates of the music in "Scylla" and in "Ithaca" are copied from Joyce's copy—and this permits the reader finally to see his hand appear in the text. While the notations are the same in all three editions, they vary in the size of their reproduction, the "Scylla" staff being larger in the Random House than in the original and smaller in Gabler. The size difference relative to the surrounding lexical text produces a different proportion in the sign systems visually presented.

As a final mark of another kind, there is the period at the end of "Ithaca," perversely a square in the original, despite Joyce's correcting the proofs by indicating "une pointe bien visible,"[8] but periods in Random House and Gabler, proportionate to their respective typefaces but still not acknowledging the artist's hand in being made more visible.

Some difference in the appearance of the page may be due to pragmatic concerns, yet deviations from the original impose a distance between what Joyce actually saw in print and what generations of his readers saw and future ones will see. And when Joyce is said to irritate his text, the difference is crucial. Such visual features would matter to a man for whom the beautiful is what pleases the sight. Whatever the flaws in the original, Joyce saw even by peering that it was good, harmonious, and balanced; it was beautiful because it fulfilled the requirements he had articulated as a youth for what is pleasing visually. The potential ideal text from the aesthetics of the *Portrait* was made actual in the coming out of his book. Aristotle, Aquinas, and Joyce would all be pleased.

When we turn from the visual form of the book to its lexical form, the question arises as to the likelihood of a definitive edition. This study has sought to demonstrate how Joyce's enterprise so puts the text at constant disruption and supplementarity that no final decision can be reached about the letters within the text, any more than there is any possibility of interpretive closure. Thus, in considering the latest edition, another part of Joyce's comment to Beach in order to have *Ulysses* published, that his "book will never come out now," should be emphasized, and that is the "never." Despite such evidence as various drafts and collated typescripts, each yielding plausible editorial choices, the possibility arises that there could never be a correct *Ulysses,* because it is governed by deceptive letters twisted and turned in their appearance.

A brief and suggestive example, touched on earlier, can here be given additional scrutiny. It is the sentence with one word different by one letter from what appears in the Rosenbach manuscript and the Random House 1961 edition: Rosenbach has "One whiff of that and you're a goner"; Random House has "One whiff . . . doner."[9] Gabler restores the earlier word, giving the precedent to the earlier text.[10] Context is no help here, as it rarely is with unstable letters. Both words are similarly problematic in semantics. "Doner" is, according to Partridge,[11] twentieth-century slang, a late date for Bloom's use; and Joyce is scrupulous about anachronistic diction. "Goner" is American slang and inappropriate. (P. W. Joyce has neither word in his book.)[12] Thus precisely in the absence of semantic meaning and in the arbitrary nature of editorial decision, it might be suggested—given the false note that either word strikes—that this sort of switch is due purely to the deceptive modalities of letters, taking into account the vertical substitutability of *d* and *g*. If Joyce playfully transforms and inverts letters in their visual possibilities, some of the difficulties and debates of editorial decisions in the new edition might arise from such intentional tricks that, earlier in their turn, befell Joyce's typists and typesetters and then were reinstituted by editors. With Joyce playing at irritating the eye with each appearance of his work in print, one might be daunted to say which version had any claim. In fact, the answer is both and neither. In regard to a definitive edition, what letters should be there in the text cannot be said to matter, only that all of their modal possibilities do, to make a text constantly shifting, proteanly eluding the editorial grasp, never to come out.

The crucial restoration, as argued in the previous chapter, which Gabler does well to recover, is the telegram Stephen remembers receiving while in Paris. This startling change from "Mother" to "Nother" in "Nother dying come home father" (3.199) reinforces Joyce's sense of the modality of language, the changing of the similar letter *m* with *n*.[13] Thus the similarity of letter shapes joins with Joyce's fictional creation of a fallible French telegraphist to make a picture puzzle of error and complexity. That very combination, however, points to the elusiveness of any textual precision: Gabler's correction actually enshrines a mistake. The presence of such an error in transcription would seem to indicate that Joyce was aware of the similar errors to which his own text is prone in the audible, phonetic confusions that we saw were part of the transcription of his English text by French typesetters. Gabler's restoration points to the inevitable gaps in which Joyce works, the voids over which his spirit and eye brood.

Misplaced letters are the stuff of literature, for Joyce in *Ulysses* long before Biddy finds hers in the midden heap. He would correct some errors; he would intend to correct others but not actually do so; he would be content to let some errors stand. His last work would be a monument to all errors, but *Ulysses* would be poised precariously at the blurred edge of correction and mistake. A dynamic of dis-lexia embraces as well as causes errors, some intentional, some fortuitous. All readings of this text should have, as the text itself does, the capacity to engage misseeing and mistake, as irritation is a consequence of Joyce's iritis and thus the inevitable feature of his *Ulysses*.

NOTES

Introduction

1. Beach, *Shakespeare and Company,* 47.
2. Ellmann, *James Joyce,* 524; Fitch, *Sylvia Beach and the Lost Generation,* 2; Beach, *Shakespeare and Company,* 113.
3. *Ulysses: A Facsimile,* 2.
4. *James Joyce Archive* 27:182.
5. Ibid., 25:102.
6. Ibid., 24:57, 132.
7. Ibid., 24:172.
8. See Ellmann, *James Joyce,* 441–42.

Chapter 1: Iritis as Cause and Effect

1. In her essay "Intentional Error: The Paradox of Editing Joyce's *Ulysses,*" Mahaffey discusses the mechanics of the Gabler edition, which she feels provides a view of writing as process rather than as product. She notes, "If we look to Joyce's texts for evidence of his intentions, we discover him minimizing the importance of authorial intentions by stressing the ways in which they are modified . . . by the variable processes of writing, transmission, and reception" (181). This study will argue that, prior to those areas of instability Mahaffey specifies, Joyce's seeing provides a locus of error and that he willfully seeks to reproduce that visual uncertainty in his text. The reception of his text by readers—and editors—will likewise be affected by the instability and density of the surface seen.
2. See Bishop, *Joyce's Book of the Dark,* specifically chapter 8, "Meoptics." Bishop also considers, however, the mechanics of dream, death, and the darkness of night as the appropriate influences on the *Wake*'s obscurity.

3. Ellmann, *James Joyce,* 649, 714.

4. On the unknowable inherent in this detailed text, see Bernard Benstock, "On the Nature of Evidence in *Ulysses.*" See also McCarthy, "Joyce's Unreliable Catechist," and van Caspel, *Bloomers on the Liffey.* Thomas, in *James Joyce's "Ulysses,"* also considers gaps in the text (53). All of these works consider obscurity in meaning; there also needs to be a recognition of another, more fundamental obscurity found immediately in Joyce's view of the text.

5. Budgen, *The Making of "Ulysses,"* 172.

6. Ibid., 173.

7. He claims to create a contrasting language when he notes of the dream world of the *Wake* that, "One great part of every human existence is passed in a state which cannot be rendered sensible by the use of wideawake language" (*Letters* 3:146).

8. For poststructuralist readings of the text, see Cixous, "Joyce: The (r)use of writing"; and Rabaté, "Lapsus ex machina." One recent book, Stewart, *Reading Voices,* particularly engages the material quality of Joyce's language and recognizes its disruptive lexical features; indeed, it strikingly considers the breaking of the letters within words as "the 'dyslexia' of the transegmental effect." Yet Stewart's focus on such space "between text and reception" is not on the page but away from the visual to "an aural activation that impedes mere scriptive processing" (103). The difficulties of Joyce's sight would suggest that the disruption of the lexemes of the text would preclude any "mere" reading, no matter what other difficulties are consequent.

9. *Ulysses: The Corrected Text.* All quotations of *Ulysses* cited in the text by chapter and line number are from this edition unless otherwise noted. In many quotations, words and especially letters within words will be italicized to make visually evident the disrupted lexical surface; it will be obvious from the critical context when the italics are used for emphasis.

10. For example, in "Intentional Error," Mahaffey notes that the *Wake* "could be described as a book composed entirely of misprints . . . carefully selected" (185).

11. See McCabe, *The Revolution of the Word.*

12. *Ulysses: A Facsimile* (Rosenbach MS), P 100, L 130–31, N 103–4, manuscript p. 16.

13. Senn has raised the issues of such disruptive gaps in his *Joyce's Dislocutions,* emphasizing the presence of diction and displacement in speech and translation. The visual aspect of disruptions at the smaller level, focusing on the placement and displacement of letters, seems necessary and fruitful.

14. If ideology is to be questioned in this hermeneutic indeterminacy, as McGee proposes in *Paperspace,* it should recognize that all such readings depend on the sight of the text itself in its material aspect. Indeed etymology reveals that "idea"

and "ideology" derive from the sight or appearance of the object: the Greek *idein*, related to the Latin *videre*. As Joyce's sight is questionable, so will hermeneutics be.

15. These views are offered in Kershner, *Joyce, Bakhtin, and Popular Literature*, and Herr, *Joyce's Anatomy of Culture*.

16. Recent examples of each are Gillespie, *Reading the Book of Himself*, and Houston, *Joyce and Prose*. Gillespie discusses Joyce's options for his creations in the "possible imaginative constructs—that is, texts—stimulated by images of a particular work" (4) but defines texts as "imaginative (re)constructions [of] perceived images . . . and not as the artifact of wood, paste, paper and ink that we have before us" (7). Inescapably, however, that status of another text as a physical printed artifact was also important to Joyce. Houston's analysis of style begins at a larger level of consideration.

17. Senn, *Joyce's Dislocutions*.

18. Katie Wales says in *The Language of James Joyce:* "'Dis-integration'; 'dis-location'; 'dis-order': the prefix *dis* is hard to avoid in any appreciation of Joyce's syntax" (110). The prefix is also applicable at a level below syntax, that of letters, and above it, at that of reading.

19. Senn, *Joyce's Dislocutions*, 64.

20. Scholes, "Observations on the Text of *Dubliners*."

21. Booth, *The Rhetoric of Fiction*, 301, esp. n.26.

22. O'Hehir, *A Gaelic Lexicon for "Finnegans Wake,"* for the *l/r* split, 392–93; for the *p/k*, 403–5. Joyce favored the *q* for either *c* or *k*, O'Hehir astutely notes, because *p* and *q* are "twin mirrors in print."

23. Bishop says in *Book of the Dark* that "most of the night does not involve vision . . . at all" (216).

Chapter 2: Illness and the Magnification of Letters

1. Gorman, *James Joyce*, 33; Ellman, *James Joyce*, 28.
2. Ellmann, *James Joyce*, 64.
3. Lyons, *Joyce and Medicine*, 186.
4. Ibid.
5. Gorman, *James Joyce*, 196.
6. Lyons, *Joyce and Medicine*, 205–6. For a fuller consideration of the consequences of syphilis, see Ferris, *The Burden of Disease*.
7. Lyons, *Joyce and Medicine*, 187.
8. Ibid.
9. Ellmann, *James Joyce*, 412.
10. Gorman, *James Joyce*, 232. Also of interest on the same page is Gorman's account of Bernan's description of Joyce, troubled again, sitting in a completely dark room, when he received the letter from Harriet Shaw Weaver's solicitors.

11. *Letters* 1:102.

12. November 1917, to Sykes. "The first episode of Telemachia has to be typed as quickly as possible so that the printers can get to work" (*Letters* 1:108).

13. Budgen, *The Making of "Ulysses,"* 172–73.

14. This activity will be described in *Finnegans Wake* as a function of the symbolic of the alphabet itself: "When a part so ptee does duty for the holos we soon grow to use of an allforabit" (19.1–2).

15. Gorman, *James Joyce,* 259; Lyons, *Joyce and Medicine,* 190.

16. Lyons, *Joyce and Medicine,* 190.

17. The picture is reproduced in Maddox, *Nora,* 204f. Joyce moved to 38 Universitaetstrasse in January 1918 (Ellmann, *James Joyce,* 421).

18. *Letters* 3:49.

19. *Letters* 2:397.

20. Snellen's test was developed in 1862.

21. Quoted in Lebensohn, ed., *An Anthology of Ophthalmic Classics,* 69.

22. *James Joyce Archive* 25:103.

23. Ibid., 25:102.

24. Ibid., 23:90; 27:151.

25. Many of these elements have been discussed to other purposes by McCarthy in "*Ulysses* and the Printed Page." McCarthy considers how Bloom's modes of thought "reveal the impact of printed texts" (61) in a Dublin culture that was primarily aural and oral.

26. Kenner's observation that "language is a Trojan horse by which the universe gets into the mind" (*Dublin's Joyce,* 117) is fortuitously reinforced here.

27. Riquelme considers the variety of letters: "alphabetical, typographical, epistolary, bellelettristic" (*Teller and Tale in Joyce's Fiction,* 28). For an especially thorough discussion of all the letters see Shari Benstock, "The Printed Letters in *Ulysses.*"

28. McGee discusses this message in *Paperspace,* 35, and reviews the debate over it on 207n.21. It is also considered by McCarthy, "*Ulysses* and the Printed Page," 69.

29. *James Joyce Archive* 16:166.

30. *James Joyce Archive* 27:195.

31. Additionally, that these abbreviations are not the actual phonetic equivalents adds to a degree of complexity. This matter of how the sound of letters is represented by the text will be discussed in chapter 6.

32. *James Joyce Archive* 27:195.

Chapter 3: The Complicit Reader and Joycean Dis-lexia

1. McCarthy, *Portals of Discovery,* discusses Bloom's active reading as a source of meaning and error.

2. Bernard Benstock, in *Narrative Con/Texts in "Ulysses"* (184), discusses Bloom's experiences in "Lotus Eaters" as visual, by noting the various ways Bloom reads and sees.

3. See chapter 5 for something more on the brand name Cantrell and Cochrane's.

4. Neel, "Reading and Writing," 154–55.

5. Senn recognizes the frequent acts of misreading. See his essay "Righting *Ulysses*," 17.

6. Even a critic uncongenial to postmodernism acknowledges the fact that *Ulysses* resists any critical formulation and recognizes that only in the act of seeing the smallest elements of the text can any understanding be derived: "*Ulysses* is a text to be deciphered but not read"; "the novel can be made intelligible but not interpreted" (Bersani, *The Culture of Redemption*, 174, 175). "Deciphered" and "intelligible but not interpreted" seem to describe the cryptogrammatic dis-lexia discussed here.

7. Miles and Miles, eds., *Dyslexia*, 7.

8. Huston, *Common Sense about Dyslexia*, 1.

9. Miles and Miles, *Dyslexia*, 30–31.

10. Barthes distinguishes between work and text: work as object, text as process ("From Work to Text," in his *The Rustle of Language*). Yet in the dis-lexia caused by Joyce's sight, both come together as the physical object that causes the uneven process.

11. For a summation and analysis of this issue, see McGee, *Paperspace*, 25–29.

Chapter 4: The Poet's Picture Puzzle

1. Ellmann, *James Joyce*, 206; *Letters* 2:88–90.

2. Senn remarks that "*Ulysses* does deceive, puzzle, mystify, trick, mislead its readers" ("Righting *Ulysses*," 17).

3. Gabler, ed., *Ulysses: A Critical and Synoptic Edition*, 964, 1746.

4. Senn, "Entering the Lists," 241–58.

5. *Ulysses: A Facsimile* (Rosenbach MS), P 117–18, L 154–55, N 121–22, manuscript p. 6.

6. *James Joyce Archive* 18:7.

7. Gilbert, *James Joyce's "Ulysses,"* 194.

8. *James Joyce Archive* 27:182. Joyce gave particular instructions to the printer to have this odd letter depicted in the text.

9. A quick glance at the index yields more than thirty numbers in her chapter—a tribute to Molly's nature as a very visually sensitive and less literate thinker. Houston notes in *Joyce and Prose* (84) that Molly's use of numbers is a replication of how she might write them, although one could stress that she thinks them because she has seen them written. Attridge, in "Molly's Flow," notes that the

chapter "accents the inseparability and interdependence of speech and writing in a literate culture" (552), although he does not discuss how something "literate" must include a visual form.

10. Kenner, *Ulysses*, 51.

11. Can the reader overlook the obvious irritation, by the possibilities of letters, of *moly* with "Molly," made from the *l* missing from "L. Boom"?

12. This issue gives an answer to Stephen's question posed in *Portrait* (166) as to whether he preferred the sight or sounds of words.

13. Houston discusses the phrase "gaunt quaywalls, gulls" and finds in their segmentation "a play of sounds" (30).

14. "Perception is perception of something absent" (Brivic, "The Other of *Ulysses*," 205). This can be a particularly visual as well as cognitive or Lacanian psychological feature.

15. Several critics have noticed how the reader is engaged by the text in a temporal way. Kenner's notion of parallax concerns the act of seeing because it begins by analyzing Bloom's view of the Ballast Office clock, but it also requires the reader to engage in a span of time, to read and recall two disparate appearances of a scene or event. ("Two different versions . . . is Joyce's normal way," Kenner says [*Ulysses*, 75]—although he is more concerned with event or information and not so much concerned with letters that happen in particular words.) His theory is called the "aesthetics of delay" because, in between the space where the scenes are read or the dialogue is seen, time is engaged. This process, Kenner notes, can take "some hundreds of pages to transverse" (80), pages in space in which the time of reading the text passes. Another view of time engaged by the material of the text is found in Senn's notion of metathesis. This "change or shift in narrative," he says, occurs when "a technique is foreshadowed that will gradually unfold a few pages later" (*Joyce's Dislocutions*, 140); this revealing of the text takes place on the page through the passage of "real" "reading" time.

16. Kenner, *Ulysses*, 81–82.

17. Shloss, "James Joyce and *The Irish Times*," 32.

18. Hart recognized a long time ago that Joyce needed to temper his sentimentality with irony; see "Joyce's Sentimentality."

19. See on these midwives Senn's *Joyce's Dislocutions*, 106–7.

20. Although it was made more material and alien there by capitalization, a diphthong, and italics: *Foetus* (*Portrait*, 89).

21. See Senn, *Joyce's Dislocutions*, 33. Such Latinate usage is a move in diction that he says takes such words out of ordinary experience.

22. The best example of an error in haplography by a typist of *Ulysses* is the "*Amor vero*" lines from "Scylla"; see chapter 6.

23. Any momentary glimpse for Joyce involves hampered vision. In the *Wake*,

"Augenblick" clearly is related to the diseased eye, "eyegonblack" (16.29).

24. Kenner makes much of this scene, suggesting that Stephen's glasses are broken in an altercation with Mulligan (*Ulysses*, 115–16). McGee reviews the issue in *Paperspace*, 221n.31, as does van Caspel in *Bloomers on the Liffey*, 211–12.

25. Thanks to Bernard Benstock for bringing this into focus.

26. In this as in so much else Senn has seen sharper and sooner: "Anagnostic Probes," 129.

27. As Hart demonstrates in his analysis of "Wandering Rocks," 181–216.

Chapter 5: Identity, Intertextuality, and Infection

1. For the original deciphering of the semantics of these names, see Adams, *Surface and Symbol,* 23n.10. Adams, however, fails to note the discrepancies: Cicero is a nickname, Podmore an augmentation (from Gaelic, *mor,* "elder"), and Napoleon only part of the body.

2. Joyce never let go of any of his words and was fiercely parsimonious with and possessive of the alphabet he used to create them. (Later in this chapter this sort of transfer of letters will be discussed as a trans-lexia.) It should come as no surprise that a configuration similar to "deedpoll" (shadowed by the playful "socalled roll") should appear in another of his texts. *Finnegans Wake* offers to sight "evidencegivers by legpoll too untrustworthily irreperible" (57.16–17). This is a legal proceeding (*poll*), a spoken testimony of questionable veracity that figures and echoes the *lex* (both orally and visually); the poll is something to be read, as written or *leg*endary. It is subject to error (*irren* in German) and cannot be fixed, although any verbal surface is malleable and transformable. And above all, language in the service of law or literature is a game, a leg-pull, confirming the ludic nature of Joyce's dislexic jumbling of letters.

3. See McGee, *Paperspace,* 39, on the *a* missing from "Daedalus" to "Dedalus." The visual—imprint in-print—aspect of the diphthong should be stressed, something that takes up space, catches the eye, especially of a myopic young man without glasses. See also Ellmann, *James Joyce,* 164, on the signing of Joyce's first story.

4. Reproduced in Magalaner, *Time of Apprenticeship,* 176–77.

5. The ads for the machinery may be seen in the *Homestead* (vol. 10, no. 51), Saturday, December 17, 1904, 1039. Even the front page has an ad for an oil engine, as if somehow substantiating Joyce's automobile story within.

6. Budgen recounts Joyce's comment in *The Making of "Ulysses,"* 20.

7. Ellmann, *James Joyce,* 308n.

8. For a discussion of the "amorous" and "intimate associations" of the moon for Bloom, see Bernard Benstock, *Narrative Con/Texts in "Ulysses,"* 78.

9. For a discussion of authority and authorship, see Mahaffey, "The Myth of the Mastermind," in her *Reauthorizing Joyce,* 23–26.

10. Lyons, *Joyce and Medicine*, 60.
11. See Lyons, *Oliver St. John Gogarty*, 41.
12. The Best account is reproduced in Ellmann, *James Joyce*, 363.
13. Scholes and Kain, *The Workshop of Daedalus*, 97.
14. Stanislaus Joyce, *The Complete Dublin Diary*, 88.
15. Ibid., 36.
16. Gogarty, *It Isn't That Time of Year at All*, 90.
17. Ibid., 89–90.
18. Stanislaus Joyce, *The Complete Dublin Diary*, 32.
19. Gogarty, *It Isn't That Time of Year at All*, 89.

Chapter 6: Ghosts, Sounds, and Errors

1. They are formed by "the internal reflections of the lens," according to the *Dictionary of Visual Science*, 1980.

2. *Woerterbuch der Medizin u. Pharmazeutik,* Dritter Auflage, 1981; *Dictionnaire des terms medicaux et biologiques*, 1974.

3. Lyons, *Joyce and Medicine*, 187; also Ellmann, *James Joyce*, 308.

4. In *The Art of James Joyce,* Litz refers to Joyce's sense of the form and the design of the work (4–5) and his visualizing its complex patterns (26).

5. In this light, one should note that early criticism saw a connection between *Ulysses* and the cinegraphic and visual, a connection made by critical metaphors. Gilbert explains to the early readership the effects of Joyce's "silent monologue," "which certainly has the air of an untouched photographic record, and has, indeed, been compared to the film of a moving-picture" (*James Joyce's "Ulysses,"* 10). The same attention to the language of the novel and the new style of the narrative led Levin to a similar observation that "in its intimacy and in its continuity, *Ulysses* has more in common with the cinema than with other fiction" (*James Joyce*, 88).

6. Ellmann, *James Joyce,* 654.

7. On the issue of ghosts, see Shari Benstock, "*Ulysses* as Ghoststory," and McGee, *Paperspace*, 52–54.

8. Gabler, ed., *Ulysses: A Critical and Synoptic Edition*, 1738.

9. On the debate about the phrase "the word known to all men," see McGee, *Paperspace*, 21, 203n.7.

10. The most aural "Sirens" has any number of uses of the word "eye"—in the singular, in the plural, and as a verb—as if substantiating the connection of what is heard to what must be seen. See particularly the essays in the chapter on "Sirens" in Beja, Herring, Harmon, and Norris, eds., *James Joyce: The Centennial Symposium*.

11. This agrees with Derrida that there is no phonemic writing per se, as writing is always subject to the sign ("Différance," in his *Margins of Philosophy,* 5).

12. See Stewart, *Reading Voices,* 237, for a discussion of this passage.

13. Stewart, in his informed theoretical discussion of what he calls the "phonotext," uses the term "discompose" to describe the place "where graphic and phonic patterns intersect each other," and he explores where "phonemic reading . . . stakes out the site of that discomposure" (15). While Stewart characterizes "phonetic reading" as something that "sensualizes the lexical interstices of . . . a ground . . . continuous with lettering as a potential space of interloping semiosis, of wording" (5), and thus recognizes a debt to the importance of the lexical features of any text, he does not consider the site of reading to be wholly visual, as has been argued here throughout. Rather, he considers that readers read phonemically in between "a rigorously linguistic attention to textual semiosis" and "a given social sphere" that includes "a conceptual but also . . . a full sensorial response" (17). Disagreeing wholly with Derrida, Stewart believes that "the phonic will not hold fast within the graphic" (4); he argues that the phonotext is "that articulatory stream which the interruption of script at the lexical borders never quite renders silent," and its "phonotextuality is inherent . . . in the very nature of so-called phonetic writing" (28). By contrast, the argument carried on here is that the phonic aspect of the text is wholly secondary to the visual aspect of the lexical surface as a visual form. In his chapter on Joyce, one filled with otherwise fruitful observations, Stewart claims that "Joycean writing takes the place in the space of its own undoing, its refusal of an exclusive or even predominantly graphic function" (233), an argument that cannot be sustained even by the *Wake*.

14. Ellmann, *James Joyce,* 624.

15. Ibid., 702.

16. Ibid., for the Beckett dictation, 649; for the proofreading, 714.

17. Ibid., 617. At the recording session Joyce was given a script with half-inch-high letters, but he could not read; he had to be prompted.

18. Ibid., 590.

19. See Heath, "Joyce in Language," 131–32.

20. Stewart discusses this pun as "entirely . . . a phonic rather than a scriptive coincidence" (235), although it could be maintained that its effect is homophanic rather than homophonic.

21. Bernard Benstock, *Narrative Con/Texts in "Ulysses,"* 196.

22. For a detailed discussion of the classical debate from Augustine onward about sounds and letters, see Weir, *Writing Joyce,* 85–91. Weir also considers that the letter is the inescapable sign in the text, although there are many nonverbal signs as well. Burgess, in *Joysprick,* chapter 2, discusses how Joyce reproduces sounds by letters.

23. In the mimicking of the song "Kelly" ("Kay ee double ell wy" [6.374]), these letters too diverge from the alphabet and from the standardized symbolic markings.

24. In this way, Joyce has taken the notion of unstable identity of character by alphabetical characters considered in chapter 5 to the extreme. Thomas, in *James Joyce's "Ulysses,"* mentions that reading re-creates the voice (142, 152–55), although here the concern is more with the tension of sound into sign.

25. For example, in the 1961 Random House edition, 93.

26. Lacan discusses speaking and absence; see Gallop, *Reading Lacan*, 120–33.

27. Derrida has drawn attention to the aural/oral dimension of the text in "Ulysses Gramophone." He particularly plays with the notions of "hearsay" and "yes," in French as *oui-dire* and *ouï-dire*, "an untranslatable homonymy [that] can be heard rather than read with the eyes." This tension leads to the interplay between what he calls grammaphony and the gramophone. Derrida remarks in passing about Bloom's reflections on the gramophone as "expressing the desire for memory" (44), particularly of the voice, and considers the presence of sounds of the affirmative in the phonographic text. Derrida focuses on the prevalence of the spoken "yes" but notes, interestingly for our purpose, that "what remains . . . inaudible, although visible, is the literal incorporation of *yes* in *eyes*" and continues discussing the "languages of eyes, of ayes" (42). What Derrida notes as "incorporation" is what is here considered as the visible letters in the materiality of what is spoken and immaterial.

28. Derrida speaks in "Ulysses Gramophone" of the doubling effect of seeing one word in another as a "ghost" (69). Kenner treats voices and shadows in *The Mechanic Muse*, 27.

29. Mahaffey discusses the wilful error in "Intentional Error," 182.

30. McGee discusses this possibility and the possibility of the telegram's reading "not her" in *Paperspace*, 58–59.

31. *James Joyce Archive* 22:346.

32. Ibid., 22:397.

33. Ibid., 22:413.

34. Ibid., 22:403.

35. Ibid., 22:419.

Appendix: What Joyce Saw in *Ulysses*

1. For a full discussion of the edition and of the criticism it generated, see Sandulescu and Hart, eds., *Assessing the 1984 "Ulysses."*

2. *Letters* 1:75.

3. Respectively, Random House, 1 inch and 1 $1/2$ inches, Shakespeare original 1 inch and 1 $5/8$ inches (taking into account the ragged edge). From top, Random House, $1/2$ inch, original 1 $1/4$ inches. Bottom margin, Random House 1 inch, original 1 $5/8$ inches.

4. Both sides $9/_{16}$ of a inch (the right margin including the line numbers); from the top $9/_{16}$ of an inch; and bottom 1 inch.

5. It seems that the original is sixteen characters per inch. No information regarding type size and font is available at the University of Texas, for example, or in the archives of Beach or Darantière.

6. Groden, "The Early Stage: 'Aeolus,'" in his *"Ulysses" in Progress,* notes that Joyce picked headline size from Darantière's type.

7. *Ulysses: A Facsimile* (Rosenbach MS), P 189–190, L 253–254, N 197–198, manuscript p. 16.

8. *James Joyce Archive* 21:140.

9. *Ulysses: A Facsimile* (Rosenbach MS), P 100, L 130–131, N 103–104, manuscript p. 16; *Ulysses* (Random House, 1961), 104.

10. Gabler, ed., *Ulysses: A Critical and Synoptic Edition,* 212.

11. *Dictionary of Slang and Unconventional English,* 7th ed.

12. P. W. Joyce, *Irish As We Speak It.*

13. Joyce takes away the middle leg from this letter to make it emasculated, restoring it perversely to the unmale despite its not reading "Mother."

BIBLIOGRAPHY

Works of James Joyce

Critical Writings. Edited by Ellsworth Mason and Richard Ellmann. New York: Viking, 1959.
Dubliners. New York: Viking, 1965.
Finnegans Wake. New York: Viking, 1966.
Letters. 3 vols. Vol. 1 edited by Stuart Gilbert. New York: Viking, 1957; reissued with corrections, 1966. Vols. 2 and 3 edited by Richard Ellmann. New York: Viking, 1966.
A Portrait of the Artist as a Young Man. Edited by Chester Anderson. New York: Viking, 1977.
Ulysses. New York: Random House, 1934.
Ulysses. New York: Random House, 1961.
Ulysses: A Facsimile of the Manuscript. Edited by Harry Levin and Clive Driver. New York: Octagon Books, 1975.
Ulysses: The Corrected Text. Edited by Hans Walter Gabler. New York: Random House, 1986.

Secondary Works

Adams, Robert. *Surface and Symbol.* New York: Oxford University Press, 1962.
Attridge, Derek. "Molly's Flow: The Writing of 'Penelope' and the Question of Women's Language." *Modern Fiction Studies* 35, no. 3 (1989): 543–65.
Attridge, Derek, and Daniel Ferrer, eds. *Post-Structuralist Joyce.* Cambridge: Cambridge University Press, 1984.
Barthes, Roland. *The Rustle of Language.* Translated by R. Howard. Berkeley and Los Angeles: University of California Press, 1986.

Beach, Sylvia. *Shakespeare and Company.* New York: Harcourt, Brace, 1959.

Beja, Morris, Phillip Herring, Maurice Harmon, and David Norris, eds. *James Joyce: The Centennial Symposium.* Urbana: University of Illinois Press, 1986.

Benstock, Bernard. *James Joyce: The Augmented Ninth.* Syracuse: Syracuse University Press, 1988.

———. *Narrative Con/Texts in "Ulysses."* Urbana: University of Illinois Press, 1991.

———. "On the Nature of Evidence in *Ulysses.*" In *James Joyce: An International Perspective,* edited by Bernard Benstock and Suheil Badi Bushrui, 46–64. Totowa, N.J.: Barnes and Noble, 1982.

Benstock, Bernard, and Suheil Badi Bushrui, eds. *James Joyce: An International Perspective.* Totowa, N.J.: Barnes and Noble, 1982.

Benstock, Shari. "The Printed Letters in *Ulysses.*" *James Joyce Quarterly* 19, no. 4 (1982): 415–27.

———. "*Ulysses* as Ghoststory." *James Joyce Quarterly* 12, no. 3 (1975): 396–413.

Bersani, Leo. *The Culture of Redemption.* Cambridge, Mass.: Harvard University Press, 1990.

Bishop, John. *Joyce's Book of the Dark.* Madison: University of Wisconsin Press, 1986.

Booth, Wayne. *The Rhetoric of Fiction.* Chicago: University of Chicago Press, 1967.

Bornstein, George, ed. *Representing Modernist Texts: Editing as Interpretation.* Ann Arbor: University of Michigan Press, 1991.

Brivic, Sheldon. "The Other of *Ulysses.*" In *Joyce's "Ulysses": The Larger Perspective,* edited by Robert D. Newman and Weldon Thornton, 187–212. Newark: University of Delaware Press, 1987.

Budgen, Frank. *The Making of "Ulysses."* Bloomington: University of Indiana Press, 1973.

Bunjes, Werner, ed. *Woerterbuch der Medizin.* Stuttgart and New York: Thieme, 1981.

Burgess, Anthony. *Joysprick.* London: Deutsch, 1973.

Cheng, Vincent, and Timothy Martin, eds. *Joyce in Context.* Cambridge: Cambridge University Press, 1992.

Cixous, Hélène. "Joyce: the (r)use of writing." In *Post-Structuralist Joyce,* edited by Derek Attridge and Daniel Ferrer, 15–30. Cambridge: Cambridge University Press, 1984.

Derrida, Jacques. *Margins of Philosophy.* Chicago: University of Chicago Press, 1982.

———. "Ulysses Gramophone." In *James Joyce: The Augmented Ninth,* edited by Bernard Benstock, 27–75. Syracuse: Syracuse University Press, 1988.

Ellmann, Richard. *James Joyce.* New York: Oxford University Press, 1982.

Ferris, Kathleen. *James Joyce and the Burden of Disease.* Lexington: University Press of Kentucky, 1995.
Fitch, Noel Riley. *Sylvia Beach and the Lost Generation.* New York: Norton, 1983.
Freund, Gisèle. *James Joyce in Paris.* New York: Harcourt, Brace, 1965.
Gabler, Hans Walter, ed. *Ulysses: A Critical and Synoptic Edition.* 3 vols. New York: Garland, 1984.
Gallop, Jane. *Reading Lacan.* Ithaca: Cornell University Press, 1985.
Gilbert, Stuart. *James Joyce's "Ulysses."* New York: Random House, 1952.
Gillespie, Michael. *Reading the Book of Himself.* Columbus: Ohio State University Press, 1989.
Gogarty, Oliver. *It Isn't That Time of Year At All.* Garden City, N.Y.: Doubleday, 1954.
Gorman, Herbert. *James Joyce.* New York: Rinehart, 1948.
Groden, Michael. *"Ulysses" in Progress.* Princeton: Princeton University Press, 1977.
——. *James Joyce Archive.* New York: Garland, 1978.
Hart, Clive. "Joyce's Sentimentality." *Philological Quarterly* 44 (1967): 516–26.
Hart, Clive, and David Hayman, eds. *James Joyce's "Ulysses."* Berkeley and Los Angeles: University of California Press, 1974.
Heath, Stephen. "Joyce in Language." In *James Joyce: New Perspectives,* edited by Colin McCabe, 129–48. Bloomington: Indiana University Press, 1982.
Herr, Cheryl. *Joyce's Anatomy of Culture.* Urbana: University of Illinois Press, 1986.
Houston, John Porter. *Joyce and Prose.* Lewisburg, Pa.: Bucknell University Press, 1989.
Huston, Anne M. *Common Sense about Dyslexia.* Lanham, Md.: Madison Books, 1987.
Joyce, P. W. *Irish as We Speak It.* Dublin: Talbot Press, 1903.
Joyce, Stanislaus. *The Complete Dublin Diary.* Edited by George Healy. Ithaca: Cornell University Press, 1971.
Kenner, Hugh. *Dublin's Joyce.* Boston: Beacon, 1962.
——. *Joyce's Voices.* Berkeley and Los Angeles: University of California Press, 1978.
——. *The Mechanic Muse.* New York: Oxford University Press, 1987.
——. *Ulysses.* London: Allen and Unwin, 1980.
Kershner, R. B. *Joyce, Bakhtin, and Popular Literature.* Chapel Hill: University of North Carolina Press, 1989.
Lebensohn, James, ed. *An Anthology of Ophthalmic Classics.* Baltimore: Williams and Wilkins, 1969.
Lepine, Pierre, ed. *Dictionnaire des terms medicaux et biologiques.* Paris: Flammarion, 1952.

Levin, Harry. *James Joyce*. New York: New Directions, 1960.

Litz, A. Walton. *The Art of James Joyce*. New York: Oxford University Press, 1964.

Lyons, J. B. *Joyce and Medicine*. Dublin: Dolmen Press, 1973.

———. *Oliver St. John Gogarty: The Man of Many Talents*. Dublin: Blackwater, 1980.

Maddox, Brenda. *Nora*. Boston: Houghton Mifflin, 1988.

Magalaner, Marvin. *Time of Apprenticeship*. New York: Abelard-Schuman, 1959.

Mahaffey, Vicki. "Intentional Error: The Paradox of Editing Joyce's *Ulysses*." In *Representing Modernist Texts: Editing as Interpretation,* edited by George Bornstein, 171–91. Ann Arbor: University of Michigan Press, 1991.

———. *Reauthorizing Joyce*. Cambridge: Cambridge University Press, 1988.

McCabe, Colin. *New Perspectives*. Bloomington: Indiana University Press, 1982.

———. *The Revolution of the Word*. New York: Barnes and Noble, 1979.

McCarthy, Patrick. "Joyce's Unreliable Catechist." *English Literary History* 51, no. 3 (1984): 605–18.

———. *Portals of Discovery*. Boston: Twayne, 1990.

———. "*Ulysses* and the Printed Page." In *Joyce's "Ulysses": The Larger Perspective,* edited by Robert D. Newman and Weldon Thornton, 59–73. Newark: University of Delaware Press, 1987.

McGee, Patrick. *Paperspace: Style as Ideology*. Lincoln: University of Nebraska Press, 1988.

Miles, T. R., and Elaine Miles, eds. *Dyslexia: A Hundred Years On*. Philadelphia: Open University Press, 1990.

Moran, Michael, and Ronald F. Lunsford, eds. *Research in Rhetoric and Composition: A Bibliographical Sourcebook*. Westport, Conn.: Greenwood Press, 1984.

Neel, Jasper. "Reading and Writing: A Survey of the Questions about Texts." In *Research in Rhetoric and Composition: A Bibliographic Sourcebook,* edited by Michael G. Moran and Ronald F. Lundsford, 153–88. Westport, Conn.: Greenwood Press, 1984.

Newman, Robert, and Wendel Thornton, eds. *Joyce's "Ulysses": The Larger Perspective*. Newark: University of Delaware Press, 1987.

O'Hehir, Brendan. *A Gaelic Lexicon for "Finnegans Wake."* Berkeley and Los Angeles: University of California Press, 1967.

Partridge, Eric. *Dictionary of Slang and Unconventional English,* 2nd edition. New York: Macmillan, 1938.

Rabaté, Jean-Michel. "Lapsus ex machina." In *Post-Structuralist Joyce,* edited by Derek Attridge and Daniel Ferrer, 79–101. Cambridge: Cambridge University Press, 1984.

Riquelme, J. P. *Teller and Tale in Joyce's Fiction*. Baltimore: Johns Hopkins University Press, 1983.

Sandulescu, George, and Clive Hart, eds. *Assessing the 1984 "Ulysses."* Totowa, N.J.: Barnes and Noble, 1986.

Schapero, Max, ed. *Dictionary of Visual Science.* Philadelphia: Chilton, 1960.

Scholes, Robert. "Observations on the Text of *Dubliners.*" *Studies in Bibliography* 17 (1964).

Scholes, Robert, and Richard M. Kain. *The Workshop of Dedalus.* Evanston, Ill.: Northwestern University Press, 1965.

Senn, Fritz. "Anagnostic Probes." *Dutch Quarterly Review* 18, no. 2 (1988).

———. "Entering the Lists: Sampling Early Catalogues." In *Joyce in Context,* edited by Vincent J. Cheng and Timothy Martin, 241–58. Cambridge: Cambridge University Press, 1992.

———. *Joyce's Dislocutions.* Baltimore: Johns Hopkins University Press, 1984.

———. "Righting *Ulysses.*" In *James Joyce: New Perspectives,* edited by Colin McCabe, 3–28. Bloomington: Indiana University Press, 1982.

Shloss, Carol. "James Joyce and *The Irish Times.*" *James Joyce Quarterly* 15, no. 4 (1978): 325–38.

Stewart, Garrett. *Reading Voices: Literature and the Phonotext.* Berkeley and Los Angeles: University of California Press, 1990.

Thomas, Brook. *James Joyce's "Ulysses": A Book of Many Happy Returns.* Baton Rouge: University of Louisiana Press, 1982.

van Caspel, Paul. *Bloomers on the Liffey.* Baltimore: Johns Hopkins University Press, 1986.

Wales, Katie. *The Language of James Joyce.* London: Macmillan, 1992.

Weir, Lorraine. *Writing Joyce: Semiotics of the Joyce System.* Bloomington: University of Indiana Press, 1989.

INDEX

Italicized entries indicate either titles of works or words from Joyce's fiction. Italics are not indicative of the typeface used in Joyce's text.

a, 34, 71, 143, 173n. 3
abbreviations, 65, 97–99
A.B.S., 98–99
Adams, Robert, 173n. 1
admirers/advisers, 79, 81
advertisements, and Joyce's publications, 103–5
A.E.I.O.U., 98
"Aeolus": letters in, 66–67; murders discussed in, 48; names in, 64–65; puzzles in, 136, 139; typography in, 28–29, 163
aesthetics, 53–54, 68, 172n. 15
afterimages: description of, 78, 86–87; examples of, 89, 91, 94, 112, 119. *See also* ghosts
"After the Race" (story), 104–5
Agendath, 91–92
alliteration, 137. *See also* letters (alphabet), repetition of
allusions, 106–8, 113
alphabet, recitation of, 141–44. *See also* letters (alphabet)
amor vero, 130
ampersands (&), 65, 97

an, 63
anagrams, 17–18
anatomy, language for, 68–69, 78–79
antonyms, 16–18
Apelles, 68
Apollo, 68
Aristotle, 33, 164; on colored signs, 73; on matter and form, 13, 29–30, 52, 55
Armstrong (character), 145
Attridge, Derek, 171–72n. 9
Augenblick, 85
aurality, uses of, 134–36. *See also* sound
authority, challenges to, 18
autobiography, 117–19, 122, 125

b, 17, 19, 28–31, 50, 62, 66, 84, 137
ba (bat), 58
Bacon, Francis, 111
Barthes, Roland, 86, 171n. 10
Beach, Sylvia, 1–2, 161, 164
"Beatitudes, British," 137
Benstock, Shari, 170n. 27
Best, Richard, 115
betweenness, concept of, 71
biography, and eyesight, 22–23
Bishop, John, 167n. 2, 169n. 23
bit/tit, 79
Black Mass, 16
blanks, uses of, 59
blind spot, 77–78, 111, 142, 148. *See also* iritis, effects of

Index

Bloom, Leopold (character): on authorial controversy, 111; books of, 3–4, 64; correspondence of, 36–39; digestion of, 145–46; and Dlugacz's porkshop, 91–92; eyesight of, 76, 86; father of, 147, 151–53; history of, 83; language of, 36, 74, 138, 146–47, 155–56; memories of, 109–10, 113–14, 148–49; misperceptions by, 79–82; name of, 100–103; observations of, 46–47, 86, 93; and phone numbers, 73; poem by, 29; reading by, 43–46, 50, 87–88, 152–53; and typesetting, 67; and unstable self/letters, 99–100

Bloom, Molly (character): features of, 69; language of, 34, 65–66, 133; and metempsychosis, 80–81; similarity to Milly, 98; singing by, 132–33, 146–47

Boardman, Edy (character), 78

bonzes, 116

books, publication of, 1–2, 5–6. *See also* print/printing; text; typography

Boom, L., 15, 34, 99, 129, 156

Booth, Wayne, 21

bottle, re-creation of reality of, 89–90

boudin, 92, 99

boustrophedonic, 40–41, 107

Boylan (character), 68–69, 89–90, 110

breadchestviousness, 60

breeks/Greeks, 116–17, 121

Bright's bright eye, 62–63

bright tubes of Agendath, 91–92

"British Beatitudes," 137

Budgen, Frank, 11, 13–14, 24–25, 108, 134

Burgess, Anthony, 175n. 22

buttock, 68–69. *See also* gallantbuttocked

c, 58, 70, 108, 144

"Calypso," 80, 92, 141–44

canal/circulation/waters, 47

Cantwell/Cantrell, 47, 56, 103–4

capitalization, 36–37, 39–40, 64, 98

Castille/cast steel, 136

Catholicism, influnce of, 15–17

characters: confusion of words by, 78–82; diminution of, 96–97; effects of unstable letters on, 96–97, 99–100; emotions of, 82–83, 109–10; errors in seeing by, 43–46; ethnicity of, 45; names of, 97–103; and real people, 114–22. *See also* identities

Chase me, Charley/Chase me ladies, 108

cheek, 117, 121

Cicero, 100

cinema, 24, 128

"Circe": afterimage in, 112; allusions in, 113; blind spot in, 78; characters' mistakes in, 79; composition of, 63; Dublin burned in, 46; and iritis attacks, 26; languages mixed in, 74; lecture in, 108; letter inversions in, 30; Mass in, 16–17; puzzles in, 82; repetition in, 72; Rudy's appearance in, 84–85; typesetters in, 155–56; watch's cadence in, 43

circulation/waters/canal, 47

Citronlemon, 73

CLEVER, VERY, 67

Clifford, Martha (character), 35, 54–55, 76

color, 73

color, for book covers, 3, 52

commercialization, and book publishing, 2

Conmee (Father) (character), 74–75, 97–98

counterwriting, 121–22

craved . . . mutely, 108

Crawford, Myles (character), 32, 48

crux, 111–13

crypt, 150

cryptograms: definition of, 49; density of, 54; and other texts, 153; uses of, 37–43, 150. *See also* puzzles

cuffedge, 15

cultural studies, and text evaluation, 19

Cunningham, Martin (character), 100–101

"Cyclops": hangman's epistle in, 36; languages in, 40, 75; lists in, 32, 113; names in, 4, 100; page proofs for, 28; puzzles in, 82; type font in, 44–45

d, 17–19, 31, 84, 142, 165

Daedalus, Stephen (aka James Joyce), 103, 105

Dante, 73

Darantière, Marcel: and page proofs, 64, 141, 154–56, 163; publications by, 3–4
dashes, uses of, 16, 59
dates, confusion of, 48
"The Dead" (story), 21
death, 148–53
Dedalus, Stephen (character): eyesight of, 22–23, 54–56, 76, 85, 109; imagination of, 61–62, 83; language of, 73–74, 155; and letters (alphabet), 24, 106; lists by, 100; memories of, 130, 149; mother of, 129–30, 147–52, 165; parable by, 112; on rhythm, 133; teaching by, 144–45; on time, 85–86; women described by, 89, 97
deedpoll, 100–103
deline the mare, 73–74, 108, 133
Derrida, Jacques, 174n. 11, 176n. 27
diacritical marks, 4
Dignam, Patrick (character), 64–65, 90, 141, 148, 155
dimensionality (time and space): absence versus presence in, 78–82, 151–52; disruption of, 75–76; and identity, 104; links in, 83–86; meaning constructed in, 77; and reading, 75–77, 85–86, 138–40
diphthong, uses of, 98, 103
dis-audia, 144–45
discourse, disruption of, 51–55. *See also* text
dis-lexia: description of, 7, 51, 132, 141; examples of, 64–65; and readers, 5, 7, 19–20, 48, 51, 77, 96; and sound, 131–32; and typography, 164. *See also* dis-audia; errors; eyesight; irritation; puzzles; trans-lexia
distance, 85–86
Dlugacz' porkshop, 68–69, 90–91
dog/god, 30, 116
Dollard, Ben (character), 57–58, 134
doner/goner, 18, 165
drawer, 36–37
dreams, 110. *See also* ghosts
Dublin, description of, 13, 30, 150
Dubliners (Joyce), 16, 23, 69, 162
dull green mass of liquid, 60
dyslexia, versus dis-lexia, 51

e, 27, 99, 142–43
editors, decisions of, 18
Eisenstein, Sergey Mikhaylovich, 128
Ellmann, Richard, 22, 128
Elvery's Elephant house, 47, 56
E.L.Y.'S, 31
Emmet, Robert, 145–46, 148–50
emotions, blurring of, 82–83, 109–10
empathy, 96
encryption. *See* cryptograms; puzzles
end, 55, 61
endlessnessnessness, 31
epigram, 146, 149
epiphany, in *Stephen Hero,* 53–54
epistemology, and Joyce's descriptions, 13
epitaph, 146, 149–50
errors: in cryptograms, 41–43; effects of, 34–35, 51, 69, 130–31, 148, 152–56; intentional, 9–10, 13–14, 49–50, 152, 154, 158–59, 165–66; and misreading of visual, 140; in page proofs, 156–58; as possible interpretation, 44–45; printer's, 9, 20, 28, 112, 147, 154; visible versus aural, 133. *See also* irritation; puzzles
ethnicity, markers for, 45
"Eumaeus," 72, 101–2, 111
eye charts, 26–27, 34, 64, 78, 91
eye diseases: glaucoma, 12, 23, 51, 78; myopia, 12, 15, 18, 23, 25, 51. *See also* iritis
eyeglasses, 22–23, 52, 90
eyesight: and alliteration, 71; as compromised, 54–56; and memory, 149; necessity of, 130; and obscurity, 81–82; and sound, in text, 132; and trickery, 68
eyetrompit, 67, 138

f, 27–28
fashion, materiality of, 80–81
felly, 15
Figatner, Aaron (character), 44–45, 49
film, 24, 128
Finnegans Wake: anagrams in, 17–18; errors in, 21; and eye difficulties, 6, 9–10, 127; ideal reader for, 20; Joyce's characterization of, 2; phonemic

quality of, 12; sound in, 134–36; and tricksters, 57; *Ulysses* referred to in, 128; words in, 59–60, 90, 151
fonts, 28, 44–45
foreign words: highlighting of, 35–36, 72, 74; sounds of, 137; uses of, 90–91, 109, 153–55
foreshadowing, 78. *See also* afterimages
fractions of phrases, 153
Freund, Gisèle, 11
funferal, 151

g, 17–19, 71, 74, 146, 165
Gallaher, Ignatius (character), 48
gallantbuttocked, 68–70, 76, 90, 108
ghosts: context for, 134; sound of, 131; of Stephen's mother, 129–30, 147–48; substantiation of, 151; types of, 127–28, 137, 150. *See also* afterimages
Gilbert, Stuart, 10, 174n. 5
Gillespie, Michael, 169n. 16
glaucoma, 12, 23, 25, 51, 78
god/dog, 30, 116
Gogarty, Oliver St. John: counterwriting by, 121–24; dis-lexia of, 7, 124–27, 154; Joyce's relationship to, 114–26
golden, 121
goner/doner, 18, 165
Gorman, Herbert, 24
Goulding, Richie (character), 61–63
gramophone, 149–50
graphe, 150
Greeks/breeks, 116–17, 121
Guillermet (Mlle.), 25
gulls/walls, 71

h, 28–30, 44–45, 50, 99, 142
ha (hat), 58
"Hades," 157–58
Hamlet (Shakespeare), 111, 113, 149
handicap, representation of, 94
haplography, 85, 131
hawker, 87–88
Hely's sandwich men, 30
Hirschwald (Darantière's assistant), 158
history, challenge to, 48
homonymy, 136, 176n. 27

Houston, John Porter, 169n. 16, 171n. 9
Htengier . . . Dog Drol Eht, 16
Hupinkoff, Borus (character), 28
Huysmans, Joris-Karl, 3

i, 98, 142, 144
identities: of characters, 95–99, 117, 119; destabilization of, 101–3, 122; and puzzles, 83; of readers, 7, 20, 114, 119, 135; of texts, 106–8; and voice, 147; of words, 95–96; of writer, 103–5, 111
-ight, 62
illness, as model for reader, 5–6. *See also* dis-lexia; irritation
images, doubled or crossed, 26. *See also* afterimages; ghosts
incense, 84
ineluctable modality of the invisible, 23, 29–30, 85
initials, misreadings of, 45–46, 50. *See also* abbreviations
interlexicality, 106–8
International Phonetic Association, 141
intertexuality, 106–9
Introibo ad altare Dei, 15–17, 116
Introibo ad altare diaboli, 16
introit, 16
invalid, 89
Irish Homestead (periodical), 103–4
Irish Nationalism, 113, 145–46
iritis: attacks of, 5, 9–11, 23–26, 28, 156; causes of, 28, 114; effects of, 6, 8–12, 14–15, 20, 23, 61, 77, 127–28; treatment for, 10–11, 18, 25
irritation: methods of, 16–17, 28, 39; of text, 14–21. *See also* dis-lexia; errors; magnification; puzzles
italics: highlighting by, 84, 88, 130, 146; and material as alien, 16–17, 136, 153; and typesetter, 131; and unstable identity, 35
"Ithaca": emotions in, 84–85; juxtapositions in, 47; languages mixed in, 155; list of lovers in, 63; names in, 100–101; titles in, 65
It Isn't That Time of Year at All (Gogarty), 118–25

j, 32–33, 142
Jerry, 78
journalism, 48, 57, 66–67, 101
Joyce, James: and ghosts, 127–28; Gogarty's relationship to, 114–26; handwriting of, 11, 13–14, 24–25, 157–58; identity in text of, 103, 105; intertexuality of, 106–8; notebooks of, 12, 25, 53–54, 115–16; and page proofs, 3–5, 26, 28, 41, 52, 130, 156–58, 162; publications by, 103–5; and reading, 25–26, 43–45, 48–50, 175n. 17; real people used as characters by, 114–19; sentimentality of, 82–83, 110; working method of, 12, 24, 39. *See also* eye diseases; iritis; syphilis; *titles of specific works*
Joyce, Lucia, eyesight of, 26
Joyce, Nora Barnacle, 22–23, 82
Joyce, P. W., 165
Joyce, Stanislaus, 23, 116–17, 124
Joyce Archive, 161

k, 175n. 23
Kearns, Anne (character), 89
Keats, John, 127
Kenner, Hugh, 80, 170n. 26, 172n. 15
KEY(E)S, 67
Kidd, John, 28
K.M.A./K.M.R.I.A., 32
knackers, 78
Kratchinabrichistich, Prhklstr (character), 4

l, 15, 34–35, 54–55, 62, 76, 99, 129, 135, 137, 139, 143
language: as alien, 35; changes in, 100–103; inadequacies of, 55, 68; and letters (alphabet), 15; materiality of, 80–82; mixtures of, 69–70, 72–75, 92, 108, 154–55, 158; opacity of, 12–13, 19, 25, 54–56; and poststructuralism, 13; spoken versus written, 121; subversion of, 122. *See also* foreign words; typography; words
lap/lapin, 73
Larbaud, Valery, 26
L. Boom, 15, 34, 99, 129, 156

Léon, Paul, 10
"Lestrygonians," 70, 80, 108–10
letters (alphabet): concatenation of, 90–91, 97; confusion of, 18–21, 43–44, 51, 55, 66, 81–82, 95–96, 156–58; context of, 46–48, 107; disruption of, 15–19, 48–50, 54–56; and fonts, 28, 44–45; functions of, 27–29, 35, 37–41, 136–40; instability of, 6–7, 13, 76, 144; inversions of, 30–31; magnification of, 8, 26–27, 36, 41, 50, 81–82, 95–97, 106; and material reality, 27–28, 51–56; modalities of, 30, 32, 47, 59, 64, 72, 79–80, 165; number used per sentence, 32–34; recitation of, 141–44; repetition of, 31–32, 63–64, 142; and sound, 70, 131–32, 138; spelled out, 37, 39, 98, 138–44, 147; substitutions of, 16–18, 21, 36, 102–3; as symbols, 29, 135; transposition of, 51, 151
letters (epistolary): cryptograms in, 37–43; disruption in, 35, 42, 97; presence of, 151–53; typography of, 36–37
Levin, Harry, 3, 174n. 5
limp/limping, 93
links/lynx, 86
liquid, 60–61
lists, 32, 63, 100, 113
literary magazines, and book publication, 2
Llandudno, 71–72
locum tenens, 71–72
loquat, 75
"Lotus Eaters," 37–39
love, 60–61, 129–30
lovemaking in Irish, 81–82
"Lycidas" (Milton), 112
Lyons, John, 23

m, 99, 142, 152, 165
MacDowell, Gerty (character), 36, 93–94, 105
Macintosh/mackintosh, 97
Maginni, Denis (character), 97
magnification: and contiguity, 30; effects of, 8, 11, 14–15, 18, 24–27; and excursive reading, 50–51; of letters

(alphabet), 36, 41, 50, 81–82, 95–97,
    106; level of, 23; of mistakes, 34–35
Mahaffey, Vicki, 167n. 1
maison Claire, 109–10
maison/moon, 110
Mallarmé, Stéphane, 3
Marha, 40
Martello, 34
mass, 60
materialist views, 13
material reality: of actual versus novel's
    world, 51–56; destabilization of, 58–59,
    61, 67, 72, 76; and ghosts, 129–30; of
    language, 80–82; and letters (alphabet),
    27–28, 51–56; manifestations of, 149–53;
    recreation of, 89–90; and sound, 144
McCarthy, Patrick, 170n. 25
merry, 122
metathesis, 172n. 15
metempsychosis, 80–81
midwives, 83
Miller, William (character), 45
Milton, John, 112
M'Intosh (character), 97–98
modality, 23, 29–30
Moly, 70
monocular occlusion, 51
moon, 109–10
mother/nother, 152–53, 165
Mulligan (character), 116–17, 123
Murphy (character), 98–100
music, combined with print, 4, 133, 163–
    64. *See also* songs
mutely craved, 108
myopia, 12, 15, 18, 23, 25, 51

n, 28–30, 44–45, 55, 61, 76, 142, 152, 165
narrative techniques: alliteration, 137;
    allusions, 106–8; anagrams, 17–18;
    antonyms, 16–18; counterwriting, 121–
    22; epiphany, 53–54; foreshadowing, 78;
    parallax, 83, 172n. 15; verisimilitude, 56.
    See also afterimages; irritation; puzzles;
    text; typography
"Nausicaa," 93, 105–6
Nelson, Horatio, 112
nepogreasymost, 136
"Nestor," 123

neumonia, 133
Newdigate poetry prize, 115
newspapers, 57, 67
N.IGS.WI.UU.OX/W.OKS.MH/Y.IM,
    38, 40–41
Nolan, John Wyse (character), 94
nother/mother, 152–53, 165
novel. *See* text
numbers, 65–66, 73

o, 34–35, 98
"Ode on Indolence" (Keats), 127
O'Hehir, Brendan, 169n. 22
onehandled, 112
ophthalmology, 26–28, 46, 127. *See also*
    eye charts; eye diseases
orthography, 3–4, 65, 141
our prize titbit, 79
"Oxen," 26, 116, 137, 151
Oxford English Dictionary, on reproduc-
    ing sound, 141

p, 27, 61–62, 66, 102, 133, 135, 142
Paddyrisky, Pan Poleaxe (character), 113
Paderewski, Ignacy Jan, 113
palindrome, in list, 64
parable, 112
parallax, 83, 172n. 15
Partridge, Eric, 165
peer/pier, 144–45
"Penelope," 156
ph, 83
phonotext, 175n. 13
photograph, 149–50
picture, 57
pills, 62
Pinker, J. B., 25
Podmore, 100
poet, definition of, 57
poets' picture puzzle, 57, 61, 97, 138
POLDY, 29
poll/roll, 102–3
polonies, 92
polylexy, 20, 47, 91, 93
polysemy, 93
Portrait of the Artist as a Young Man, A:
    aesthetics in, 53–54; *bous* used in, 41;
    chronology in, 23; and eyesight, 22,

54, 109; lecture in, 108; publication of, 164; shop signs in, 44; *That Time* compared to, 125
postmodernism, 52
POST NO BILLS. POST 110 PILLS, 66
poststructuralism, 13, 19, 52, 168n. 8
Pound, Ezra, 24, 132
Pprrpffrrppffff, 145–46
priest, initials on robe of, 45–46, 50
print/printing: disruption of, 154–55; and editors' decisions, 18; finality of, 156; versus hearsay, 101; possibilities for, 118–19; process of, 2–5, 64; product of, 64, 104. *See also* typography
prolepsis, 85
pronunciati, 74
"Proteus": and existence of universe, 85; identities blurred in, 83; languages in, 35, 73–74; and letters (alphabet), 29–30
publication, of books, 1–2, 5–6
publish, 2
punctuation, letters substituted for, 37, 39
puzzles: allusions as, 107–8; answers to, 58–59, 81, 91–92, 139; approaches to, 85–88; definition of, 57–58; emotions blurred by, 82–83; and letters (alphabet), 58; and sound, 138; types of, 60–61, 86–90, 111; and undoing the picture, 68. *See also* cryptograms; irritation
Pyatt/Tay Pay, 67
Pyrrhus, 144–46

q, 17, 19, 32–33, 71, 135
quorum, 71–72

r, 102, 135, 138–39, 141–42
Rahat, 75
readers: blind spot of, 80; challenges to, 38–42, 46–47, 71–74, 86–90, 94, 109, 165; confusion of, 15, 19, 47–50, 131; and disruption of text, 14, 19, 39, 93; empathy of, 96; and errors, 9, 43–46, 57, 67–68; "hearing" of, 133–34, 140; identity of, 7, 20, 114, 119, 135; and obscurity of text, 5–6, 10, 13–14, 26. *See also* dis-lexia; puzzles
reading: and arrested eye, 67–68; dimensionality of, 75–77, 85–86, 138–40; disruption of, 50, 58–59, 77–78, 111; as excursive, 50–51; process of, 49–50, 64, 86–87
representation, 51–55, 66, 68, 89
retrospection, 85, 87, 150
rheumatism, 24
Richards, Grant, 16, 162
Rider, John, 163
Riquelme, J. P., 170n. 27
roll/poll, 102–3
Rosenbach, Abraham Simon Wolf. *See Ulysses,* Rosenbach manuscript of
rose/roses, 93
Rose/rows, 136
rotto, 72
Rudy (character), 65, 149
Rudy/Ruby/ruddy, 83–85, 95, 135
runefal, 151
Russell, George William (Æ), 103
rutilance, 84, 95

s, 97, 142–43
s___, 59
s, antiquated, 4, 65, 141
scanned, 87
"Scylla," 130
sea, 73–74
see, 136
see blank tee, 57–58, 138
self-definition, 46
Senn, Fritz, 20, 168n. 13, 172n. 15
sentimentality, 82–83, 110
shadows, 86. *See also* afterimages; ghosts
Shakespeare, William, 42, 105, 111, 113, 127
Shakespeare and Co., 161–62
shaving, 120–21
Sherlock, Lorcan (character), 71–72
sights, as sound, 140
signs (shop), 44–45, 47–48
sin, 74–75
"Sirens": aurality of, 174n. 10; Bloom's letter in, 99; introduction in, 4; mistakes in, 44; names in, 90–91; song in, 131–32
"Sisters, The" (story), 103–5
slut combs, 88
Snellen, Herman, 27

songs, 131–32, 146–47
sound: of Bloom's digestion, 145–46; confusions of, 141–43; effects of, 132–34; gaps in, 139; of ghosts, 131; glyphic aspect of, 155; immateriality of, 144; letters read as, 59, 137; lexical representation of, 132–40; rhyming of, 113, 116; as sight, 140; transcription of, 137–44, 147
space, as dimension, 75–78, 86
spellingbee conundrum, 139, 141, 148
spellings, errors in, 34–35. *See also* letters (alphabet)
stag, 78
Stephen Hero, 53–54
Stewart, Garrett, 168n. 8, 175n. 13
style, studies of, 19
substitution, 16–18, 21
suicide note, 151–53
Sullivan, John (singer), 134
Sykes, Claud, 24, 135
symbols, 135
syphilis, 24, 70, 114

t, 27, 58, 62, 138, 140, 142–43
Tay Pay/Pyatt, 67
telegram, 151–53, 165
"Telemachus," 24, 118, 121
text: arrangement of, 4–6, 51; challenges to meaning of, 95–96, 111, 113, 122, 159; confusion of, 65, 86–87; density of, 32; dimensionality of pages in, 77–78; encrytion of, 38–42; intertexuality of, 106–9; misreading of, 43–46, 131; parallels in, 83, 91–93, 107–8, 172n. 14; qualities of, 30, 133; reality in, 58–59, 152–53; stability of, 14, 18, 105, 144; substitution in, 16–18; types of, 150; visual versus phonic aspects in, 133–36, 175n. 13; and writer's identity, 103–5, 111, 154. *See also* dimensionality (time and space); irritation; readers; typography; words
Thomas Aquinas, 53, 60, 129–30, 141, 164
throwaway, 43–44
thrush/thrust, 146–47, 154
tightpacked pills, 62

time, 48, 75–77, 85–86, 93
time/term, 113–14
titbit, 79
trans-lexia, 107–10, 112, 117–19
typesetters, 155–58
typography: and abbreviations, 65, 97–99; and ampersands, 65, 97; appearance of, 3, 16, 28–29, 64; blanks, 59; and capitalization, 36–37, 39–40, 64, 98; changes in, 95; dashes, 16, 59; and diacritical marks, 4; and fonts, 28, 44–45; jumbled, 67; and language, 36–37; and letters as punctuation, 37, 39; and musical notation, 4, 133, 163–64; and orthography, 3–4, 65, 141; and reversed visual signs, 72; and underlining, 36. *See also* italics; magnification

u, 28–30, 55, 61, 71, 76, 142
Ulysses: absence in, 59, 148–54, 159; characterization of, 1–2, 118; and cinematic techniques, 128; color of covers for, 3, 52; composition of, 24; and counterwriting, 121–24; descriptions in, 10, 13, 30; Gabler edition of, 18, 63, 130, 147, 152, 163–65, 167n. 1; graphemic quality of, 12, 21, 39, 134–36; and lexicality, 20, 28, 33, 50, 164; as object of sight, 5–6; page proofs for, 3–5, 26, 28, 30, 41, 52, 130, 156–58, 162; printing of, 1–3, 154–55, 161; Random House editions of, 18, 31, 162–65; Rosenbach manuscript of, 3, 18, 63–64, 164–65; *That Time* compared to, 119–25; visual form of, 51–54. *See also* ghosts; puzzles; readers; sound; text; typography; *titles of specific chapters*
Ulysses (in text), 105
underlining, as magnification, 36
U.P., 35
useless/usylessly, 128–29
usurper, 124

v, 32–33
Venus Kallipyge, 69–70
verisimilitude, 56

Verlaine, Paul, 109–10
Vidi aquam egredientem de templo a latere dextro, 16–17, 61
visa, 53
voglio, 74, 146
Volta cinema, 24, 128
vowels, double, 45

w, 142
waaaaaaalk, 31
Wales, Katie, 169n. 18
walls/gulls, 71
"Wandering Rocks": advertisements in, 105; characters in, 97; identities blurred in, 83; language in, 71–72, 110; letter inversions in, 30; location shifts in, 93–94; paragraphs added in, 4
waters/canal/circulation, 47
wavyavyeavyheavyeavyevyevyhair, 31
wayawayawayawayaway, 31
Weaver, Harriet Shaw, 9, 11, 20, 24, 26, 28, 134, 154, 158
Weir, Lorraine, 175n. 22
wheeze, 136
Wilde, Oscar, 115

word-blindness, 51
words: absence of, 130; aurality of, 148; characters and people as, 115–16; disarranged, 151; fragments of, 11–12; genealogy of, 61; identity of, 95–96; metonymic function of, 91; odd or disruptive, 68–69; opacity of, 18, 26; physical gestures as, 117; processing of, 14–15, 59–60; as puzzles, 59–60; repetition of, 71, 109–10; resistance of, 19; reversed, 64, 104–5; substitution of, 102–3; visual quality of, 71. *See also* foreign words; letters (alphabet); magnification
word/world, 15, 34–35, 54, 76, 129

x, 32–33, 81

y, 32, 99, 143
Y.M.C.A. young man, 43, 99
you, 55, 61

z, 24, 27, 32
Zeuxis, 68